EMPLOYMENT AND WORK RELATIONS IN CONTEXT SERIES

Series Editors

Tony Elger
Centre for Comparative Labour Studies
Department of Sociology
University of Warwick

Peter Fairbrother
School of Social Sciences
Cardiff University

The aim of the *Employment and Work Relations in Context* series is to address questions relating to the evolving patterns and politics of work, employment management and industrial relations. There is a concern to trace out the ways in which wider policy-making, especially by national governments and transnational corporations, impinges upon specific workplaces, occupations, labour markets, localities and regions. This invites attention to developments at an international level, tracing out patterns of globalization, state policy and practice in this context, and the impact of these processes on labour. A particular feature of the series is the consideration of forms of worker and citizen organization and mobilization in these circumstances. Thus the studies address major analytical and policy issues through case study and comparative research.

WOMEN, WORK AND TRADE UNIONS

Anne Munro

Routledge
Taylor & Francis Group

LONDON AND NEW YORK

First published 1991 by Mansell Publishing

2 Park Square, Milton Park, Abingdon, Oxfordshire OX14 4RN
711 Third Avenue, New York, NY 10017

Routledge is an imprint of the Taylor & Francis Group, an informa business

First issued in paperback 2017

British Library Cataloguing in Publication Data
A catalogue record for this book is available from the British Library

Library of Congress Cataloging-in-Publication Data
Munro, Anne.
    Women, work and trade unions/Anne Munro.
      p. cm.—(Employment and work relations in context series)
    Includes bibliographical references and index.
    ISBN 0–7201–2328–3 (hb.)
    1. Women in trade-unions—Great Britain. 2. Women—Employment—
Great Britain. 3. Trades-unions—Health facilities—Great Britain.
I. Title. II. Series: Employment and work relations in context.
HD6079.2.G7M86 1999
331.4'7'0941—dc21
                                                99-25910
                                                CIP

Typeset by York House Typographic Ltd

ISBN 13: 978-0-7201-2328-9 (hbk)
ISBN 13: 978-1-138-99752-3 (pbk)

CONTENTS

Acknowledgements

This research has spanned more than seventeen years and an enormous number of people have given valuable support and encouragement at various points during that time. Thanks must go to the trade union activists who have given time as well as access to documents and meetings. The research would not have been possible without the help and co-operation of ancillary staff and managers at the hospitals involved. The original research which forms the basis for this book was funded by an ESRC studentship during the early 1980s. During the research support has been given by colleagues at various institutions, including: the Departments of Sociology and Applied Social Studies at the University of Warwick, the West Mercia district of the WEA, Coventry Business School, and particularly the University College Northampton, where I was allowed time to complete this book. Numerous people have contributed directly or indirectly to the completion of this book over the years; particular thanks go to Tony Elger, Ruth Elkan, Peter Fairbrother, Jane Martin and Helen Rainbird. Finally, but by no means least, my thanks to Stuart Graham for his support.

TABLES

ABBREVIATIONS

AEEU	Amalgamated Engineering and Electrical Union
ASC	Ancillary Services Council
BDC	Branch District Committee
BMA	British Medical Association
CCT	Compulsory Competitive Tendering
COHSE	Confederation of Health Service Employees
CWU	Communication Workers' Union
DBFO	Design, Build, Finance and Operate
DMU	Directly Managed Unit
DHA	District Health Authority
EOC	Equal Opportunities Commission
ESRC	Economic and Social Research Council
GMU/	General and Municipal Workers' Union
GMWU/	
GMB/	
GMBATU	
GPMU	Graphical, Paper and Media Union
HWSU	Hospitals and Welfare Services Union
JSCC	Joint Steward Consultative Committee
LCCEPS	London County Councils Employees' Protection Society
LRD	Labour Research Department
MEA	Municipal Employees' Association
MHIWU	Mental Hospital and Institutional Workers' Union
MSF	Manufacturing, Science and Finance
NALGO	National and Local Government Officers
NASUWT	National Association of Schoolmasters & Union of Women Teachers
NAWU	National Asylum Workers' Union
NBPI	National Board for Prices and Incomes
NEC	National Executive Committee
NHS	National Health Service
NS	New Statesman
NUCW	National Union of Corporation Workers

NUPE	National Union of Public Employees
NUT	National Union of Teachers
PFI	Private Finance Initiative
PLWTU	Poor Law Workers' Trade Union
RCM	Royal College of Midwives
RCN	Royal College of Nursing
SEN	State Enrolled Nurse
TGWU	Transport and General Workers' Union
TUC	Trades Union Congress
UKCC	United Kingdom Central Council (for nurses, midwives and health visitors)
USDAW	Union of Shop, Distributive and Allied Workers
WEA	Workers' Educational Association
WTE	Whole Time Equivalent

To J. M. Munro and D. W. Munro

Introduction

This book is about working-class women and the way in which their interests are represented in trade unions. It explores the position and role of women in trade unions, focusing on the internal relations of participation and representation. The central argument is that there operates an institutional mobilization of bias which sets a trade union 'agenda' and which excludes a number of issues which are specific to women workers. This agenda not only serves to limit the articulation and representation of women's interests within unions, but also to direct women's activity away from collective organization in unions.

A second argument is developed that the major difference of interest between men and women in the labour market stems from the hierarchical division of the labour market by sex. Furthermore, the trade union agenda has a material basis in the organization of work, reflecting and reproducing the hierarchical divisions by sex. Underlying this, is an argument that an understanding of trade unions requires an examination of the processes which operate in the workplace itself. It is only possible to identify what is excluded from the trade union agenda by a detailed analysis of women's concerns within the workplace. This study, therefore, investigates the racial and gender composition of employment and how it results in women having specific interests, and the ways in which they develop strategies for dealing with these interests, often outside of trade unions.

This research has been approached from a position of critical support for trade unions. The conclusions suggest that there is considerable scope for improving participation and representation of women members. They also indicate underlying limitations to this process, which cannot be challenged through structural change to unions alone. On the one hand the enduring nature of the resistance to change in local trade union organization is highlighted, while an argument is also developed that a long-term challenge to the trade union agenda has to come through workplace organization. These arguments have a general relevance to forms of collective organization and trade union activity across different labour markets, areas of employment or indeed industrial relations systems. However, the force of these arguments has to be demonstrated in relation to specific patterns of trade union experience, and this book uses a case study of work and union activity in the health sector in Britain as the substantive setting for this more general analysis.

The initial empirical research which forms the basis for this book was carried out during the mid 1980s, at four trade union branches, two National Union of Public Employees (NUPE) and two Confederation of Health Service Employees (COHSE), recruiting women hospital ancillary workers in the National Health Service in the West Midlands. Three of these union branches were revisited during the mid 1990s, after the formation of UNISON in 1993 and the establishment of NHS trust status from 1991. The research therefore spans a period of more than seventeen years, enabling an analysis of continuity and change at the workplace level.

In order to give a contextual background to the book, this introductory chapter begins with a discussion of the way in which the concept of the trade union agenda·is used. Secondly there is a consideration of why the study of women in unions is important, followed by a discussion which locates the work within the debates around gender and race. Finally the main areas covered by each chapter are outlined.

The Trade Union Agenda

The concept of a trade union agenda used here does not refer to a written or formally acknowledged agenda. It is used to indicate the range of issues which are generally recognized as part of the appropriate business of trade unions. It is not merely a function of the structure of trade unions which prevents the articulation of certain interests. Rather, the accepted trade union agenda hinders the development of potential issues and interests.

The arguments presented here draw on Lukes' (1974) work on the three-dimensional view of power. The one-dimensional view of power has a behavioural focus, based on decision-making where there is observable conflict. This is extended by the two-dimensional view of power to include the process by which decisions are prevented from being taken. Lukes argues, however, that this view retains a behavioural focus because non-decision-making is seen as a form of decision-making. There are three key aspects which Lukes develops in the three-dimension view: he includes not only decision-making, but also control over the political agenda; not only observable conflict, but also latent conflict; not only subjective interests, but also real interests.

Lukes describes how the mobilization of bias may exclude potential issues from the political process:

Decisions are choices consciously and intentionally made by individuals
between alternatives, whereas the bias of the system can be mobilised,
recreated and reinforced in ways that are neither consciously chosen nor the
intended result of particular individuals' choices. (Lukes 1974: 21)

In this way power may be exercised through the limitation of choice by a
restriction of the political agenda. Lukes suggests that this process may take
place either through collective action as in political parties or 'there is the
phenomenon of "systematic" or organisational effects, where the mobilisation
of bias results . . . from the form of organisation' (Lukes 1974: 22). This form of
the exercise of power is not maintained merely by the chosen acts of certain
individuals, but through the nature and practices of institutions. This concept
of power can be applied to the setting of a trade union agenda. It is not based
on a conspiratorial view of trade unions, rather that the trade union agenda
has developed in a particular historical context. It has been set, over time, in
the context of sectional organization with the dominance of male, skilled, full-
time, white manufacturing workers. This agenda has developed and changed
with changes to the workforce, yet many issues specific to women workers
remain largely excluded. Women frequently fail to identify the trade union as
a route for certain workplace problems because they too accept this union
agenda, and the limited role of unions.

Lukes suggests that the shaping of expectations through control of the
political agenda constitutes the extreme exercise of power:

... is it not the supreme and most insidious exercise of power to prevent
people, to whatever degree, from having grievances by shaping their
perceptions, cognitions and preferences in such a way that they accept their
role in the existing order of things, either because they can see or imagine
no alternative to it, or because they value it as divinely ordained and
beneficial? (Lukes 1974: 24)

It is not only that women accept the trade union agenda, but the way in which
they identify and define issues or problems at work is shaped by this agenda.
Their expectations are limited by their experience of trade unions.

Lukes' concept of potential issues which never reach the agenda also opens
the possibility for potential conflict. There is potential conflict around a number
of issues specifically relevant to women, for example around the definition of
skill and labour market hierarchies in grading structures. Since union organization is based on the maintenance of differentials, a challenge to the value placed
on the skills involved in women's work would provide a threat to male labour.
This suggests that the gendered construction of work raises potential conflicts
between men and women. The difficulty is that the mobilization of bias through

the trade union agenda prevents the articulation of that conflict. While there are complex debates around the identification and definition of interests (Somerville 1997), here the nature of women's interests are defined through the substance of the research rather than on an *a priori* basis. Those issues affecting women in their day-to-day experience of the workplace are identified and these concerns are related to the responses the women make, their articulated demands and the organized demands expressed through their trade unions.

The trade union agenda reflects and reproduces the dominant position of men within the labour market and within trade unions. It defines both the appropriate business for trade unions to engage in, and the appropriate processes by which unions operate. Yet during the 1980s and 1990s there have been changes in many unions in terms of the processes and procedures for the involvement and representation of women members. These changes may lead to an overly optimistic prognosis for the future of unions. The story of equal opportunities in trade unions is not one of systematic progress. Initiatives at national level, such as the commitment to proportionality in UNISON seem to indicate the development of what Cockburn (1989) describes as the long equal opportunities agenda. This research highlights the uneven nature of change and resistance from local union organizations.

Why Study Women and Trade Unions?

Increasing involvement in waged-labour has had a limited effect on women's subordinate position in society. The labour market is divided horizontally and vertically by sex, with women disproportionately represented in the less secure areas of employment (Mackie and Pattullo 1977, Hakim 1979, Aldred 1981, Coote and Campbell 1982, Martin and Roberts 1984, Bradley 1989, Rees 1992, Crompton 1997). While women have moved in greater numbers into professional and administrative jobs (Crompton 1997, Walby 1997), they remain concentrated in low-paid work, in part-time work, in low-grade work and in home-working. Despite the introduction of legislation in the fields of equal pay and sex discrimination, the distance between men and women workers in terms of pay and skill levels has changed very little in recent years. This situation has led to many attempts to analyse and understand the persistence of women's subordinate position in wage-labour and in this the attention is focused on the role of workers' collective organizations, the trade unions. Questions are raised about the degree to which women participate in trade unions in order to maintain or improve their conditions of employment, and

Table 1. *Percentages of women in senior positions in largest 10 unions 1997–8*

Position	Union									
	UNISON	TGWU	AEEU	GMB	MSF	USDAW	CWU	NUT	GPMU	NASUWT
Membership	78	20	6	36	31	59	19	75	17	59
NEC delegates	65	13	0	41	32	53	20	43	22	24
TUC delegates	61	25	16	33	45	59	25	43	15	8
National officers	38	4	0	8	30	25	10	14	13	22
Regional officers	26	8	2	13	16	24	na	11	5	18

Source: *Labour Research*, March 1998: 13.

the degree to which unions are able and willing to represent their women members. Further questions are raised about whether trade unions serve to reproduce gender inequalities, or whether they challenge them. As more women become engaged in wage-labour, as trade unions become more reliant on women's membership, and as feminist analysis of employment relations has developed, the specific study of the relationship between women and trade unions has become more important for social scientists and for trade unionists. This research aims to develop the theoretical background to this area of study, and to indicate realistic possibilities for change.

By 1996 women made up 45 per cent of the United Kingdom workforce, and had a union density of 29 per cent compared with 33 per cent for men (Labour Research 1997b). There is, however, a general problem in the lack of statistical information available about the position of women in unions. Until recently few unions collected information on the sex of post-holders within their organizations. Where this information is available, it usually only covers senior posts. Unions also find it difficult to maintain up-to-date information on membership numbers as workers move jobs and unions.

In 1980, Coote produced information on ten major unions which demonstrated that women were under-represented in a number of senior positions, including executive members, as full-time officials and as delegates to the TUC (Coote and Kellner 1980). Since 1980 there have been considerable improvements in the collection of data. Labour Research now regularly produces figures on women's post-holding in the ten unions with the largest female memberships. During the 1980s and 1990s almost all of the unions included in the survey had made some improvements in the proportion of women holding posts. There have been particular improvements in the proportion of women NEC members and the proportion of women TUC delegates. Least progress was made among full-time national and regional officers (Labour Research 1998b).

One implication of the argument put forward here that there exists a restricted trade union agenda, is that the election or appointment of women to senior posts within trade unions does not necessarily result in the representation of women members' interests. Some writers suggest that women officials bring a different style of leadership (Dorgan and Grieco 1993); Heery and Kelly (1988) argue that women officers do make a significant difference to the representation of women's interests. They indicate that women officials are able to 'tilt the union towards a much fuller engagement with specific interests and needs of women workers' (Heery and Kelly 1989: 201). Phillips (1991), in a general debate about democracy, advises that getting more women elected may be necessary to the inclusion of women's concerns on the political agenda, but that it is not sufficient to ensure it. There is, it seems, a need for some caution in assuming such a link.

There are no equivalent statistics available on the position of black women in unions. The TUC (1987) suggested that there was no significant difference between the proportion of black and white women in elected posts in unions, although in 1992 it highlighted the problems of gaining reliable information and of monitoring race (TUC 1992). Black workers are more likely to be union members than white workers, and among black workers, women are more likely to be unionized than men (Labour Research 1996b). However, union density is now declining more rapidly among black members (Labour Research 1997c, Labour Research Department 1998). There is little data available to show how far membership figures are reflected in post-holding. Modood (1997) found that Caribbean men were under-represented in union posts compared to white men, while all women were equally under-represented. It is this persistent under-representation which has focused debate on the relationship between women and their trade unions. The question arises about why this under-representation exists and persists. Less information is available on women's involvement at local level in unions and this is the area which will be covered in this book, through a study of UNISON and two of its former constituent unions, NUPE and COHSE. Having outlined the general position of women within trade unions it is necessary to locate the research in terms of the literature on gender and race.

Gender

The aim here is to link the discussion about women's role in trade unions to the body of feminist literature which investigates women's oppression and the ways in which gender divisions are reproduced. To date much of the literature on women and unions has failed to make links with the literature concerned with explaining the nature of women's oppression. In early debates there was a lack of agreement on the nature of women's oppression and on the definition of patriarchy. In the most general terms it is used to refer to the 'power relations by which men dominate women' (Millett, in Beechey 1979: 66). From this basic understanding of patriarchy, the debates about its nature have led in two main directions. Firstly there has been an attempt to analyse the relationship between patriarchy and capitalism, and secondly an attempt to identify the base of reproduction of patriarchal relations. The latter has primarily been identified as the family, sexuality and childbearing, while some writers have extended the debate to include the state and employment (Beechey 1979, Walby 1986 and 1990). Walby (1986) describes a number of different approaches to patriarchy, herself adopting a position which regards patriarchy and capitalism as independent and autonomous social systems. The starting point here is that any analysis of social relations must take account of women's oppression and that class relations and gender relations are inextricably intertwined. In her more recent work (1997), Walby too has moved away from using the term patriarchy, preferring 'gender regimes', which is a concept sensitive to the diversity in gender relations, yet maintains her general theoretical framework.

In their research on part-time work, Beechey and Perkins (1987) have been more concerned with understanding the relationship between gender and the social organization of employment. Here, gender 'refers to a process in which social relationships which are based on perceived differences between the sexes are constituted' (Beechey and Perkins 1987: 147) Using this concept of gender it is possible to investigate how gender relations are produced and reproduced within specific institutions, in this case in trade unions. Increasing attention has been given to the processes of gendering of work and organizations (Ledwith and Colgan 1996, Halford, Savage and Witz 1997, Bradley 1999). Much of this literature has focused on professional and managerial occupations, whereas my research aims to address these issues in the context of manual work in the public sector.

Race

This book is primarily about the relationship between women and trade unions. However, it is essential that the analysis includes an integrated discussion of the relationship between black women and unions. The term 'black' will be used to indicate groups of people who are likely to suffer forms of oppression due to perceived differences based on racial origin. It is important not to assume homogeneity among black groups. Where appropriate, specific groups will be referred to by their ethnic origins, for example, 'those of Asian origin', 'those of Afro-Caribbean origin'. Reference to ethnic origin is not intended to imply nationality, since many of the groups covered in the research are black UK subjects. White groups will mainly be referred to as of white UK origin. Where appropriate, specific groups, for example 'those of Irish origin', will be identified as such.

The concept of race potentially has as many pitfalls as that of patriarchy. Although it is not the intention here to enter a debate on the relative importance of the overall subordination based on class, gender and race, there is an assumption that an understanding of social relations must encompass all of these areas and that they are necessarily interconnected (Phizacklea and Miles 1980, Miles 1982, Sivanandan 1982, Gilroy 1987). The aim of this research is to retain a structural analysis which is also sensitive to difference (Bradley 1996). There are important differences between issues of race and of gender. However, using the framework of Beechey and Perkins' (1987) approach to the construction and reconstruction of gender provides a useful tool for considering the construction and reconstruction of racial divisions. Gilroy's approach to race shares much with Beechey and Perkins' understanding of gender:

> 'Race' has to be socially and politically constructed and elaborate ideological work is done to secure and maintain the different forms of 'racialization' which have characterized capitalist development. Recognising this makes it all the more important to compare and evaluate the different historical situations in which 'race' has become politically pertinent. (Gilroy 1987: 38)

This book is particularly concerned with the way in which divisions based on race are constructed and reconstructed in the context of work. It considers the process by which stereotypes are applied to certain groups of workers to differentiate them and to legitimate discriminatory treatment. This is discussed primarily in relation to women of Asian origin, large numbers of whom worked in the hospital ancillary departments covered in the empirical research. Chapter 6 identifies the centrality of race to the process of recruitment and the way in which racial stereotypes have been used to justify an expressed preference for the employment of white workers. There is also an examination of the way in which divisions based on race serve to hinder the development of a collective identity among women workers, resulting in separate forms of resistance among the women of Asian origin. Chapter 6 also discusses how the restructuring of ancillary work poses a particular threat to women of Asian origin. It is argued that black women, in this case women of Asian origin, have particular interests in the workplace and that the trade union agenda excludes these interests and undervalues the forms of resistance that these women encounter. The concept of the trade union agenda provides a particularly useful means for understanding the failure of trade unionism to reflect black women's experience in the workplace.

There are other important divisions among workers, for example based on age, sexuality, disability and so on. However, the argument developed here is that gender and race are fundamental to the structuring and restructuring of the labour market, and best illustrate the operation of the trade union agenda. The concept could, however, be developed to explain the exclusion of other interests.

Structure

The book is divided into three parts. The first part reviews the literature and theoretical arguments, and provides a background to the empirical research; the second looks in detail at the nature of work; and the third examines the nature of trade unionism.

There are three chapters in Part I. In Chapter 1 the literature which is specifically concerned with women and trade unions is reviewed. Chapter 2 develops an argument around the divisions in the labour market, and discusses the specific interests of women. This is linked to a discussion of the role of trade unions in the maintenance of divisions through the operation of a restricted trade union agenda. Chapter 3 gives a general background to hospital work, in particular ancillary work, and introduces the hospitals and union branches involved in the research.

Part II involves a detailed analysis of women's ancillary work. Chapter 4 highlights the factors which affect unity and division among workers, looking in detail at catering and cleaning work. Drawing on this material, Chapter 5 demonstrates the centrality of gender to the construction and reconstruction of work, and the resulting gendered nature of workplace interests. Chapter 6 shows that race is also central to the construction of work, giving rise to specific interests and specific forms of resistance.

Part III focuses on how trade unions respond to the interests of women ancillary workers. Chapter 7 considers branch organization, analysing post-holding, shop-steward systems and union meetings. It argues that certain structures are necessary to enable the involvement of women ancillary members, although structural changes alone cannot guarantee their involvement. Chapter 8 analyses the representation of women's interests. It argues that through the operation of the restricted trade union agenda, many of women's specific interests are excluded. Many of women's concerns in the workplace are seen as inappropriate issues for trade unions, not only by shop stewards and union officers, but also by the women themselves. This argument is developed in Chapter 9, which shows that the restricted agenda discourages union participation, meaning that women's involvement does not guarantee better representation of women's interests. This chapter also highlights the way in which women's activities in the workplace are frequently underestimated. However, despite the obstacles identified, this chapter suggests that there is considerable potential for increased participation through structural change, in particular better workplace organization.

The central argument which is discussed in the concluding chapter is that the restricted trade union agenda is crucial in hindering the representation and participation of women members. It has developed over time and can be challenged and altered, although because of the way in which it is reproduced, any change is likely to be very slow.

Part One
The Context

1 WOMEN IN TRADE UNIONS

In this chapter, the literature which directly addresses the issues of women's roles in trade unions is reviewed. Much of the literature from the early 1980s provides valuable insights into aspects of this area, although it tends to lack a clear theoretical framework. The desire to conclude optimistically about the future of trade unions leads many writers to ignore the evidence of their own research (Aldred 1981, Beale 1982). Recently a number of writers have engaged in a more thorough analysis (Rees 1990 and 1992, Cunnison and Stageman 1993, Briskin and McDermott 1993, Lawrence 1994, Colgan and Ledwith 1996, Bradley 1999).

For the purpose of analysis it is necessary to distinguish between the reasons why people do or do not join trade unions, and secondly why they are either active or inactive within the union. The first set of issues will be addressed in terms of organization and recruitment, while the second set of issues will be addressed in terms of participation and representation. These headings will form the basis for the structure of this chapter. While it is the latter area which will be particularly developed, a review of the whole field provides the context for the material.

Organization and Recruitment

The main growth of union membership during the 1970s was among women workers and the decline in union membership during the 1980s and 1990s has been least rapid among women workers (Labour Research 1996b). However, there are still proportionally fewer women in trade unions than men. This has raised the question of whether women are more difficult to organize into unions, and if so why? In an attempt to respond to this question, the discussion is divided into issues of organization and issues of recruitment. Organization refers to the process by which workers develop a collective and specifically trade union response to improving working conditions. It focuses on workers themselves and their position within the labour market. In contrast, recruitment focuses attention on the actions of trade unions, not on the actions of workers. Under recruitment, the focus is on the role of trade unions in actively enrolling women members.

Organization

There are four main arguments developed in the literature on organization, linked to workplace, skill levels, part-time working and job attachment. Each of these arguments will be assessed in turn.

Firstly, it has been argued that women tend to work in small scattered workplaces, where it is generally more difficult to organize (Aldred 1981, Ellis 1981, Beale 1982). Many women are employed in small firms, in isolated groups, in the informal economy and in home-working. Because of the nature of women's jobs, many women are employed in small work groups even where the employing organization is large, for example as office cleaners or canteen staff in a large factory. In small work groups, daily and close contact with the employer or management may make worker organization uncomfortable and difficult. This discomfort may be experienced as disloyalty where control is both patriarchal and paternalistic. Communication with wider union structures can be difficult. Employers frequently adopt policies of favouritism or higher wages as a reward for passivity, which lead to distrust and jealousy between workers. They may bar workers who attempt any sort of organization (Hoel 1982, Beale 1982).

The evidence from the literature appears to support the argument that women tend to work in those areas of employment where organization is more difficult. However, despite these problems, there is also evidence, both historical and contemporary, which suggests that organization is possible where the trade unions are prepared to invest the necessary time and energy. Drake (1984) describes the organization of domestic servants in the 19th century, while there have been some more recent successes with home-workers (Wrench and Virdee 1996).

Secondly, Ellis and Aldred argue that organization has always been greater among skilled workers who have greater bargaining power, whereas women are concentrated in unskilled and low-grade work (Ellis 1981, Aldred 1981). This viewpoint is problematic. Trade unions have their roots in craft organizations, and have always been strongest where workers have vital positions within the economy. However, the concept of 'skill' cannot be understood without reference to social definitions in the context of a sexually segregated labour market. Are men better organized because they are more skilled, or are they defined as more skilled because they are better organized? Does women's work involve less objective skill content, or is women's work defined as unskilled because women are less well organized? Despite the potential problems with this argument, the relationship between skill and organization is an important one which is addressed during the discussion of this research.

Thirdly, Beale and Aldred argue that it is more difficult to organize part-time workers, and that 40 per cent of women work part-time (Aldred 1981, Beale 1982). Part-time workers have fewer legal protections than full-time workers, which may make organization more risky for part-timers. Where they work on twilight shifts, communication with other workers or the union may be difficult. While this does point to added difficulties to organization, part-time working alone is not necessarily a good indicator of the level of union organization. Where a firm or organization is unionized, part-time workers are just as likely as full-time workers to be union members, as is the case in the public sector. This suggests that part-time working in itself does not prevent union membership; in fact union density has been more stable among part-time workers during the 1990s (Labour Research 1996b).

Fourthly, Ellis (1981) argues that job attachment is likely to coincide with involvement in unions. She suggests that job attachment is a reflection of continuity of work, job control and commitment to the job for its intrinsic satisfaction. She further argues that women tend to be in those jobs without control, low-grade work, unskilled work and individual repetition (boring) work. This argument is based on a male definition of job attachment, for example, with attachment being linked to length of service, and with satisfaction being linked to skill level. However job attachment is defined, it is difficult to substantiate a relationship between it and trade union involvement. Research such as Coyle's work on unemployment (1984), has found that women workers frequently do feel a high level of job attachment. Many women work in the service sector where workers have a strong sense of the intrinsic value of their jobs, which may promote job attachment. Indeed in this research among hospital cleaners, a group with little control, and defined as unskilled, there was considerable commitment to the job, to the health service and to the patients.

Lawrence (1994) cautions against using a different explanatory framework to account for women's involvement in trade unions compared to men. The increases and decreases in union density for both men and women may be better understood with reference to factors outlined by Bain and Price – industrial structure and potential membership, employer and government policies towards trade unions and so on (Bain and Price 1983). However, there is some indication that because of the vulnerability of women workers in certain sectors of the labour market, organization may require greater time, effort, and support from trade unions. This leads on to the second aspect of this section, considering the role unions have played in recruiting women members.

Recruitment

Historically, some unions have actually barred women from membership and many have only reluctantly admitted women members (Lewenhak 1977, Boston 1980, Drake 1984). Although actual bars to membership no longer exist, until recently comparatively little effort has been devoted to the recruitment of women. The increase of women union members has been most marked in the public sector, where less effort was required from unions themselves. In the public sector groups of women workers tend to be larger and less isolated than many in the private sector, especially in service industries, and management in the 1970s acquiesced with union growth. The comparative failure to recruit more women in the private sector may be linked to the problems discussed earlier, of small isolated work groups. Recruitment in small workplaces may not be regarded as 'cost-effective'; or recruitment among groups such as home-workers might actually cause a clash of interests between new and existing members (Munro 1982).

Beale (1982) argues that the recession in the early 1980s, with its resulting loss of members, forced the unions to recruit women. There is indeed evidence that the union membership crisis is causing the union movement to consider ways of recruiting more women members (Cunnison and Stageman 1993). Unions such as the TGWU have run specific campaigns to recruit women members. In 1996 the TUC launched the New Unionism project, which aims to focus resources on recruitment, particularly trying to appeal to women and young workers (IRS Employment Trends 1997). Training for lay officers and full-time officials is central to this development, with an objective of enabling them to 'take ownership of regenerating the union in the workplace' (IRS Employment Trends 1997: 7). Underlying such attention to women's membership of unions, however, there seems to be an assumption that increased union density among women workers will automatically improve the representation of their interests. Evidence from the historical literature, and from the more recent experience of unions with a majority of women members, suggests that this assumption should not be made.

Participation and Representation

The concepts of participation and representation are sometimes conflated, but need to be analytically separated, reflecting the distinction between participative democracy and representative democracy. This is particularly important because of the explanatory framework attached to each. The literature which can be linked to participation primarily focuses attention on the actions of women members themselves. In contrast, that which can be linked to representation looks at the actions of trade unions – the extent to which women's interests appear in the bargaining agenda (although this area has received less attention in much of the literature). This difference of focus is obviously of great importance in terms of prescriptions for future policy.

The concept of participation is problematic in terms of how it is identified, how the significance of different forms of participation is compared, and how it is quantified. Most studies assess participation in terms of the formal structures of unions, post-holding and attendance at meetings being two of the key indicators used. There is, however, a need for a wider notion of participation which takes account of activities outside of formal structures. In a number of texts 'representation' is used to denote the proportion of women holding posts within unions. In this analysis, however, representation is used to signify take-up and presentation of interests, while post-holding is considered as an aspect of participation.

Women's participation in trade unions

There are two main bodies of literature which are relevant to this discussion. There is the literature that comes from the general area of the sociology of work, and which focuses on women's employment and in particular on notions of women's 'work-consciousness'. There is another body of literature that is less theoretically based, which will be called the 'practical' literature, and which comes from some of the texts already mentioned and from the considerable literature emerging from trade unions themselves.

A number of valuable workplace studies attempt to link empirical research to broader theoretical issues in the context of women's work (Pollert 1981, Cavendish 1982, Wajcman 1983). The issue of work-consciousness is posed in the light of the potential for women to act to change their disadvantaged position in employment – do women have an awareness of the unequal social relations of production and do they seek collective responses to challenging them? However, the concept of consciousness and how it relates in complex and contradictory ways to work and the family are problematic. Does women's role in the home result in a different form of consciousness in the workplace? Beechey raises a number of other questions which are not adequately addressed in the literature.

> What do we mean by the term 'consciousness'? Is there such a thing as women's consciousness? Is women's consciousness essentially the same as men's or different from it? If women's consciousness is different from men's, how can we account for the differences? How can we develop a framework for analysing consciousness which is appropriate to women? (Beechey 1983: 39)

The particular danger in this literature, as Beechey points out, is that of assuming an 'ideal type' of feminist consciousness. This may result in the pathologizing of women who do not achieve this 'ideal' consciousness. This becomes particularly problematic when we consider participation in trade unions. The concept of work-consciousness seems frequently to assume a notion of 'union-consciousness', that is, an awareness that the route to changing and improving present work situations lies in active involvement in trade unions. Thus, if women are not active in their trade union, they must lack the 'proper' work-consciousness. However, as the studies referred to above show, male trade union officers and activists frequently act in ways which make active involvement very difficult for women. Therefore, it seems impossible to consider work-consciousness or union-consciousness without looking at the constraints placed on women's involvement and activity, and the possible limitations on improving their position in work.

As Lawrence points out (1994), activism within trade unions has always been a minority activity among both men and women. She argues that reasons for participation should be studied as well as barriers to participation. While this is an important point, it is necessary to look specifically at the problems women face in the light of the widespread acceptance of 'the passive woman worker' thesis:

> It is one of those taken-for-granted assumptions that women, and particularly women workers, are generally more placid, stable, fundamentally exploitable than men. (Purcell 1984: 54)

Purcell critically considers the arguments in this debate and attempts to reappraise the relationship between the concepts of militancy and militant trade unionism. She concludes that variables related to work and market position are far better indicators of militancy than gender, although this has to be understood in the context of a sexually segregated labour market:

> From a consideration of the industries and unions, it seems to me that situational variables can be used to give plausible explanations of both women's militancy and women's acquiescence in industrial relations, which rely very little on sex or even gender *per se*. (Purcell 1984: 67)

The 'passive woman worker' thesis has been further applied to black women, in particular women of Asian origin. When discussing older Indian women, Westwood (1984: 77) says that there 'was nothing in their experience or the ideology of their community which lent support to trade unionism'. While this observation may be accurate in the context of this case study, Parmar (1982) criticizes any assumed link between passivity among Asian women and their cultural background. She discusses strategies of resistance outside of 'traditional trade union activities', and argues for an acceptance of the relevance of other forms of organizing. Thus there is a need to be sensitive to alternative forms of activity and organization in which women may be involved.

The literature divides into two contradictory lines of argument, the one claiming a distinct women's work-consciousness and the other claiming that differences between men and women result from differences in their situations, not from their sex. Although this research does not focus primarily on issues of work-consciousness, any arguments that suggest that women's union-consciousness is in any way 'lacking' or 'undeveloped' is rejected, and it is argued that the assumed link between work-consciousness and union-consciousness is problematic. Attempts to identify a specific women's work-consciousness obscure more than they reveal. In the light of these points this research is particularly concerned with understanding the constraints and limitations on women's activities within unions which relate to trade unions themselves and the nature of work organization.

Barriers to participation

There are obviously many factors which will affect women's ability to participate in trade unions. These many factors are presented in what has been termed the 'practical literature'. To clarify a little what these factors are, Stageman's categories of obstacles of a practical nature, of an institutional nature and of male dominance can be used as a starting point (Stageman 1980a).

Obstacles of a practical nature

Most commentators point to the problem of union meeting times and places not suiting women members, especially part-time workers (Stagemen 1980a and 1980b, Ellis 1981, Beale 1982, Coote and Campbell 1982). They suggest that women have particular difficulty attending meetings outside of work time, because of their domestic responsibilities. Also, it is contended that the venues of meetings, particularly those in the evening, are inappropriate for some women, for example rooms in public houses. Another frequent argument is that women, especially if they have children, lack time and energy to become involved with their unions. They are also deterred by the prospect of union responsibilities on top of domestic responsibilities (Aldred 1981, Beale 1982, Coote and Campbell 1982). Beale suggests that taking time off for union business during work hours may be more difficult for women, for example for part-time workers or workers on piece rates for whom it may mean a reduction in wages. Coote and Campbell also point out that because of the organization of women's work, women lack the opportunity for informal discussions, which they suggest are essential for the development of collective organization.

Obstacles of an institutional nature

A common theme in the literature is that women lack confidence and experience within trade unions. This is seen to be exacerbated by a failure of communication within unions about how basic union procedures work, which results in unions appearing remote from the workforce (Beale 1982, Coote and Campbell 1982).

Obstacles of male dominance

Beale perceives trade union procedures to be based on the assumption of the 'typical man's working life' and therefore to discriminate indirectly against women. This view can be linked to the argument for the significance of a limited trade union agenda, which is presented in this book. In addition some male unionists often act in a sexist way, directly discriminating against women.

While the arguments in this literature appear convincing, the main problem with them is that none of the writers offer either any indication of the relative importance of each of these factors, or any method for assessing their relevance. The result is that when it comes to prescriptions for change, they can offer no set of priorities for action, or means to assess progress. However, there is one issue which is given considerable weight by all of the writers on women and unions, and this is the importance of the extent of women's domestic responsibilities in limiting their involvement. Lawrence (1994) draws on Wertheimer and Nelson's 1975 study of participation, and this provides a useful route for considering this range of factors. Their study identifies three groups of barriers to participation – work-related, union-related and cultural-societal-personal. It was the emphasis in much of the literature on women's domestic responsibilities, which fits into the last category, which initially led to the development of this research which focuses on work and union-related issues.

Cunnison suggests that researchers should be wary about how much weight is given to domestic responsibilities in explaining women's level of union participation:

> This is an oversimplification and misses an important point: it is not so much the extent of domestic obligations which matters, as the way in which they are perceived, the priority accorded to them in competition with obligations connected with work and wage earning . . . and the willingness or not of women to organise their lives so that these latter interests and obligations can be accommodated. Indeed I have been surprised in the course of my research by the number of women with family responsibilities – though rarely women with babies and very small children – who still find time for union work. (Cunnison 1983: 78)

In their later work, Cunnison and Stageman (1993: 3) emphasize the subordination of women's concerns through the culture of masculinity which pervades the union movement and supports structures of male power. They argue that women operate through their own culture of feminity in which they have specific sets of values and different ways of doing things. In contrast, this research attempts to locate explanations for the level of women's participation in unions in their experience of the workplace and trade union activity. It will be argued that some obstacles to participation can be removed, particularly some union-related factors, yet it also points to the enduring nature of work-related factors which cannot easily be removed.

Participation is examined in the context of how members perceive the union and appropriate issues for discussion within it. The argument will be developed that the nature of problems raised within the union is to a large extent defined by the perceived accessibility of the union, which is in turn defined by a trade union agenda. This restricted trade union agenda results in women seeking individual solutions outside of the structures of trade unions for many of their problems and grievances.

Representation of women's interests in trade unions

The issue of interest representation forms a major focus for this research. Little attention is given in the literature to individual representation, more attention being given to general debates about the nature of women's interests, and why the interests of women have been neglected within trade unions (Beale 1982, Coote and Campbell 1982, Cunnison and Stagemen 1993, Briskin and McDermott 1993, Forrest 1993). The latter area forms the basis for the following chapter.

In the existing literature there seems to be difficulty in moving between debates which are concerned with the local workplace and union representation, and those which are concerned with more general theoretical issues. However, the importance of developing this connection is clear from the methodological issues raised in substantive research. Questions can be raised about whether trade union representatives spend proportionately as much time and energy representing women members as men members in individual case work, such as disciplinary and grievance handling. Although this seems to be an easily quantifiable question, it is actually very difficult to assess the extent of take-up by members and shop stewards. Certain groups of workers may have many more problems as a result of their position in the labour force. Certain groups of workers may have more 'small-scale' problems which are dealt with without having recourse to the formal procedures, and thus are not recorded. These questions will be considered in detail in this research. In particular they are pursued through comparisons between the case studies in relation to the nature of individual problems raised, the form of response from union officers, and alternative means of dealing with problems. This also leads to a consideration of whether having more women shop stewards results in better take-up, and/or better representation.

Many trade unionists spoken to in the course of this research commented on the problem of members, both male and female, regarding the union as a 'service agency'. That is, they felt that members expected officers to carry out individual representational work, while feeling no necessity or obligation for their own participation in the union. However, it will be suggested that many women members do not even see unions as a service agency, but as something even more external. This was also found by Cunnison (1983), who writes that the women in her research saw the union as something they used only in extreme circumstances. Rather than seeing the use of the union for individual representational work as a negative indicator of participation, it can be seen as the reverse. This research suggests that many of the women members did see the union as an external agency. However, this is not merely a function of women's union awareness, but also of the form and nature of trade unionism.

Summary

This chapter has outlined the broad discussions concerning reasons for women's union membership, and explanations for the level of women's activity within trade unions. A need for caution has been identified in explaining patterns of participation only by reference to factors related to women's domestic roles. The concept of participation used in the literature has been challenged as being too narrow, and the failure to address the nature of representation has been criticized. It has been suggested that there is some potential to enable greater participation and representation, but there are underlying limitations to this process which relate to the wider issues of representation of interests, and this forms the focus of the next chapter.

2 DIVISIONS IN THE LABOUR MARKET AND TRADE UNIONISM

This chapter develops the argument that there is a fundamental difference of interest between men and women in employment which is related to the nature of the hierarchical labour market, that being a market divided by sex. This has important implications for the nature of trade unionism, which is based on the maintenance of division and operates through a restricted trade union agenda. Siltanen (1994) has argued that because of the diversity in women's employment experiences, it is overly simplistic to talk of 'women's interests' as such. Bradley (1999) also points out that men's and women's interests converge to a considerable extent. Nonetheless, the argument is developed in this chapter that there are sufficient commonalities between women in the labour market to make gender a useful category of analysis. However, as this research demonstrates, class and race cut across gender in the structuring and restructuring of work. The way in which interests emerge and are articulated in the workplace depends on the context of the particular work situation. Equally, while the notion of women as a distinct interest group within trade unions should not be regarded as unproblematic (Bradley 1999: 188), a further argument is developed here that the reproduction of gender divisions is central to the nature of trade unionism.

There is an ongoing debate concerning the extent to which occupational gender segregation in the labour market still continues. Some writers have suggested a decline in overall levels of segregation (Walby 1997), whereas Blackburn, Jarman and Siltanen (1993) have indicated problems based on statistical analysis, concluding that segregation has been stable. In her recent work, Bradley (1999) found gender segregation widespread; this view is supported by the research for this book. To address these issues, this chapter considers the debate around the nature of the interests of men and women; it continues with an historical overview of the development of trade unions and an assessment of the scope and limitations of trade unionism. There follows a discussion of the implications of racial divisions in the labour market. Finally, the implications of these arguments for this research are outlined.

The Identification of Interests

The concept of interests is used at two levels. Firstly, there is an argument that at a general level women workers share certain interests which result from the hierarchy of labour which is divided by sex. Secondly, the divisions of the labour market are reflected in individual workplaces, although they may be overlaid by other divisions such as race, and result in specific interests which are often regarded as sectional. Kelly (1987: 34) defines sectional interests as being where the 'interests of a particular group of workers were placed by that group above the interests of the working class as a whole'. There are problems with the notion of 'interests of the working class as a whole' where it does not take account of differences based on gender or race – where it actually means the interests of white male skilled workers. British unionism is based on the maintenance of divisions among the working class, or more accurately on the maintenance of a hierarchy of labour which is divided by sex. The maintenance of this hierarchy underwrites and reinforces a fundamental difference of interests between men and women in the labour market. There is a bottom layer in the hierarchy of labour, differentiated by grading structures, made up of women. For unions to challenge this hierarchy of labour they would have to challenge the whole concept of British unionism. This position is supported by Forrest, who argues that:

> What has emerged is a profound identity between the interests of [white] working-class men and the meaning of trade unionism, so that, now, it is seemingly impossible to disentangle the ways in which trade unions act to protect the narrow economic interests of a particular group of men and industrial relations' conceptualization of trade unionism as a social force. (Forrest 1993: 331)

There is, therefore, an inherent contradiction for unions in their representation of women members.

The labour market as a whole is divided by sex, and this is reflected in individual workplaces, where most men and women work in jobs segregated by sex. Individual work groups will have specific interests reflecting this sexual division of labour. As Colling and Dickens (1989: 33–4) point out, there is a problem of 'particular industrial/occupational interests being categorised, and then marginalised or ignored, as "women's interests" '. Beale (1982) argues that in the pursuit of sectional interests it is men's sectional interests which predominate, because men predominate in the senior positions in the trade union hierarchy:

> Women and men tend to do different jobs, and compete with each other in the pursuit of sectional interests. Sexist attitudes within trade unions can make this worse. Some men still think women workers are less important than themselves. They under-rate women's potential power, and they are unwilling to give up their own privileged position. The result is that employers exploit this lack of solidarity to their own advantage. (Beale 1982: 6)

Although this research broadly supports this argument, it could be added that men dominate in local union hierarchies because they also dominate in the hierarchy of labour. Sectional interests within the workplace are not necessarily conflicting, but where they are, unions are less likely to support women's interests. Sometimes, even when interests are not in conflict, women's interests are less likely to be taken up than men's. The representation of women's interests may be improved by increasing the number of women shop stewards and branch officers, but such measures do not guarantee an improvement. As Colling and Dickens found (1989: 34), 'serving men's interests and upholding existing structures and arrangements which favour men tended to be equated not with sectional concerns but with serving *members'* interests'. Thus what has passed as the collective interest has frequently been men's interests, while anything specifically relating to women has been regarded as sectional.

Beale (1982) concludes optimistically that because unions need women in terms of membership, they will be forced to address women's interests. However, this optimistic outlook seems unsupported by her own evidence or by women's experience of unions, which have historically preferred exclusion of some sections of the workforce to unity of the whole workforce. There has in recent years been a considerable change in the way in which unions have approached the organization and representation of women members. Ellis (1988) argues that the trade union agenda has changed to meet women's needs. This may in part be a result of the restructuring of industry and the increased importance of women to trade unions, and in part a result of the efforts of the women's movement. However, there remain underlying limitations to the representation of women's interests.

Coote and Campbell argue that the central division of interest between men and women lies in male workers' claim to a right to a family wage:

> As long as the myth of the family wage persists, there is bound to be a
> conflict between women and men in the trade union movement. For if men
> see themselves as breadwinners-in-chief, how are they to view the prospect
> of women gaining equal opportunity and equal access to all jobs? (Coote and
> Campbell 1982: 155)

They argue that the self-protection role of unions prevents them taking up
interests in conflict with their own, 'for men to champion women's cause
whole-heartedly requires a degree of altruism that has no part in the tradition
of British trade unionism' (Coote and Campbell, 1982:155). The previous
discussion of the hierarchy of labour supports their contention that there is a
contradiction in the nature of trade unionism. However, Coote and Campbell's emphasis on the family wage is too narrow. Despite the ideology of the
family wage sitting uncomfortably alongside demands for equal pay, it is still a
concept that underpins the approach of many trade unions. However, as Coote
and Campbell point out themselves, the family wage has always been a reality
for only a small proportion of the workforce. It has also been significantly
undermined by high male unemployment and an increasing number of
female 'breadwinners-in-chief'. Rather than seeing the ideology of the family
wage as the one key cause of division, it should be seen as one of the important
factors which support the hierarchical divisions of the labour market.
Although the hierarchical divisions of the labour market may be legitimized by
the ideology of the family wage, the divisions cannot be totally explained by
it.

This is to suggest that the key difference of interests between men and
women results from the hierarchy of labour based on gender divisions. The
labour market is divided with a bottom layer made up of those occupations
classed as manual unskilled work, such as hospital ancillary work. This layer is
internally divided within employment by grading structures which enable the
maintenance of a bottom tier of jobs occupied solely by women. In the case of
hospital ancillary workers, this consists of the catering assistants and domestic
service assistants or cleaners. While there may be some mobility at the margins,
with some possibilities for promotion within grading structures, the detailed
analysis of the ancillary grading structures will demonstrate that although
there are divisions among male workers, there is for men the possibility of
moving up this hierarchy, even without formally gaining promotion. In contrast, women workers never move up the grading structure without gaining
formal promotion, and have very rare opportunities for promotion. Moreover,
in the case of hospital ancillary work, men never enter the hierarchy of the
grading structure at the very bottom, whatever their skills or lack of skills.

There is a band of occupations at the bottom of this hierarchy of labour from which there is no route upwards, where skills are undervalued, where pay is the lowest, where there is much part-time work – where women work. This pattern within hospital ancillary work exemplifies a general pattern to be found in employment.

This hierarchy of labour has been developed and maintained through two processes in which male-dominated trade unions have played a key part. These two processes are the systematic exclusion of women from certain occupations and the definition of skill which is in part socially constructed and which devalues the skills that women hold (Phillips and Taylor 1980, Coyle 1982, Lever 1988).

The debate around the nature of skill is not the prime focus here, although it is a key feature in the maintenance of a hierarchically divided workforce. This work broadly supports the position of Phillips and Taylor who argue that:

> ... the classification of women's jobs as unskilled and men's jobs as skilled or semi-skilled frequently bears little relation to the actual amount of training or ability required for them. Skill definitions are saturated with sexual bias. The work of women is often deemed inferior simply because it is women who do it. Women workers carry into the workplace their status as subordinate individuals, and this status comes to define the value of the work they do. Far from being an objective economic fact, skill is often an ideological category imposed on certain types of work by virtue of the sex and power of the workers who perform it. (Phillips and Taylor 1980: 79)

Obviously not all women work in the band of occupations at the bottom of the labour market hierarchy. With the growth of female professions such as teaching and nursing, there are sectors of employment where women may move up internal professional hierarchies. However, even in professions numerically dominated by women, the internal hierarchies reflect and reproduce the hierarchies of the whole labour market, with men in the most senior positions and frequently women from ethnic minorities in the lowest positions without a career structure. Equally, some women do progress within male-dominated occupations. Proposals for positive action in employment have been specifically aimed at increasing the employment of women within male-dominated occupations (Robarts, Coote and Ball 1981, Stamp and Robarts 1986, Coyle and Skinner 1988). However, such a programme is unlikely to cause a challenge to the basic structure of the labour market.

Individual firms and individual occupations or professions reflect the hierarchical structure of the labour market as a whole. Trade unions played a role in establishing this hierarchical structure, and operate on an assumption of its maintenance. Beale (1982) argues that differentials are often maintained by men at women's expense. Colling and Dickens found resistance among men to changes to the traditional division of labour:

> We came across instances where changes had been made, particularly in respect of regrading of jobs to better reflect women's skills, which had upset the men who had been made relatively worse off. (Colling and Dickens 1989: 37)

In short, the fundamental difference lies in the hierarchy of labour divided by sex. It follows from this that trade unionism has developed in such a way as to reflect and reproduce that labour market.

Historical background

This particular form of the labour market developed with industrial capitalism, in part shaped by early trade unions, and based on pre-existing sexual divisions. As trade unions grew they reflected and reproduced a labour market divided by sex. Thus the two strands of this argument, the fundamental difference of interest and the restricted trade union agenda are interconnected and have long historical roots.

Hartmann's argument pays significant attention to the issue of job segregation in explaining the continuing subordination of women (Hartmann 1979a). She argues that the form of the labour market cannot be seen as a pure function of capital, and identifies the need to look at the role of organized male labour in shaping it.

> Historically, male workers have been instrumental in limiting the participation of women in the labour market. Male unions have carried out the policies and attitudes of the earlier guilds, and have continued to reap benefits for male workers. Capitalists inherited job segregation by sex, but they have quite often been able to use it to their own advantage. If they can supersede experienced men with cheaper women, so much the better; if they can weaken labor by threatening to do so, that's good too; or, if failing that, they can use those status differences to reward men, and buy their allegiance to capitalism with patriarchal benefits, that's okay too. (Hartmann 1979a: 229)

While not suggesting a simple functional relationship, or that male workers are totally responsible for the divisions in the labour market, it can be noted that they have played a key role in its development and that trade unionism has been shaped by this process. The maintenance of control in the early craft organizations necessitated the maintenance of divisions within the working class. Power for the craft worker lay in control over the supply of labour and exclusion of all unskilled labour. However, capitalist relations were based in pre-existing sexual hierarchies of power. Gender relations were transformed, but not destroyed. It could be argued that with the rise of capitalist production, the necessity to exclude unskilled labour became largely synonymous with the necessity to exclude female labour. Marx (1977) argues that the development of machinery enabled employers to replace male workers with cheap female and child labour. This misunderstands the importance of gender in mediating capitalist developments. In most industries this simple substitution did not take place, yet the threat of substitution did provide employers with a tool to break down the resistance of male workers to capitalist developments (Drake 1984).

In feudal society, women's entry into certain craft work had been carefully controlled and restricted (Hutchins 1978, Pinchbeck 1981, Clark 1982). The separation of home and work reinforced the difference between male and female labour. From the point of view of the organized male worker, female labour threatened wage levels and the ability to combine against the introduction of new technology. Male workers were faced with a choice to fight for equal pay for women, or to fight to exclude women. In the context of the developing middle-class Victorian ideology of domesticity, it is not surprising that the majority of male workers chose the latter (Liddington and Norris 1978, Drake 1984, Bradley 1989). Although working men sometimes attempted to emulate the middle class Victorian ideal of the dependent wife in the home, the reality for most women was endless childbearing, taking in of work and poverty.

While the basic division among the working class underpinned by craft organization was that between skilled and unskilled workers, the almost total exclusion of women from skilled work and from craft organizations created women workers as an easily identifiable threat. The concepts of skilled and unskilled cannot be understood by reference to gender alone, but equally they cannot be understood outside of an historical context in which female labour meant unskilled labour, even if unskilled labour did not necessarily mean female labour. Where women were employed in auxiliary occupations, craft workers frequently encouraged them to form their own unions or to form women's sections of the craft union. However, this was often used as a better means of controlling the supply of women's labour, rather than to represent their interests and improve working conditions (Gurnham 1976).

Hartmann shows how the development of the hierarchical labour market was very much the result of struggle, with the various groups having a different impact at different stages in the process:

> Thus, in periods of economic change, capitalists' actions may be more instrumental in instituting or changing a sex-segregated labor force – while workers fight a defensive battle. In other periods male workers may be more important in maintaining sex-segregated jobs; they may be able to prevent the encroachment of, or even drive out, cheaper female labor, thus increasing the benefits to their sex. (Hartmann 1979a: 230)

The representation of women's interests was by definition excluded from the early craft unions. For women, organization was based on control, not representation. Even when unions considered questions of health and propriety, it was usually used to exclude women from certain industries, not to improve conditions (John 1984). The organization of unskilled workers in the 1880s into the massive general unions was predominantly the organization of male unskilled workers in the industrial sectors where few women were employed, although here too female labour was regarded as a threat, and attempts were made to exclude women. However, there was a growth in unionization among women workers at this time. Many small unions of women workers were organized with the assistance of the Women's Trade Union League (Drake 1984). It could be argued that these unions did articulate the interests of women workers and they achieved some improvements in wages and conditions of work. As they were absorbed into mixed unions, so women's interests were gradually submerged into a more general framework based on male interests (Drake 1984 and Boston 1980). Few of the male and mixed trade unions articulated the interests of women workers, who were regarded as presenting a potential threat to wage levels. An agenda of issues appropriate to trade unions had always excluded women's interests and developed around the maintenance of division among the working class.

This brief history of trade unionism obviously offers a simplified account of a complex situation. It points to the relationship between two processes and their gender-specific nature, that is, the development of a form of unionism based on divisions within the working class, and the development of a hierarchical, gender-divided labour market. This is a claim that the hierarchic nature of the labour market based on gender divisions is the underlying problem of women's employment. Further, the nature of trade unionism does not enable a challenge to that structure. In other words, the difference of interests between men and women stems from the nature of the labour market, and trade unionism has developed on the basis of its maintenance. The aim of the remainder of this chapter is to consider the implications of this argument.

The Scope and Limitations of Trade Unionism

This section connects the arguments made in this chapter so far with those in the previous chapter, linking the argument about the representation of women's concerns in the workplace to wider theoretical issues. As indicated, the labour market is divided by sex, with women disproportionately occupying those jobs which are defined as unskilled, and which are low paid and part-time. Occupational segregation has been particularly persistent in manual work (Hakim 1981, Rees 1992). In these circumstances, trade unions, at best, are only prepared to take up issues specifically relevant to women where they do not challenge the basic structure of the labour market. This then frequently excludes challenges to grading structures and equal value claims which question the skill definitions which undervalue women's skills.

There is no attempt to denigrate either the real attempts of some male trade unionists to represent women members, or the importance of the women's movement in affecting trade union practice. However, it is important to make a realistic assessment of the importance of union reforms so far, and the future potential of unions in their representation of women's interests. There is a vast array of very important issues which do not challenge the basic structure of the labour market but which have important implications for women workers. In these areas there is some potential to improve the representation of women's interests. However, the restricted trade union agenda also results in the exclusion of a whole range of issues relevant to women workers.

It could be contended that there are examples which suggest that the argument of the exclusion of women's interests is overstated. Such an example might be the trade union demonstration in support of women's rights to abortions.

> One of the most dramatic manifestations of union support for women's demands was the TUC's official demonstration against the restrictive abortion Bill introduced into Parliament by John Corrie, Conservative MP for Bute and Ayrshire North. When some 80,000 women and men marched from Marble Arch to Trafalgar Square on 31 October 1979, it was the largest trade union demonstration ever held for a cause which lay beyond the traditional scope of collective bargaining; it was also the biggest ever pro-abortion march. (Coote and Campbell 1982: 147)

Such supportive actions are very rare, but do show that there is potential to extend the trade union agenda, although it could be claimed that this action was possible because it was not linked to the workplace and therefore entailed no challenge to the hierarchy of labour. While it appears unlikely that such numbers of trade unionists could be mobilized on such an issue in the 1990s, the nature of trade unionism does not totally preclude such action. Coote and Campbell's conclusions are in line with the argument made here:

> The defeat of Corrie's Bill has been one of the trade unions' few *major, tangible* achievements for women ... But we have yet to see convincing signs that they have the capacity to mount an effective challenge to the traditional distribution of jobs and pay between women and men. [their emphasis] (Coote and Campbell 1982: 148–9)

Trade unions cannot mount this challenge to the distribution of jobs and pay, because such a challenge would in itself challenge the nature of trade unionism. It could be argued that trade unions are indeed taking on this challenge, by negotiating the removal of the lowest grades and negotiating for flat-rate pay increases. Such strategies may reduce differentials and have been forced on unions keen to recruit women members; however, such measures do not affect the basic form of the labour market, as will be demonstrated with reference to hospital ancillary workers. In some cases there is now slightly less distance between men and women at the bottom of the labour market hierarchy, although women are still located at the bottom of the hierarchy. In this way unions are able to support equal pay claims which in no way challenge the structure of the labour market, but have greater difficulty with equal value claims which may begin to challenge this structure and the nature of skill.

Divisions of Race

The prevalence of racism, both institutionally and individually in employment and trade unions, is generally acknowledged. So far this chapter has outlined the process by which men dominate in the hierarchies of labour and men's interests dominate within trade unions. However, it is necessary to integrate an understanding of the implications of racial and sexual divisions in the workplace, and the ways in which trade unions play a role in reproducing both forms of division.

Much of the literature on women and unions referred to previously either ignores the position of black women, or briefly concludes that whatever the situation for women in general, it will be worse for black women (Coote and Kellner 1980, Aldred 1981, Ellis 1981, Beale 1982). Moreover, the literature on black workers and trade unions deals almost solely with male black workers (Labour Research Department 1985, Wrench 1986a, Gow 1987, Allen 1987, Labour Research 1988b). Few studies incorporate discussions of both gender and race (Hoel 1982, Phizacklea 1983, Westwood 1984, Cunnison and Stagemen 1993, Leah 1993, Wrench and Virdee 1996).

It has been argued previously that there are certain ways in which unions can improve their representation of women members and other areas where there has been less progress because of underlying contradictions. In relation to black women, one issue which unions can take up is recognition. Union recognition is obviously beneficial for the union, because it offers the potential for increasing membership numbers. Recognition disputes provide unions with the opportunity to show their support of workers in the more insecure sectors of the labour market at relatively little cost, although they provide no challenge to the structure of the labour market. This is not to underestimate the importance of such recognition disputes. Such disputes may also be important in dismissing stereotypical assumptions about the submissiveness of black women. However, it is important to recognize that much of the literature which does refer to black women concentrates on one or two well-known recognition disputes (Dromey and Taylor 1978, Wrench and Virdee 1996).

As already indicated, the hierarchical sexual divisions of the labour market have crucial implications for unionism. In a similar vein it should be noted that the labour market is also divided racially. It is, however, necessary to understand that racial divisions exist in a context of a sexually segregated labour market. Research has provided evidence of a number of effects of racism in the labour market, some of these with trade union collusion or even instigation (Wrench 1986b, Ohri and Faruqi 1988). Black workers have to make more job applications than white workers before they get accepted for a job; black workers on average earn less than white workers and are more likely to work unsocial hours than white workers; black workers are more likely to be working on unpleasant or arduous tasks than white workers, and suffer disproportionately from unemployment (Smith 1977, Brown 1984, Ohri and Faruqi 1988, Modood 1997). The literature, however, fails to investigate whether all these factors affect black men and black women equally. In the 1970s Smith argued that the distance, in terms of pay, between white and black male workers was greater than the distance between white and black female workers (Smith 1977). A TUC report concludes that black and white women tend to receive the same low pay in relation to white men (TUC 1987). This conclusion has been challenged by Bruegel, who argues that

> ... where black women are concerned other factors, primarily racism as it affects unemployment and the earning levels of both black men and women, are at least as important in determining women's place in the labour market. The existing literature structured as it is by standard categorizations of occupations and by standard approaches to gathering information, especially through household surveys, presents a false picture of the position of black women in relation to white. Both groups of women are affected by sexual discrimination in labour markets, but black women are also subject to racial discrimination, much of which remains hidden by conventional approaches to the gathering and analysis of labour market information. (Bruegel 1989: 63)

Bruegel thus offers a very useful contribution to the debate, and provides an important warning against the assumption of similar experiences of black and white women.

Wrench indicates that active struggle over the attempted exclusion of black workers is most prevalent in skilled male areas of work:

> ... members of craft unions in particular have long been willing to practise racial discrimination. Lee and Wrench (1983) found resistance to black co-workers particularly strong in skilled areas, for example, in toolroom, maintenance and sheet metal working areas. (Wrench 1986a: 10)

It is here that there is most to lose and most to gain by the exclusion of black workers; it is here that male workers are practised at using exclusionary tactics and protection of sectional interests. The sorts of strategies used may include word-of-mouth recruitment to control labour supply, skill differentials to maintain an under-class of workers, or grading divisions to force one group to absorb fluctuations in 'manpower' requirements.

Structural effects of racism in the labour market may in certain situations be different for black men and black women. In the manual labour force, there may be a tendency for greater horizontal racial segregation of the female labour force, and greater vertical racial segregation of the male labour force. This means black and white women are more likely to be segregated by shift, department or factory, while black and white men are more likely to be segregated by grade and pay levels. This situation results from the lack of hierarchy in women's manual work, which means that there is little to fight for or defend. It is important, however, to remember that this argument is not intended to deny the racial discrimination which black women experience in the labour market.

This discussion suggests that among men there is more struggle over access to better jobs, therefore in terms of fighting racism, the issues raised for trade unions are those of recruitment, promotion and training. However, for women, the issues raised are more concerned with concentration within an already concentrated labour market:

> ... there are regional and racial variations whereby Asian women are confined to even more specific sections of the labour market. They are over-represented in the low paid unskilled and semi-skilled sector, where most Asian women are to be found working as machinists in the clothing industry, in laundries, light engineering factories, the hosiery industry, in canteens, as cleaners, and also as homeworkers. (Parmar 1982: 247)

Having argued that there is an underlying limitation to the representation of women's interests in trade unions based on conflicts over the sexual segregation of the labour market, the concentration of black women in this bottom section of the labour market makes this limitation of particular significance to black women. Wrench (1986a) argues that trade unions are only tackling the problems of black workers if they are those also faced by white workers. This may be true for male workers; however, unions tend not to tackle problems faced by white women workers. This suggests that issues specifically affecting black women workers may be even further from the union agenda. Wrench criticizes unions for failing to act 'on issues such as under-representation in certain areas of work, promotion, the differential impact of redundancies or racial abuse' (Wrench 1986a: 10).

Of course, these are very important issues for black men and women. What is of crucial importance to women generally, and particularly to black women, however, is the over-representation at the bottom of the labour market. As Wrench and Virdee (1996: 241) describe, black women workers are 'concentrated in these "poor work" sectors, and they raise a whole extra set of issues with regard to union policies'. Where the workforce is divided hierarchically on gender and race lines, there is also the possibility that white women workers may form coalitions with male workers in the defence of their interests at the expense of black women workers. Even if unions were to act on all of the issues discussed by Wrench, it would not challenge the basic structure of the labour market which keeps women at the bottom of a hierarchy with no route out of it.

Unions are beginning to tackle some of the issues identified by Wrench. In 1996 a group of male Asian and Afro-Caribbean workers at Ford of Dagenham won a case on the grounds of racial discrimination. They had been excluded from the well-paid truck drivers' jobs through a 'fathers and sons' recruitment policy. The case was supported by the TGWU, despite the white drivers also being TGWU members. They have since left the union to join the small United Road Transport Union. This indicates how the racialization of job hierarchies feeds divisions between workers and between union members. Yet this example also illustrates a case in which a trade union has been prepared to challenge the structure of the labour market.

Despite the many common interests of black and white women, the degree of racial conflict among women at the bottom of the labour market should not be underestimated. Because one aspect of the restructuring of the labour force is the shift from full-time to part-time working, black women who are more likely than white women to work full-time, are a particular target. Also, as unemployment rises, there are struggles occurring at the bottom of the labour market, not over who gets which job, but who gets any job. While black and white women workers may share an interest in challenging the hierarchically divided labour market, they are also divided. In some situations they have different interests and there is a need for an awareness of the specific effects of racism on the occupational structure. This obviously has important implications for trade unions, especially in the way which they represent sectional interests which reflect divisions based on race in the workplace.

Summary

In this chapter the argument has been outlined that trade unionism operates in a way which maintains a hierarchy of labour, in which women are disadvantaged and which precludes the full representation of women's interests. Any understanding of trade unionism also requires an examination of the racial and gender composition of employment. Since the central aim of this research is to investigate the relationship between divisions in the workplace and trade union organization, it will look in detail at the racial and gender composition of a number of workplaces, investigating the causes of division and unity. It also considers local union organization at each of these workplaces, assessing the degree to which union organizations reflect and reproduce divisions in the workplace, and investigating how these divisions are reproduced through a restricted trade union agenda.

In practice, it is likely that only certain types of interest will be taken up within unions. To make the case, the research looks in detail at the organization of local union branches, critically examining the way in which issues are defined and raised, relating representation to divisions among the workforce.

The effectiveness of the representation of women members' problems in the different union branches is compared. Despite underlying limitations, there is considerable scope for the improvement of the representation of women's interests. The research concludes with a consideration of how that improvement might be achieved. The wider theoretical issues discussed in this chapter are linked to the experience of individual workplace organization.

3 HOSPITAL WORK AND TRADE UNIONS

This chapter provides the setting for the empirical research discussed in the remainder of the book. The first section describes hospital work generally, identifying the hierarchical nature of all occupations in the NHS. In the second part the detail of hospital ancillary work is examined, including the historical background to the organization of ancillary work. This discussion highlights the way in which the continual pressure on the cost of wages within the NHS has led to a particular focus on women's ancillary work. The initial research was based around two branches of NUPE and two branches of COHSE, and the background to each of these unions is discussed. Finally a description of the case study hospitals and union branches involved in this research is provided.

The rationale for studying hospital ancillary work is that it provides an ideal setting for an analysis of the problems raised in Chapters 1 and 2. Prior to the formation of NHS trusts from 1991, the NHS was the largest single employer of manual women workers in work which is low paid, regarded as unskilled and low grade, and where there are also high levels of part-time working. The focus of the study is on two ancillary occupations, catering and cleaning, which also reflect the types of work women perform unpaid as domestic labour. A study of representation within unions of women members requires high levels of union membership among women, and this too is found among hospital ancillary workers.

Hospitals vary vastly depending on location, size and specialty which makes the comparative approach, basing the research at a number of carefully selected hospitals, necessary. In addition, the main recruiting union among ancillary workers varies from area to area. Therefore, the initial choice of hospitals also provided the basis for a comparison of trade union branches, initially involving two trade unions. In 1993, NUPE and COHSE combined with the National and Local Government Officers Association (NALGO) to form UNISON, which provides a particularly interesting context in which to research women's involvement, since equal opportunities were established as one of its central policy issues. The early 1990s also saw the development of NHS trusts. Three of the union branches were revisited during the 1990s, enabling a long-term study of workplace organization spanning a period of dramatic change to both work and trade unions.

Hospital Work

Hospitals differ enormously, not only for medical and nursing staff, but also for ancillary staff. For example, where there is an outpatients department it cannot be cleaned during the day and this necessitates the employment of many evening staff. Where there is an accident and emergency department large numbers of nursing and medical staff working in the evening need adequate catering facilities at all hours. Further, if a hospital is located in the country-side, staff cannot be brought in for a couple of hours a day to cover peaks of activity such as meal times, rather they are employed over a longer period of the working day. The one constant feature of the health service is its clearly delineated hierarchical structure. There is a status hierarchy among specialties with general and acute at the top, and psychiatric, geriatric and mental handicap care at the bottom. More importantly, there is a very clear occupational hierarchy within the hospital. At the top of this structure are the senior administrators, managers and consultants, often preoccupied with professional autonomy and authority, how money is allocated and how the hospital is run. They are closely followed by the remainder of the 'curing' medical profession, who are separated in power and status from the 'caring' nursing staff. A variety of clerical, and professional and technical staff exist on the fringe of this hierarchy, while at the bottom are the ancillary workers.

In 1980 there was a total of 835,582 staff employed in the NHS in England, nursing staff accounting for nearly half of this. Ancillary workers were the next largest group with over a fifth of the total, in terms of whole time equivalents (WTE). By 1986, the total number of staff had risen, yet the proportion of ancillary staff had dropped to 15.5 per cent. It should be noted that if the figures are translated into actual numbers rather than whole time equivalents, ancillary workers would appear to constitute a larger proportion of the workforce and the reduction of ancillary jobs would appear even larger. Because of the frequency of part-time work among these groups, the use of whole time equivalent figures masks the actual numbers of workers. There was a general shift towards part-time working during the mid 1980s. By 1992 an

Table 2. *NHS Workforce – England WTE*

	Total staff	Ancillary staff	Ancillary staff as percentage of total
1980	835,582	171,967	20.6
1986	850,000	124,267	15.5
1992	849,408	78,995	9.3

Source: Health and Personal Social Statistics.

enormous loss of jobs in NHS ancillary work resulted in a whole time equivalent staff of 78,995, down to 9.3 per cent of total staffing in the NHS (Health and Personal Social Statistics).

The workforce is divided by class, race and gender, and each profession has its own very complex internal hierarchies, again based on class, race and gender. On the basis of family and educational background, Doyal (1979) identified doctors as predominantly 'upper middle-class', and the unskilled and semi-skilled ancillary workers as 'working-class'. Although 75 per cent of workers in the Health Service are women, only about 20 per cent of doctors are women. Within the medical profession, women are disproportionately represented in the lower level posts (Doyal 1979). Nursing has traditionally been a female occupation, although now approximately 10 per cent of nurses are male (Witz 1992). There have always been more men in psychiatric nursing, but their numbers are also increasing in general nursing, and despite their small numbers, men are disproportionately represented in the higher posts in nursing.

During the post-war years of full employment and health service expansion, migrant workers were drawn into the NHS labour force in all occupations. Doyal found that in 1978 more than a third of NHS doctors were born overseas, but that they were disproportionately represented in the lower level posts and in the low-status specialties (Doyal *et al.* 1980). Despite the lack of statistical information on nurses, Doyal suggests that overseas-born nurse learners are more likely to be found in the low-status psychiatric and geriatric hospitals. They were also more likely to have been State Enrolled Nurses (SENs), the less prestigious qualification which did not automatically lead to a place in the career structure of the nursing hierarchy, a grade which has now been removed.

There is even less information on the racial composition of the ancillary workforce. No national figures are available, and it seems that regional variations are so great that individual ancillary departments may have no staff

Table 3. *NHS Ancillary staff – England WTE*

	Total 1980	Total 1990	Percentage reduction
Domestics	68,579	33,861	50.6
Catering	40,436	20,815	48.5
Porters	23,639	16,821	28.8

Source: Health and Personal Social Statistics.

born overseas, or they may have 100 per cent staff born overseas. Manual work tends to be sensitive to local labour markets, resulting in such sharp differences. This makes generalizations from small-scale research almost impossible. Despite these problems research indicates that each occupation within the NHS is composed predominantly of one group delineated according to gender and place of birth, thus indicating the importance of divisions based on race and gender to employment in the NHS (Cousins 1988).

Hospital Ancillary Work

In the past ancillary workers ranged in occupations from laundry workers to shoemakers, from telephonists to waitresses, but the largest single group are the cleaners, in domestic services departments, with catering staff and porters the next largest groups. Catering staff are less homogeneous than the domestic services departments, with a greater range of grades, from dining room assistants (waitresses) to head cooks and superintendents. While domestic services departments tend to be overwhelmingly female, there are usually some men employed in catering departments, usually as cooks/chefs or superintendents. The next largest group under the ancillary umbrella are the porters, the largest group which is predominantly male and where part-time work is rare. Total ancillary staff numbers were increasing up to 1982, and thereafter declined.

All three departments experienced considerable declines in staffing. In domestic service departments, despite an increase up to 1982, staffing had fallen dramatically by 1986. Because of the preponderance of part-time working, this represents an enormous loss of actual jobs – 30,000 cleaners' jobs were lost between 1982 and 1986. Among those still with jobs, the general trend towards part-time working also had the most significant effect within cleaning departments. Since 1990 statistics on the make-up of the ancillary workforce are no longer regularly produced. The reorganization of ancillary work, particularly generic working and privatization, makes it increasingly difficult to accurately identify specific groups of ancillary workers.

Historical background to ancillary work

From the formation of the National Health Service in 1948 (following the National Health Service Act in 1946), the cost of funding has escalated, a major source of concern to all governments. The bulk of these rising costs were made up of increasing wage bills as the labour force grew (National Board for Prices and Incomes (NBPI) 1971, Manson 1977, Dimmock 1977). A dual problem developed: the need to cut expenditure and also the need to be seen to be responding to problems of low pay. This remained the central issue in the health service up to the 1980s. During the 1980s rising unemployment and a hostile industrial relations climate transformed power relations in the health service, enabling a series of managerial reorganizations and cost-cutting exercises aimed primarily at ancillary staff. The 1990s heralded some of the most dramatic organizational changes to the NHS as a whole.

The 1960s

Hospital work is labour-intensive, and nowhere is this more evident than in the patterns of expansion of nurses and ancillary workers. Between 1949 and 1953, staffing levels of nurses and ancillary workers were rising proportionately faster than the number of occupied beds in the health service (Williams *et al.* 1977). The hospital sector was becoming more labour-intensive. As Manson points out, in such a labour-intensive service, if costs were to be cut, staffing levels had to be a prime target, especially those of nurses and ancillary workers, the two largest groups of workers (Manson 1977). As a part of the 'Hospital Plan' of 1962, capital expenditure was more than doubled in an attempt to reduce labour costs. Although this did put more pressure on management to maximize labour efficiency, it did not have the desired effect of reducing staffing levels. By the mid 1960s, the Labour Government was under pressure to cut public expenditure through the reorganization of various sections of the Welfare State (Balfour 1972). At the same time, workers in the public sector took the brunt of a series of statutory incomes policies and wage freezes. It was these same public sector workers who were suffering not only from very low pay, but from falling wages in real terms.

In 1966, the government referred to the National Board for Prices and

Incomes the question of the pay and conditions of service of ancillary workers in the NHS (Balfour 1972). At the time, there were 266,000 ancillary staff in England, Wales and Scotland with an annual wage bill of £142 million. The report revealed that full-time male workers in the NHS ancillary sector had fared badly compared with comparable workers in the private sector, and compared with other public sector workers. They were, in fact, among the lowest paid male workers in the country. The report suggested that the main reason for low pay was the lack of opportunity to extend basic pay through overtime or incentive bonuses (National Board for Prices and Incomes 1966). The report also found that women ancillary workers were better paid than men ancillary workers in relation to the average for all industries. Although within the health service women were paid much less than men, they were actually better off than women with comparable jobs in the private sector. So the concern with low pay became a concern with men's low pay.

The report recommended that improvements in pay and productivity should be achieved through incentive bonus schemes. It may not have been an overt intention of the report, but the implication of it was to improve the pay of men ancillary workers by rationalizing the work of women ancillary workers. This is one of the first indications of the particular vulnerability of women's ancillary work to rationalization. The report also criticized management techniques, or lack of them, in the NHS, and the conflict in authority between administrative, medical and nursing services. Through a number of reorganizations, this conflict over the 'right to manage' has been an enduring controversy.

Although the report did not have an immediate wide-ranging effect, it was important, firstly, in identifying management inefficiency as a problem, and, secondly, in establishing a basis for local negotiations in a service where all previous negotiations had been handled at national level in the Whitley Councils. Another implication of the introduction of work study and incentive schemes was the need for greater functional control of ancillary work. The Salmon Report had already recommended that nurses should be relieved of non-nursing duties, such as supervising ancillary workers on the ward (Manson 1977). The creation of separate departments with functional management transformed the nature of control and organization in ancillary work. It meant that ancillary staff were controlled through departmental line management rather than by the ward matrons to whom they had been responsible previously. This gave ancillary workers, especially the cleaners, greater identification with their ancillary department than with individual wards.

Despite the recommendations, very few incentive schemes were introduced, or fully introduced. The unions had an ambivalent attitude towards them.

They began very much in favour, but as the progress remained slow and increases in pay minimal, they retracted their co-operation. Manson (1977) argues that the bonus schemes also provided workers with a new sense of 'group consciousness' and 'awareness of their job' which were important in the stimulation of a trade union consciousness. Trade union membership did increase rapidly during this period among ancillary workers. However, there needs to be some caution about seeing this growth of membership as an outburst of work consciousness. Mailly, Dimmock and Sethi (1989) suggest that it was not the introduction of bonus schemes alone that led to local bargaining, while Fryer (1989) outlines a variety of reasons for the growth of union membership at this time. The functional departments created clear work groups, but served to highlight certain divisions among staff. Furthermore, it is important to remember the role of management in the development of trade unionism. The introduction of a bonus scheme depended on the co-operation of the workforce, and management recognized the advantages of a friendly trade union with which to negotiate and which would explain the system to the workforce. The growth of unionism at this time cannot be seen merely as a result of a more widespread trade union consciousness among workers. The introduction of bonus schemes meant an increased role for local negotiations between management and unions, and enhanced the position of local union officers. Industrial relations were transformed in the health service; but it would be a mistake to overemphasize the impact on most ancillary workers.

The 1970s

By the end of the 1960s, it was obvious that neither incomes policies nor plans for incentive schemes were going to do much for the low-paid ancillary workers. The hoped for cuts in expenditure on staff wages had not been achieved, while anger increased among public sector workers, whose wages had been further eroded by pay policies (Balfour 1972). With ancillary workers now better organized in trade unions and through the threat of industrial action, their case was again referred to the National Board for Prices and Incomes in 1970. The new Conservative Government aimed to keep wage increases below ten per cent, and took a particularly firm stand in the public sector. However, there was a wage explosion in the private sector, and as prices rose rapidly, demands for high increases in the public sector rose. The miners claimed 33 per cent and received 12 per cent, electricity workers claimed 25 per cent and obtained a productivity deal which meant 10–15 per cent.

The NBPI report assessed progress on the introduction of incentive schemes and work study, and concluded by criticizing both management and unions for their failure to speed up progress towards improvements in pay and efficiency (National Board for Prices and Incomes 1971). The report criticized the structure of NHS budgeting for not providing a stimulus to greater efficiency, and the lack of clearly defined managerial responsibility, with administrators lacking personnel experience and functional managers lacking training in management techniques. Scientific management had yet to take off in the health service. Where incentive schemes had been introduced, managers were again criticized for a failure to follow through with continued control.

Where an incentive scheme was not continually reviewed and re-negotiated, the impetus to active trade unionism also faded. Some areas already had a nucleus of active trade unionists, typically white and male, and this continued, but the spread of 'active trade unionism' to the bulk of ancillary workers was limited. At one of the hospitals studied in this research, an interim bonus scheme had been introduced for the domestic services department during the early 1970s. However, it was never followed up by a fully work-studied scheme, and the impact on trade unionism among domestic staff was minimal.

The NBPI report is important because it articulates the desire to gain the co-operation of trade unions, and criticizes them for their lack of enthusiasm. The report estimates union membership among hospital ancillary workers to be 70 per cent for full-time male workers, 60 per cent for full-time women workers and 40 per cent for part-time women workers. As with previous government reports, concern is expressed about the men ancillary workers only, despite the fact that three-quarters of the workforce are women. The report argues that active trade unionism was limited by the lack of scope for local negotiations, which would be increased by the introduction of local incentive schemes. Both managers and trade unionists were encouraged to become involved with joint consultation and discussion at local levels.

Although the spread of a union consciousness among ancillary workers should not be overestimated, that is not to say that it had not happened at all. There was evidence of increased industrial militancy among these workers, and particularly in the large city hospitals (Carpenter 1988). This develop-ment, however, should not be related too closely to the introduction of bonus schemes. The Industrial Relations Act 1971 had also led to an increase in local negotiations in the NHS, and the number of shop stewards was gradually increasing. The evidence from the hospitals in this research suggests that there was no significant increase in the number of women shop-stewards until the late 1970s and early 1980s.

Ancillary workers' dissatisfaction over pay culminated in what most commentators agree to be a watershed for industrial relations in the NHS, the strike of 1972/73. This first national strike of ancillary workers proved to the workers, to the public and to the government that they had the industrial power not only to close down departments, but whole hospitals. This was later to encourage an industrial relations approach by administrators, which in turn gave administrators more power vis-à-vis the medical profession. Dimmock (1977) argues that the strike also represented the first major challenge by ancillary workers to the medical autonomy of doctors. During the strike, manual workers were deciding what constituted an emergency case, and local discussions over admissions and cover led to an increase in local negotiations. Manual workers' unions were to take a more involved position on the nature of the service (Carpenter 1988). The unions were active in restricting private medicine. In 1974, ancillary staff at Charing Cross Hospital withdrew domestic and hotel facilities in support of their demand that the private wing be closed (Carpenter 1988). During the 1970s other groups of staff also used the strike as a weapon to increase their pay and improve the service. In 1974, nurses, and in 1974/75, junior doctors went on strike. The ancillary workers' pay reached 82 per cent of average male earnings in 1974, the highest point it was to reach. From this point onwards, their pay was to decline relative to the average and dissatisfaction was to continue (Carpenter 1988).

In 1979, the Standing Commission on Pay Comparability produced its first report, the Clegg Report, on Local Authority and University Manual Workers, NHS Ancillary Staffs and Ambulancemen (Clegg 1979). At the time of the report there were 270,000 ancillary workers in Britain, in eighteen separate pay groups. Over 95 per cent of ancillary staff were in the bottom seven grades, and 75 per cent in the bottom three grades. The bottom grade was made up of domestic and catering workers and was completely female. Like previous reports, this one was not concerned with the levels of pay received by women. Women's pay in the private sector was so low that any comparison made public sector pay levels appear high. Militancy was associated with male workers and the concern expressed in the Clegg Report was to satisfy male claims to increase differentials. Despite this, the unions did mount their first real defence of their women members, arguing that the method of pay comparability served to maintain low pay for women. The report rejected the criticism of the unions and largely went on to confirm the arguments of the employers. Its recommendations were mainly in terms of the structure of the grading system and the inefficiency of the 'old' incentive schemes, which it described as being used to supplement low pay but without any true incentive. This meant that the concerns and situation of women ancillary workers were disregarded.

The 1980s

Dissatisfaction over wages erupted again in the 1979/80 'winter of discontent' and continued into the 1980s. Carpenter describes struggles during this period, such as the campaign to keep open the Elizabeth Garrett Anderson Hospital for women. He argues that as soon as the Conservative Government was elected, NHS management felt free to take a more aggressive stance towards unions (Carpenter 1988). The new Conservative Government was to transform industrial relations in the NHS, although the main impact of the changes did not take hold until 1983/84. This turning point was preceded by the largest national strike of all hospital workers, in 1981/82, concerned not only with their pay levels but also the quality of services provided and national funding to the NHS. Pay review bodies were established for nurses, midwives and health visitors, removing them from the Whitley structures (Mailly, Dimmock and Sethi 1989). Although many union activists representing ancillary workers felt demoralized by the strike, which they believed they had lost, and felt they had been let down by their national leadership, ordinary union members became more involved than they had ever been in union activities. Carpenter (1988) claims that thousands of women ancillary workers took their first industrial action ever during this strike and that many women became shop-stewards for the first time. Evidence from this research suggests that local organization was in places strengthened after this dispute, rather than being weakened as Mailly, Dimmock and Sethi suggest.

Although hospital administrators and personnel officers frequently had considerable sympathy with their staff's demands, they were now under increased pressure from the government to cut costs. Management began to take a more adversarial position towards local trade unions (Carpenter 1988). There is an indication from this research that some ancillary services began to be streamlined, with staff hours being cut and new bonus schemes introduced. Pressure from the government to consider the privatization of certain services was also increased (Leedham 1986). Despite a generally more active membership, unions were in a weak position as growing levels of unemployment led members to fear for their jobs.

In the mid 1980s the main tool used by government to force NHS managers to streamline services was privatization, or competitive tendering as it became known. In 1983 the Secretary of State for Social Services issued a circular requiring all health authorities to put hospital cleaning, catering and laundry services out to private tender (Coyle 1985). Health authorities, particularly in Labour areas, were reluctant to move in this direction and frequently placed restrictions on contracts in relation to pay and conditions. In September 1983 the government repealed the Fair Wages Resolutions (which required government contractors to comply with pay and conditions of employment within state enterprises) and instructed authorities not to stipulate pay or conditions of services in contract specifications (Mailly 1986). Where private companies did win contracts, they had some difficulty maintaining quality and profitability (Rees and Fielder 1992). Managers often recognized a certain level of inefficiency in existing departments, yet felt sympathy for their staff. As attempts to privatize led to newspaper reports highlighting industrial disputes, dirty hospitals and even the use of schoolchildren, in-house tenders enabled the reconciliation of conflicting pressures (Cousins 1990). The managers in Cousins' study also saw the contracting-out of ancillary work as a less politically sensitive means of cutting costs, because of the lower public profile of ancillary workers compared to nurses (Cousins 1990). Mailly, Dimmock and Sethi (1989) identify competitive tendering as an effective lever for management to persuade unions to accept a wide range of changes to work organization, intensification, redundancies, cuts in hours and so on. Cousins also describes the dilemma facing trade unions at the time: to negotiate with management over in-house tenders meant the acceptance of new forms of management control and 'self-exploitation', while not to co-operate meant the possibility of loss of jobs and loss of members. A key aspect of the management drive to retain in-house tenders has been an associated desire to increase flexibility of employment (Beechey and Perkins 1987, Fairbrother 1988). In the context of hospital ancillary work, flexibility has meant more bonus schemes and a reduction of hours for women staff, and a speed up in the shift to part-time working. Competitive tendering in the NHS focused particularly on women's ancillary work and has served to reinforce existing gender divisions. The use of competitive tendering has been seen as the key method of reducing costs among ancillary workers, yet, ironically, some managers now see contracted services as hindering the development of generic ancillary work (Lloyd and Seifert 1995, Corby 1996).

During the 1980s there was a considerable shift in power between national government, NHS administrators and senior consultants. The power of the last had been eroded in a number of reorganizations in the NHS, but the introduction of general managers, following the Griffiths Report in 1983, represented a more direct attack on their position. The government's aim to introduce a private sector model of efficiency and productivity was taken a step further with the publication in 1989 of the white papers on the NHS, which introduced the concept of an internal 'free market' of health care. These proposals represented a potential attack on trade unionism in the NHS through the possible removal of national negotiations.

The 1990s

The early 1990s saw the most significant changes to the NHS since 1948. A distinction between purchasers and providers was created with an aim of introducing the freedoms and efficiencies of market relationships. The purchasers, health authorities and GP fund holders, now buy care on behalf of patients. The providers, NHS trusts or directly managed units (DMUs, still under health authority control) compete with one another to provide services at the cheapest price. In 1991, 57 English trusts became operational, and further waves have followed each April since. By April 1995, 98 per cent of NHS services were provided through 502 trusts (Labour Research 1995a). The nature of services provided by trusts varies: they may provide acute care, ambulance services, mental health, community health or a combination of services (Corby 1996). Trusts are run by boards of directors and were given the freedom to determine their own terms and conditions outside of the national system of Whitley Councils and pay review bodies (Lloyd and Seifert 1995). Corby (1996) identifies a number of features which have limited the development of radical changes in relation to terms and conditions. Trusts have found it difficult to move away from Whitley Council structures and the tradition of working with trade unions (IRS Employment Trends 1993). Alongside this, the formation of UNISON in 1993 overcame some divisions between unions, enabling a more coherent union response to trust initiatives. In addition, the political sensitivity to change in the NHS led the government in 1995 to agree with the unions that national awards would continue to provide the framework for local deals until 1998 (Corby 1996). As Transfer of Undertakings (Protection of Employment) Regulations (TUPE) were extended to the public sector, contractors were prevented from changing the terms and conditions of existing staff. However, it is as yet unclear how long they will wait before negotiating changes to terms and conditions (Colling 1995). In the affected departments in the case study organizations, most union concern was focused on changes to pension entitlements.

Despite the restrictions on the actions of human resource managers, a small number of trusts have derecognized trade unions or moved away from national pay arrangements. More common has been the development of a wide range of less sweeping but significant changes such as the development of generic ancillary work and the use of cheaper support workers to carry out work previously done by nurses. Seifert (1992) argues that attempts to introduce payment by results and job evaluation schemes will stimulate local bargaining and predicts a burgeoning of workplace trade union activity. Lilley and Wilson (1994), however, predict that developments in medical technology will enable a 'job massacre', with up to 100,000 redundancies by the year 2000. It is as yet uncertain how these developments will be affected by the election of the Labour Government in May 1997, but as some trusts run into financial difficulties, trust mergers and rationalization seem likely.

Another development affecting the NHS has been the Private Finance Initiative, announced in 1992, aiming to encourage private sector investment in capital projects across the public services (Labour Research 1995b). In return for the investment, the company would gain some benefit, for example the contract to run hotel services in a hospital. In 1995 the government supported the 'DBFO' option, in which the private company would 'design, build, finance and operate' entire projects such as building and running a new hospital including medical services (Labour Research 1996d). Despite considerable initial interest, however, there has been limited progression with this initiative.

These developments raise important questions about the role of NHS trade unions in the 1990s regarding the representation of their women members. It is a context of change, both for the trade unions, and for the organization of work. It is a time when management are attempting to transform the nature of jobs primarily undertaken by women.

Unions in the NHS

Workers in the NHS are represented by a vast array of trade unions and professional associations, where membership size does not necessarily equate with power and influence. The most influential professional associations are the British Medical Association (BMA), the Royal College of Nursing (RCN), and the Royal College of Midwives (RCM). The most powerful of these is the BMA, representing consultants and other doctors. The RCN has begun to span the trade union/professional association divide, by taking on an increasing amount of representational work in the workplace (Carpenter *et al.* 1987, Carpenter 1988).

NALGO was the largest recruiting union for clerical and administrative staff, as well as nursing staff in some areas. The various works and maintenance staff employed in the NHS have their own occupational unions. Ancillary staff were recruited by NUPE and COHSE, and also by the Transport and General Workers' Union (TGWU) and the General, Municipal and Boilermakers Union (GMB). UNISON is now the largest health union, having brought together COHSE, NALGO and NUPE.

There have always been considerable regional variations in union recruitment among nurses and ancillary workers. COHSE recruited all NHS staff, including nursing staff, but only NHS staff. NUPE recruited all staff within the NHS, but tended to be concentrated among ancillary staff. In addition, it recruited public employees outside of the NHS. The two general unions, TGWU and GMB, again are concentrated among ancillary staff, and recruit in the public and private sectors. These latter two unions had only very small memberships among ancillary staffs in the hospitals covered by this research. MSF (Manufacturing, Science and Finance) recruit NHS technical staff, while there is a wide range of professional associations and specialist unions representing smaller groups of workers.

As this description of unions reveals, there is a very complex pattern of union and professional association membership within the NHS. The relative strength of individual unions is much affected by local labour market traditions in union membership. This complex pattern of membership is reflected in a complicated national bargaining machinery. When the NHS was established in 1948, the Ministry of Health organized provision for the national negotiation and representation on behalf of health service employees by the use of Whitley Councils (Vulliamy and Moore 1979). Negotiations concerning pay and conditions of service for all NHS employees take place within these Whitley Councils. There is a total of ten functional Whitley Councils covering all NHS employees, one being the Ancillary Staffs Council. Each council is made up of representatives from management and from staff.

Background to NUPE

NUPE's roots lie in the London County Councils Employees' Protection Society (LCCEPS), which was formed in 1888 with Albin Taylor as president. In 1894 the LCCEPS changed its name to the Municipal Employees' Association (MEA) and in 1907 the MEA split into two parts after conflict between Taylor and the National Executive (Dix and Williams 1987). One part formed a section of what is now the GMB, and the other part with Albin Taylor as General Secretary became the National Union of Corporation Workers (NUCW). In 1928, after another change of name, the National Union of Public Employees (NUPE) was formed.

The union had an enormous expansion of its membership from 11,500 members in 1928 to a peak of 693,097 members in 1978. This growth was particularly dramatic during the 1970s. Between 1968 and 1978, NUPE's membership increased by over 170 per cent. Not only did the union as a whole increase rapidly, but there was also a dramatic rise in female membership. The proportion of women members rose from 24 per cent in 1950 to two-thirds by 1978. Approximately one-third of NUPE's members worked within the NHS, the vast majority of these being ancillary staff, predominantly women workers.

The organization of the membership had been a long-standing concern of the union. A shop-steward system was set up in NUPE in 1967, in response to the NBPI Report 29, in order to deal with workplace negotiations on incentive payment schemes. In 1973 the NUPE National Executive commissioned a report to investigate the structure of NUPE and consider how effective that structure was (Fryer, Fairclough and Manson 1974). As a result, in 1974 a reorganization took place, with the main aims of improving branch level participation and of better reflecting the changing structures of local government. There was a concern with local level organization and how it linked in with the national structures, which demonstrated NUPE's commitment to developing in a way which maximized participation at all levels. This made NUPE a particularly interesting union to study in terms of women's participation.

Background to COHSE

COHSE originated among nursing staff of mental hospitals, an association which continues today with a considerable membership among psychiatric nurses in the NHS. COHSE was formed in 1946 after an amalgamation of the Hospitals and Welfare Services Union (HWSU) and the Mental Hospital and Institutional Workers' Union (MHIWU). The HWSU, formed in 1943, had originated from the Poor Law Workers' Trade Union (PLWTU). The MHIWU had been the National Asylum Workers' Union (NAWU), formed in 1910, which had changed its name after the Mental Treatment Act of 1930 (Carpenter 1988).

In 1980 77 per cent of the members were women. Although COHSE is often associated with nursing members, it claimed 100,000 ancillary members in 1980 and 66,000 in 1989. Individual COHSE branches are usually dominated by either ancillary or nursing staff. A union steward system was introduced in 1972, as a response to the incentive payment schemes for ancillary workers. COHSE estimated that in 1981, 43 per cent of members were nurses and midwives, and 35 per cent ancillary workers (Confederation of Health Service Employees undated a). COHSE's total membership had risen from 64,035 in 1965 to 235,362 by 1982.

Women in NUPE and COHSE

Women's participation within trade unions is increasing, although women's participation rates decrease in the upper levels of union hierarchies. In this section, the position of women in NUPE and COHSE is considered in more detail. Both unions had high proportions of women members. Up to 1981 women's membership of both NUPE and COHSE was growing dramatically, while women as a proportion of the whole membership was also rising. Figures from Labour Research in March 1988 show that the total number of women members in COHSE had continued to rise to 182,000 and the proportion of women members rose to 83 per cent. However, in NUPE the total number of women members had actually fallen to 438,422 and the proportion of women members had slightly fallen to 66 per cent. It is likely that COHSE has maintained its increase in women members through the recruitment of nurse members, while NUPE lost some women members through the rationalization of ancillary services.

Despite the rise in the number of women members up to the early 1980s, the proportion of women at higher levels in both unions was still low in 1981. COHSE had no women on the National Executive Committee. Generally NUPE had higher levels of post-holding by women, although both unions had very small proportions of women full-time officers (Labour Research 1982). Between 1981 and 1985, both unions had made improvements in the proportion of women at these levels, although NUPE actually had a decrease in the percentage of full-time women officials. There appears no obvious explanation for this decrease and it runs counter to initiatives in NUPE at the time (National Union of Public Employees 1984).

Between 1985 and 1988 the number of women post-holders increased, although the rate of increased incumbency slowed down. There was a decline in the proportion of women delegates to the TUC in NUPE. Figures from COHSE in 1989 indicate that the proportion of women full-time officers, including Head Office, was 20 per cent in 1985, rising to 27 per cent by 1989. Also by 1988 both unions had Women's Officers at regional and national levels. It remained the case that at national levels, both NUPE and COHSE were largely dominated and run by men.

Since the formation of UNISON in 1993, considerable attention has been given to the position of women and there have been considerable improvements. By 1997/98, when over a million women members accounted for 78 per cent of the membership, they were 65 per cent of NEC members and 61 per cent of TUC delegates (Labour Research, 1998a). Because of the difficulties of rapidly changing the profile of union employees, women only accounted for

38 per cent of national and 24 per cent of regional full-time officials. However, there are limitations to what participation in such senior posts can indicate about women's participation at lower levels in the union. It is equally, if not more, important to look at the participation of women at lower levels in the union hierarchy. This will also allow the different structures of the organizations to be taken into account.

NUPE

The position of women in NUPE has to be seen in the light of the reorganization in 1975 which resulted from the Warwick Report, which had focused attention on the participation of women members (Fryer, Fairclough and Manson 1974). In 1981, NUPE carried out a survey of Branch District Committees (BDCs) to investigate the impact of the reorganization on women's participation (National Union of Public Employees undated a). It revealed a dramatic increase in the proportion of women shop stewards during the late 1970s, although overall they were still under-represented in proportion to membership figures. In the division covered by this research, the West Midlands, under-representation was only very slight, with 60 per cent of shop-stewards being women and at that time 67 per cent of members being women.

The survey also found that in 1981, 18 per cent of BDC secretaries and 19 per cent of branch chairs were women, whereas in 1977 only 11 per cent of BDC secretaries had been women. At this level too, although still under-represented, women's participation had increased considerably. In 1982, two seats were reserved for women on Divisional Councils. Nationally, women accounted for 53 of the 176 Divisional Council seats, that is 30 per cent. Of a total of 16 seats on each Divisional Council, the number of women varied from two in the Southern and Eastern District, to seven in Northern Ireland. There were five women on the West Midlands Divisional Council, 31 per cent of the total.

In 1982 the National Conference passed a resolution calling on the Executive Council to 'encourage Divisions to set up Women's Advisory Committees'. At this time six of the 11 Divisions had Women's Committees, although the West Midlands Division did not. On the Health Service National Committee in 1983, there were only two women out of a total of 21 seats.

A picture emerges within NUPE of major increases in the participation of women at the level of shop steward, smaller increases at the level of national and divisional posts, and least progress in branch offices and full-time posts, with the West Midlands achieving larger increases than some of the other NUPE regions. A report from the NUPE Women's Working Party in 1984 outlines some of the actions NUPE took to encourage women's participation. These include the appointment of a National Women's Officer and 12 women to the organizing staff, the development of Divisional Women's Advisory Committees and the extension of education courses for women members. It seems likely that these initiatives have been crucial in the increase in women's participation. This increase may also be linked to the growth in industrial action, particularly among hospital ancillary workers in the early 1980s.

COHSE

The number of women members in COHSE exceeded the number of men members for the first time in 1963. Since that time the proportion of women members has increased considerably. In 1976 an Equal Opportunities Committee was set up as well as a special working party of the National Executive Committee to consider women's involvement in the union. COHSE carried out a survey of women's participation above shop steward level (Confederation of Health Service Employees undated b). This report shows that in the 13 regions, the percentage of women acting as branch secretary in 1979 varied from 15 per cent in Northern Ireland and North East Thames and East Anglia, to 37 per cent in the North West. In the West Midlands there were 52 male and 15 female branch secretaries, women making up 22 per cent of the total, which was slightly under the national average. Nationally, there were 601 male and 187 female branch secretaries, making women 24 per cent of the total. In 1989 COHSE claimed further progress with the proportion of women branch secretaries rising from 28 per cent in 1985 to 32 per cent. Women accounted for 40 per cent of branch chairs.

The Equal Opportunities Committee Report included a more detailed study of the North Western Region, which found that the branches with women branch secretaries had an average of 90 per cent women's membership. This is considerably higher than average, and this finding raises a number of questions about the process by which women become or do not become branch officers. The report concluded that

> It could be argued that it is only when a branch has an overwhelming number of women, that women branch secretaries are elected ... women only come forward to be branch secretaries when there is virtually no male

> alternative to take on the job. (Confederation of Health Service Employees
> undated b: 4–5)

In 1985 women accounted for 42 per cent of shop stewards, a statistic that rose to 52 per cent by 1989. This indicates a considerable increase over the period. At branch secretary level, COHSE has had higher percentages of women than NUPE, while COHSE appears to have a poorer record at regional level. One interesting feature is that within COHSE, the West Midlands appears to be average for the whole country, while women's post-holding in NUPE in the West Midlands is significantly above average. COHSE had a greater proportion of women members, which should have led to higher levels of participation by women. In contrast NUPE appears to have given greater attention to the ways in which organization may improve participation.

Both unions were active in attempts to increase the level of participation of their women members. One route this has taken has been the encouragement of women to attend educational courses. COHSE claimed a considerable increase in women's participation on educational courses and NUPE was particularly active in the development of women-only courses and weekend schools for women members.

> NUPE recognises that women need the opportunity of getting together to
> talk about why they are reluctant to become active in the Union and what
> can be done to remedy this ... Special educational facilities for women
> members, which offer an informal, supportive environment run by women
> tutors, are seen by the Union as a way of helping women to play a greater
> part inside NUPE. (National Union of Public Employees undated c: 9)

During the 1980s policy statements coming from the unions at national level certainly indicated a growing concern for improving the participation of their women members.

> More attention is also being placed on the needs of women with regards to
> timing of meetings. It is recognised that more child care facilities are needed
> and meeting times should be adapted to enable parents, and particularly
> single parents, to attend. Discussion of women's questions and issues is
> also encouraged at branch and regional level. (Confederation of Health
> Service Employees undated a: 8)

Within NUPE there were proposals about organizational changes which were needed in order to increase women's participation.

Women's involvement will obviously begin at the workplace. In order for
NUPE to meet the needs of women members who are often in part-time
jobs, working in small dispersed groups, sometimes in shifts there is a need
for a sub-branch structure to be developed to encourage direct involvement
in the Union's business by women members. (Nation Union of Public
Employees undated a: 4)

UNISON

A commitment to equal opportunities is embedded in the constitution of
UNISON. Its core aims are to work for equality of opportunity at work and in
the community, and fair representation in all union structures for all members. The Director of Equal Opportunities described how putting the union's
equality commitment into practice involves three equality objectives:

Proportional representation for women and fair representation for all
members at every level of the union structure; self-organisation for women,
black members, lesbians and gay men and members with disabilities; and
the integration of equality issues in the core bargaining agenda. (Equal
Opportunities Review 1993: 34)

'Proportionality' was developed to enable the number of men and women
on every union body to reflect their proportions in the electorate. The union
set a target of achieving proportionality at all levels by the year 2000. The policy
is considered successful, the proportion of women on UNISON's NEC having
risen from 42 per cent in 1994 to 65 per cent in 1996 (Labour Research 1996a).
Proportionality has now been adopted in a number of other trade unions and
is being acknowledged as a key mechanism for increasing post-holding levels
for women. In addition, there is a separate provision for representation of low-
paid members. UNISON has an objective of achieving fair representation for
all groups within the union, full or part-time workers, manual or non-manual
workers, different occupations, skills, race, sexuality and disability (Equal
Opportunities Review 1993). The principle of self-organization is aimed at
providing women members, black members, lesbian and gay members, and
members with disabilities opportunities to meet together, share concerns and
develop their agenda for the union (McBride 1996).

This chapter has demonstrated the vulnerability of women's work in the
NHS. It has outlined the varying degrees of involvement by women at the
different levels within NUPE and COHSE and the developments since the
formation of UNISON, which is committed to widening the union agenda and

prioritizing equality issues. It appears that UNISON has taken on board the 'long equal opportunities agenda' (Cockburn 1989). However, McBride (1998) highlights some of the limitations of these developments, with self-organized groups failing to develop at branch level. She argues that they remain a top-down initiative with no structural link into decision-making processes. To assess these developments in relation to the issues raised in Chapters 1 and 2, the union branches studied in the 1980s were revisited during the 1990s. To prepare the ground for an analysis of these issues, the final section will look at the case studies included in the research.

The Case Studies

The original research during the 1980s was based on case studies of four hospitals. One closed in 1994 and the remaining three have been revisited during the mid 1990s. NUPE was the main organizing union at two of the hospitals, and COHSE at the other two. Since its formation in 1993, UNISON has become the largest union at all of the hospitals, although locally many active personnel have come from the previously dominant union.

A wide range of research techniques were used during the research. Interviews were carried out with senior and middle management, union branch officers, shop stewards and full-time officials. Surveys were carried out with those shop stewards not directly interviewed and membership surveys were conducted at two of the case study hospitals. Documentation was gathered wherever available from both management and unions. Finally, a series of observations were completed in the hospitals and during union meetings. The hospitals have been given fictitious names in order to preserve the anonymity of those who took part in the research.

Shire General Hospital

Shire is a general hospital in a small town, which was expanding throughout the 1980s having been designated as the District General Hospital. The hospital is made up of a number of low-level buildings, with unimposing entrance, and it appears deceptively small. Newer and older buildings are mixed together, showing the gradual growth of the hospital. Shire General has its roots in the 1834 Poor Law, the Guardians erecting the initial buildings in 1849. The nurses' home was built in 1902 and the main treatment wards and medical staff quarters were added in 1940.

Despite its growth, staffing levels remained stable until the mid to late 1980s at about 500, with 110 ancillary staff (21 per cent), and about 290 beds. Staffing levels grew rapidly during the late 1980s and early 1990s to a peak in 1994. The introduction of day surgery has enabled a reduction of 120 staff to its present level of 1600, with 414 beds. This hospital formed an NHS trust in the third wave, in 1993, along with a smaller hospital. In 1996 there were 170 ancillary staff on the main site, about 11 per cent of all staff. In 1996, after the market testing exercise, contracts for portering and domestic service were awarded to private contractors Mediguard, and contracts for catering were awarded to Mediclean.

In the 1980s this hospital had a small NUPE branch, which was dominated by the regional full-time official, who was also married to a previous branch secretary. Branch leadership was split between female nursing members and male works department members. The branch covered the geographical area of the south part of the county, and branch meetings were held monthly, alternating between Shire and another town fifteen miles away. The senior steward at Shire thought that membership numbers were generally declining, particularly after the 1982 pay dispute. Meetings were held for stewards at Shire as well as the BDC meetings. At the time of the initial research, there were seven shop-stewards at Shire, five ancillary stewards, one from administration and one from the works department. Very little consideration had been given to the involvement of members in this branch; in fact, greatest concern seemed to be about how to restrain the demands of members who had been pushing for more militant action during the 1982 dispute.

By the 1990s most branch officers were women, from nursing or technical backgrounds, although there were shop stewards from all departments. Here a part-time convenor role had just been established, although the person, an ex-clerical worker, was chosen by management rather than by the union.

County Psychiatric Hospital – St Stephen's

County was a traditional style psychiatric hospital, in a rural location two miles from the nearest town. It served an area beyond its Health Authority boundary, having a secure ward as well as usual inpatient and outpatient facilities. County was approached through a Victorian gatehouse and dark tree-lined avenue, which led to the large overbearing buildings of the hospital. It retained a certain Gothic splendour and physically dominated the landscape – a grand Victorian 'madhouse'. County was built in 1849, following the 1845 Lunacy Act, which directed every county to erect asylums and led to the great 19th-century expansion of asylums.

Because of its isolated position, the hospital had traditionally recruited staff from two nearby towns, as well as the nearest city, approximately 12 miles away. A free transport service had been provided by the hospital. In line with the general trend to close psychiatric hospitals in the mid 1980s, there was an expectation that County would be closed. However, it remained open until 1995, although a reduction in the number of inpatient beds had begun, declining from about 600 in the early 1980s to 500 by 1986. As a result of the 1987 Care in the Community Act, a decision was made to increase the role of community services, and to build a new hospital to deal with the most serious cases. St Stephens, the new 90-bed hospital, was built in the town, a comfortable and compact red-brick building with small landscaped gardens. It formed an NHS Trust in 1994. The Trust now has a staff of 600, including the community staff. Along with the dramatic reduction in hospital-based care, the role for ancillary staff, who now make up 2.4 per cent of the total staff, has also decreased.

In the 1980s County had an active COHSE branch with a membership of approximately 500. Some ancillary staff were in a NUPE branch, although COHSE was the largest union for ancillary and nursing staff. The branch officers were all young male student nurses, although they were keen to organize among ancillary workers. Locally, the branch was considered radical because it had been active in the 1982 dispute, and initiated local campaigns linked to NHS services. There were a total of 12 shop stewards, all nursing staff except for one occupational therapist, eight men and four women. Time-off arrangements for union work were frowned upon by management, and shop steward meetings were held monthly, usually in the house of the branch secretary in the evening. Branch meetings were held at various times, such as lunchtime and after work. The branch had been making an effort to find a time when more members would attend, but attendance remained low.

This branch was the least formal in terms of the way in which it operated. The main problem for organization in this branch was its reliance on student activists. Once qualified, there was no guarantee that they would be able to get jobs at County and so it was impossible to achieve any stability in union organization. This was a branch which reflected very strongly the union's tradition in psychiatric nursing, with no ancillary stewards, despite a considerable ancillary membership. Branch officers were involved in trying to increase membership involvement and develop the shop steward base, although they were finding this process difficult. By the 1990s there had been a shift toward professional staff in branch officer positions and a considerable growth in the number of shop-stewards throughout the departments. During the 1980s management had been resistant to the development of formal negotiating or consultative machinery. By the 1990s relationships had been formalized, and both senior management and union representatives described the management style as autocratic.

City Centre Hospital

City Centre is a large general hospital, the second largest in its Health Authority. The first City Centre Hospital opened in 1840, on the other side of the city. It was a voluntary hospital, funded mainly through voluntary subscriptions. The congested conditions of the original site became a problem as the number of patients increased, and the present location was found. It now occupies the area behind the city's bus station. The central hospital block is a relatively modern, post World War II building, while additional buildings date back to the 19th century. It retains buildings either side of a busy main road which leads from the city centre. It is located close to the neighbourhood where many of the city's Asian community live, which might be expected to be an important source of labour at the hospital.

City Centre's role was becoming more specialized during the 1980s, as general surgery was increasingly moved to the larger hospital, Walton. City Centre had a large outpatient department, and a relatively small number of beds, consistent at about 190 during the 1980s. Staffing levels have remained stable to the present day at about 1000. Ancillary staff accounted for a third of total staff in the mid 1980s, a very high proportion. Walton Hospital gained trust status in 1992, and in 1993 a new trust was formed including City Centre. Centralization of services at Walton Hospital is likely to mean the closure of City Centre. The trust is investigating PFI (Private Finance Initiative) as a means to build a new hospital on its main site. As a result comparatively little is being done at City Centre. At Walton there has been a development toward generic ancillary services. Overall in the trust, ancillary staff now account for about 15 per cent of staff. Despite being located close to the area in which many of the city's Asian population live, none of the ancillary staff at City Centre in the 1980s were Asian, and this is still the case in the mid 1990s.

City Centre was covered by a large and very active NUPE branch which recruited at all hospitals in the city. This was the only branch in the study where branch officers were able to provide detailed information on membership numbers and branch history, which indicates the comparatively extensive organization of this branch. The branch was formed in 1969, with a small number of members drawn mainly from the cleaning and works departments. Membership began to rise dramatically after the pay dispute of 1973/74, with membership concentrated at Walton. City Centre Hospital had the second largest group of members. By the mid 1970s, total membership had risen to 600 and by 1983 it grew to over 1900. Branch officers put their success down to a combination of national campaigns against low pay, and the willingness of shop stewards to pursue grievances. In 1983 there were 337 members at City Centre, 17 per cent of total branch membership. Approximately half of these members were from ancillary departments.

As the NUPE branch grew in size, so its importance in negotiations with management grew. NUPE branch officers played a major role in establishing trade union offices at three hospitals, including City Centre. They achieved full-time release for the branch secretary, large proportions of time-off for senior stewards, paid release for stewards to attend monthly meetings and the right for members to have paid time-off for meetings. During the 1980s there was increasing pressure from management to restrict the amount of time-off for union work. At the time of the research, the branch secretary and the chair of the shop stewards' committee (the BDC) were both men from the works department of Walton Hospital. The deputy branch secretary was a male porter and the branch chair a female auxiliary nurse, both from City Centre Hospital. NUPE had 78 shop-stewards in 1983, of whom just over 50 were women. About half of the women stewards worked part-time. In this branch the incumbency of women at shop steward level was higher than the national and regional levels. The implications of this high proportion of women stewards will be considered below in relation to women's participation and representation. At the time of the initial research both shop steward meetings and branch meetings were held monthly. However, shortly after the first phase of fieldwork was completed, branch meetings in effect ceased as a result of persistent low attendance. The new arrangement was for occasional meetings to be held for specific purposes.

During the fieldwork, the Health Authority reorganized its own management structure, dividing the authority into four units. After debate, NUPE decided to reflect this structure, encouraging a competent steward in each unit to become a senior steward for their own unit. The branch secretary argued that this was a means of devolving power from the centre of the branch. They found, however, that ordinary stewards were passing on much of their work to the unit level stewards. Far from devolving power from the centre, activity at the level of the workplace began to decline, and because of the workloads the unit level stewards were unable to take on any of the tasks of the branch officers. The system was then rejected and they returned to the original organization. This branch provided an example of a large and growing membership. It had an extensive shop steward body with high levels of participation by women in shop-steward posts. The branch leadership was dominated by men, but there had been attempts to devolve power and experiment with different forms of organization within the branch.

A rather charismatic branch secretary left in the late 1980s and was replaced briefly by a woman nursing auxiliary. She was soon to be replaced by the present branch secretary who has now been in post for more than ten years. Since he has held the post, power has been concentrated in his hands. He describes his relationship with management as less confrontational and based on mutual trust. The number of shop stewards has declined dramatically and shop steward meetings have ceased.

Community Hospital

Community was a small general hospital, situated in the less affluent south part of a rural town, on a main residential road running from the centre. It had an imposing two- and three-storey Victorian frontage, hiding the modern additions behind. It was smaller and more compact than the other hospitals studied. The hospital site was close to small industrial units, near to the main housing estates of the town. The town's sizable Asian population lived mostly in areas close to the hospital. Like City Centre Hospital, Community began as a voluntary hospital, first opened in 1832.

Community was increasingly specializing in a small number of areas. It maintained a large outpatient department, dealing with 44,000 outpatients a year in the mid 1980s, and had about 200 inpatient beds. A contract for cleaning had been won by a private contractor in the late 1980s, and in 1994 the hospital was closed. A housing estate now stands on its site.

In the 1980s it had a small COHSE branch, with approximately 150 members. It had six shop stewards from ancillary and nursing services. During the research a new branch secretary was elected. The previous branch secretary had been a young male auxiliary nurse, politically active. The new branch secretary was a man from the works department, and the branch subsequently became dominated by him and his wife, a nurse who was a senior steward. Branch and shop steward meetings were held during work time and both were well attended. This was the smallest union branch covered by the research and relatively inactive despite the good meeting attendance.

Having provided both the theoretical and empirical background to the research, the remainder of the book is divided into two parts. The next part, chapters 4 to 6, examines women's employment in more detail and the final part, chapters 7 to 9, analyses women's participation and representation in those trade union branches.

Part Two
Women's Ancillary Work

4 THE ORGANIZATION OF WOMEN'S ANCILLARY WORK: CATERING AND CLEANING

The aim of this chapter is to highlight the factors which affect division and unity among groups of workers. It has been argued that an understanding of trade unions essentially requires a detailed analysis of the organization of work. This chapter will concentrate on the organization of women's ancillary work, focusing on three catering and four cleaning departments from the case study hospitals. Divisions based on gender and race will be identified as the key factors in this discussion, issues which will be considered in more detail in the following two chapters. Through the examples of catering and cleaning departments it is demonstrated how a bottom stratum of labour is created within the grading structure. This layer is made up of women workers, and where women of Asian origin are employed they are concentrated in this lower level. Although women within the bottom stratum have specific interests, racial divisions cut across interests based on gender.

The importance of gender to the construction and organization of ancillary work will be demonstrated. Only by reference to gender is it possible to understand the construction of certain jobs as women's jobs, the construction of certain jobs as part-time jobs, and the organization of the grading structure. The analysis will explore the complex way in which this has implications for pay, status and skill definitions. This also allows an understanding of the way different jobs are being reorganized and the implications of the introduction of initiatives on flexibility for different groups of workers. In this context, attention will be given to managerial strategies in relation to women's ancillary work and the way in which work organization and reorganization are mediated by gender and race.

This chapter begins with a general review of ancillary grading structures, then looks at the organization of catering work and the organization of cleaning work through a discussion of the case studies. Finally it provides a summary of the key features of work organization.

Grading Structures

At the time of the initial research all ancillary staffs were divided between 18 pay groups, pay group 1 being the lowest and 18 the highest. Pay group 1 consisted only of catering assistants and cleaners/domestic assistants. Pay groups 17 and 18 consisted only of gardens superintendents. The vast majority of occupations were placed in pay groups 2 to 6, but pay group 1 accounted for well over half of all ancillary workers. It was an entirely female grade. In no other occupations, whether defined as skilled or unskilled, did workers enter the service in pay group 1. For the vast majority of domestic assistants there were no opportunities beyond pay group 1. The only exceptions were small numbers of cleaners in the pathology laboratories and supervisors who were in higher grades. In catering departments, the catering assistants were divided into two sections, the kitchen assistants and the dining room assistants. There were some opportunities for advancement in the dining room where catering assistants who handled cash, senior catering assistants and dining room supervisors were in higher grades. In the kitchen there was no promotion ladder providing for advancement from kitchen assistant. In contrast, general labourers, garden labourers, sewage labourers and porters all entered the service in pay group 2. These occupations were almost entirely male.

All NHS ancillary workers, male and female, were and still are low paid. The distance, in terms of money between pay groups 1 and 2 was a matter of pennies. However, the significant feature of the grading structure was the concentration of women in pay group 1. This form of pay structure, with a bottom grade consisting totally of women, was at the time of the research common to the whole of public sector manual workers, and to much of the private sector.

During the 1980s public sector grading structures were reorganized. In NHS ancillary work, Local Authority manual work and Universities' ancillary work the bottom grade was removed. The basic structure remains, however, although in a less obvious fashion. In 1986 the 18 ancillary grades in the NHS were reorganized into two separate pay scales, one for non-supervisory grades and one for supervisory grades. The non-supervisory staff were divided from Scale A (the lowest) to Scale D (the highest). Supervisory staff were divided from Scale I (the lowest) to Scale IV (the highest). This reorganization did mean some improvement for workers in certain occupations. However, the new scales had internal point systems and the only staff on Scale A Point 1 were catering assistants and cleaners/domestic assistants, made up entirely of women. Comparing the rates of pay between 1983 and 1986, it is evident that the distance between the lowest paid and highest paid ancillary staffs had actually increased slightly. On the basis of pay rates, the position of women on the bottom grade had been worsening, despite an apparent equalizing of the grading structure.

The grading structure indicates a bottom stratum of workers, entirely female, which is also almost completely part-time and defined as unskilled. However, this group is not insignificant in number, accounting for more than half of the whole ancillary staff. In the 1980s this meant up to 100,000 workers in England. Unskilled male workers never enter the workforce on this lowest grade, and in none of the ancillary jobs predominantly performed by men is there the almost total lack of opportunity for advancement which is found in women's low grade work. The ancillary workforce is one clearly segregated by sex, both vertically and horizontally. Escott and Whitfield (1995) present a similar picture for local authority employment, with part-time women workers in the lowest grade work. There is, however, increasing recognition that inequalities may be 'hidden' in the complexities of grading structures (Labour Research 1998a).

Certain grades have been constructed as women's grades. Even when men enter work in a job classed as unskilled, they do not enter the lowest grade or grades, which are reserved for women. Thus there are three problems: why women's skills are given less value, how certain work is constructed as women's work, and how grading structures are constructed to differentiate between men and women. These questions are addressed in chapters 5 and 6, drawing on the empirical material presented in this chapter.

Catering Work

Huws (1982) estimates that about a quarter of all employed women are doing jobs which she calls 'other people's housework'. In this category she includes cleaners, canteen assistants, counter-hands, cooks, kitchen hands, general servants, waitresses and launderers. Despite the significance of the service sector, most studies of women's employment have concentrated on factory work. This suggests that the lack of academic attention to areas such as cleaning and catering is a reflection of the low status of the work itself. A significant exception is Gabriel's valuable analysis of a range of catering workplaces (Gabriel 1988). Only with the national restructuring of such work, particularly through privatization of public services, has it become 'visible'.

Catering work as a general term includes the work performed by kitchen, restaurant and bar staff. In the NHS the relevant groups are the kitchen and restaurant staff, the chefs, cooks, kitchen assistants, waitresses and canteen staff.

Catering staff make up the second largest group of workers in NHS ancillary services. Cost cutting has been a persistent feature in NHS catering, and as in other departments, staffing levels have been seen as a prime target. However, catering departments were initially less likely than domestic service departments to have been identified for privatization. Why the two departments have had such different experiences will be discussed in subsequent chapters.

Catering departments are responsible for the purchase, preparation and distribution of food in the hospital for patients and staff. The centre of the catering department is the kitchen. Staff work in close proximity in relatively small areas in often very hot or very cold and uncomfortable conditions. There is a range of occupations, and the distinctive characteristics of catering departments compared with domestic services departments are the hierarchical grading structure and the employment of men. However, as in domestic services there is a low grade job performed solely by women – catering assistant. Catering assistants are divided into two main groups, the kitchen assistants and the dining room assistants. Kitchen assistants mainly perform routine food preparation, and dining room assistants are involved in the serving and clearing of food. In this section, the organization of the three catering departments in the study will be examined.

Shire General Hospital

During the 1980s Shire General had the largest catering department covered in the research, with a total of 52 members of staff. The manager was a young college-trained man. The department was situated in the centre of the hospital buildings, with light and airy conditions. Staff ranged from the male head cook on the highest ancillary grade, to the catering assistants on the lowest. Most of the men employed in the department were on higher grades, and most of the women were on the lower grades, although there were some women employed on middle grades. Of the total, there were seven men on the staff, half of the staff worked part-time and three-quarters of the staff were on Grade 1. Unlike the other two catering departments, this department had a large staff responsible for serving food to patients in the ward, the ward waitresses. Most of the part-time staff in the department were in fact the ward waitresses, which reflected the demand for staff at the peak meal times of lunch and dinner. The duties of other catering assistants were defined as:

> General duties in the kitchen, dining room and associated areas, including
> the serving of food, cleaning of premises and equipment, preparation of

vegetables, fruit, salad, sandwiches, toast and beverages. May be required to collect pre-paid meal tickets. (Shire General job description)

Staff worked on a five-day week, with a rota system for shifts. Full-time staff worked from early morning to mid-afternoon or mid-morning to early evening. The main shifts for the part-time staff were 11.30 am to 2.30 pm and 5.30 pm to 8.00 pm. This shows clearly that women's part-time labour was being used to cover the peaks of activity, mid-day and evening meal periods. Among the full-time staff peak periods were covered by overlapping shifts and overtime. This finding supports the arguments made by Beechey and Perkins (1987) that men's and women's labour is used differently to achieve flexibility.

All of the men employed in this department worked full-time while only six per cent of the women worked full-time. The three most senior positions were held by men and there were no men on Grade 1. The job of catering assistant was a completely female job. Thus the grading structure, patterns of working and occupations were all defined around gender. There were two women cooks and the particular nature of the gendering of cooking occupations will be discussed further during this chapter.

Detailed information was not available on the ethnic origin of staff in this department, although it was estimated that approximately half of the women staff were of Asian origin, and all of these women were employed on Grade 1 work. The manager commented on the good relations among all of the staff in the department and felt that there were generally harmonious working relations among staff. There were occupational divisions linked to gender and race, but these divisions did not appear to have developed into overt conflict in the department.

When revisited in 1996, a surprising level of continuity was found at Shire General, where overall staffing levels had increased by seven, and work was organized in much the same way. One development was the employment of four young male school leavers in part-time work. Many of the same staff were still employed in the department, 17 of the catering assistants having worked there for more than ten years. The contract for catering was awarded in 1996 to a private company, Mediclean.

Community Hospital

The catering department at Community Hospital was the smallest one included in the study, with a total of 21 staff, and a woman manager who had been in post for many years. The kitchen was situated in the basement of the hospital. Of the total staff, three were men, all senior cooks. There were seven part-time staff, one part-time cook and the rest catering assistants. Thirteen of the staff were employed on Grade 1. These were the dining room and kitchen assistants, and the washing up machine staff. All of these staff were women.

Most of the staff worked a five-day week, with a four-week rota in the kitchen and a two-week rota in the dining room. This department had a comparatively high level of full-time working among women staff compared with the previous department. This was also the case for domestic services at Community. The three men in the department worked regular overtime.

This department had operated an interim bonus scheme for many years, which had not been fully work-studied. In 1982 this had been updated and a bonus of 15 per cent awarded to all staff in the department. The introduction of the bonus had been achieved by a reduction in total staff hours. The manager described the ease of cutting the overall hours. One of the cooks had left, and had not been replaced. The remaining three men cooks had taken a reduction of two hours a week and some catering assistants had moved from full-time to part-time working. Despite the three men having taken a cut in hours, they continued to regularly work over the normal full-time hours.

Although there was no expressed policy of moving from full-time to part-time working in this department, this had been used as an important aspect of achieving the cut in hours required for the introduction of the bonus scheme. The manager described this shift as a 'natural' response to the situation, although she did not seem to have a policy to continue this trend. The issues of what is regarded as natural in terms of women's labour is a theme that will be developed in subsequent chapters.

The three male members of staff held the three senior positions in the department. All three were cooks, and as mentioned above, all regularly worked overtime. There were two women cooks, although they were differentiated from the men cooks, one being the diet cook and one working part-time. All but one of the catering assistants were of Asian origin. This group of workers were identified as a distinct group by the manager, who claimed that they had higher absenteeism and sickness levels and that they could speak and write little English, although this was not perceived as a problem. This was a small department which had already gone through a degree of rationalization with little resistance from staff. It retained a comparatively high level of full-time working among Grade 1 women workers, which may in part explain this lack of resistance. The department ceased to operate with the closure of the hospital in 1994.

County Psychiatric Hospital

The County Catering Department had a total of 37 staff in the 1980s. It had the largest staff of cooks, 12 plus a superintendent who was in effect kitchen manager. It also had five male staff employed as kitchen porters, a post which did not exist in the other two catering departments in the study. The manager of the department was a young college-trained woman. This department had the lowest proportion of staff employed on the bottom Grade 1, 40 per cent of the total. It also had the lowest proportion of part-time working and the highest proportion of male staff, in part reflecting the difficulties of recruiting part-time staff in an isolated rural location.

In this department cooks worked either of two shifts, 7.00 am to 4.00 pm or 10.00 am to 7.00 pm. They worked a complicated rota system of 10 days on, 4 days off, 8 days on, 2 days off. This meant working two weekends out of every three. Full-time catering assistants worked two shifts, 7.00 am to 4.00 pm or 9.00 am to 6.00 pm, on alternate days. For the main part of the day most staff were on duty. Part-time catering assistants worked from 5.00 pm to 8.15 pm. The evening meal period for assistants was covered by a permanent evening shift. The ordinary shift system ensured that cooking staff were on duty to cover this period. In this way a distinctive method was used to cover peak periods for predominantly male jobs compared to that used in women's jobs. There was comparatively little part-time working in this department, and the manager said that her aim was to move towards more part-time working. However, because of the geographical isolation of County, and because most staff were tied to the hospital transport system, the potential for an increase in part-time working was limited.

There was no distinct pattern in terms of age, although the part-time catering assistants tended to be slightly younger and to have held their jobs for a shorter period of time than the full-time catering assistants. From the length of service of some of the catering assistants it becomes apparent that the lowest grade staff remained in their jobs for considerable periods of time, the longest-serving member of staff having been in her job for 27 years. In this department internal promotion was very rare, so this meant 27 years on Grade 1 for one female member of staff with no hope of promotion. Staff turnover was greater among the cooks and the manager joked that the catering assistants 'stayed for life'. For the cooks there was opportunity for higher pay outside of the NHS, but for the catering assistants comparable work in the private sector paid no more and had much less security.

The department had been operating an interim bonus scheme for ten years with a bonus of 10 per cent. At the time of the initial research they were expecting to have a new work study carried out and a new bonus scheme introduced. However, it was expected that the new bonus might not be any higher than the existing bonus, yet it would require a cut in staff and hours. There was an assumption by the manager that cuts would be achieved by the full-time catering assistants moving to part-time working, a loss of ten hours a week each. The catering assistants did not want to move to part-time working and there were bad relations in the kitchen between them and the cooks, who seemed to expect increased pay at the expense of the catering assistants. This division was further deepened by the racial division of these two groups of workers, with the majority of the full-time assistants being women of Asian origin.

The familiar picture emerges of women occupying the bottom grade jobs, men the most senior positions, and a few women in the middle grade positions. The post of kitchen porter, which was found in this department, illustrates how men are differentiated from women even when employed on work formally regarded as equally unskilled. A job description from Shire General Hospital, where the separate male job of kitchen porter was not used, defined the job as synonymous with the job of catering assistant. However, a general Health Authority job description which was used at County Psychiatric gave the role of kitchen porter specific duties:

> Function and Responsibilities – Simple preparation of vegetables, and fish. Removal of swill rubbish. Carrying out of heavy lifting, collection of stores items. Operation of mechanical scrubbing machines. (Health Authority job description: kitchen porter)

The main difference in this description was the specification of heavy lifting and use of machinery. This then justified the payment of this job on Grade 2 and suggests that the job description cited above was constructed to differentiate between male and female labour rather than reflecting actual differences in the work. Heavy lifting in women's jobs is usually ignored or underestimated, a theme that will be developed in the following chapters.

In this department more detailed information was gained on the racial origin of staff, and the age and length of service of the women staff. Although there was a greater mix of ethnic origin in this department, there was a pattern of white men in most senior positions and Asian women in the lowest grade work. The division in this department was not solely a racial split (between black and white staff), but one based on both race and gender (between Asian women staff and all other staff). There appeared to be overt conflict between these groups, which extended to rest periods, when the Asian women took their breaks in the rest room separately from all other staff. The divisions in the department were increased by the attitude of the manager who claimed that the Asian women had higher absenteeism than other staff and did not work hard enough. The manager was also annoyed that they usually came back to work after taking maternity leave. From a managerial point of view, women leaving to have children presented a useful possibility for cutting or changing staffing levels. This was a department where divisions of race were particularly evident. The disunity was further enhanced by the disagreements over the introduction of the new bonus scheme.

When County Psychiatric moved to St Stephen's, management took the opportunity to transform work organization. Despite the labour-intensive nature of much ancillary work, there is potential for significant technological intervention. In catering, one of the key developments has been that of cook/chill, which enables the centralization of cooking for a wide geographical area. Cook/chill was introduced at St Stephen's and the staff of 37 was reduced to two directly employed staff in the kitchen preparing salads. Two further staff worked behind the servery, although these were usually agency staff. Service of food on wards had been taken over by the new category of Service Assistant, who were generic support staff.

Comparison of catering departments

It should firstly be noted that none of the catering departments studied during the 1980s still exist with NHS employees. Where catering departments appeared in the 1980s to be slightly protected from reorganization, the situation in the 1990s has been transformed. It is now possible to remove local kitchens altogether. Changes to the nature and delivery of health care have also enabled the radical transformation of ancillary work. In the case of psychiatric care, the shift to care in the community has resulted in significant reductions in size, or the closure of the traditional psychiatric hospitals. Equally, the growing use of day surgery in general and acute medicine makes a large reduction in the need for inpatient beds and the number of support staff needed to service them. Despite these recent changes, useful material can be drawn from an examination of the similarities and differences between the departments. There are five areas that will be examined: shift patterns, bonus schemes, hours of work, and racial and gender divisions.

Shift patterns

All of the departments used similar types of shift pattern. The peak periods for catering departments were mid-day and evening meal times. Theoretically, these two periods could be covered by separate workers on different shifts. In fact, in all the catering departments the peak periods were covered by the same staff working different shifts on a rota basis, for example from 7.00 am to 4.00 pm and from 10.00 am to 7.00 pm. Therefore, during the middle period of the day, all full-time staff were on duty at the same time. The shifts of the part-time evening catering assistants did not overlap with full-time staff on an early shift. However, because the full-time staff rotated their shifts, even the part-time staff worked with all other staff at some point.

The implication of this shift organization is that, with all staff coming into contact with each other, there was potential for the development of group cohesion and solidarity which would enhance trade union organization. This, however, was hindered because of the way that the hierarchical divisions within catering departments were augmented by sexual and racial divisions, preventing such unity developing.

Bonus schemes

A single bonus covered all staff in each catering department. This indicated another area which might be expected to enhance the unity in catering departments. However, the way in which bonuses had been introduced made this less likely. At County Psychiatric there had been a bonus scheme in operation for many years, although there were plans at the time of the research to introduce a new scheme with a higher bonus. The basis for the necessary savings that would have to be found in order to maintain a higher bonus had been identified as a ten-hour a week cut to the catering assistants, a strategy which had caused considerable disagreement. Community Hospital had introduced a new bonus scheme in the catering department shortly before the research commenced, achieved by considerable staff cuts. One cook left and was not replaced, the other cooks took a cut of two hours a week and some catering assistants moved from full to part-time working. As with shift patterns, the bonus schemes too provided a potential basis for conflict between staff.

Grading structures

A general picture emerged from these three catering departments, of a hierarchy divided into three main groups. The top group consisted of a small number of higher grade staff doing skilled work, mainly men of white British origin and a few women of white British origin. The small intermediary group was exclusively female, carrying out jobs with some supervisory tasks or responsibility for cash, and from a variety of racial origins. The largest group of staff were all on Grade 1, classed as unskilled, all women and mainly of Asian origin.

Among the cooks there was a promotion structure, with staff entering at a position appropriate to their experience and qualifications, with the head cook at the top of this career structure. The largest group of staff, the catering assistants, had virtually no opportunities for promotion or training. Staff turnover was lower among lower grade staff, and the lower grade staff tended to be older than other staff. It has been argued that the hierarchical grading structure in catering departments was one of its most distinctive and important characteristics. It was a hierarchical structure constructed around gender mediated by racial divisions.

Hours of work

Although part-time working was evident at all three hospitals, the extent was varied. At Shire County General 25 of the total of 52 staff (48 per cent) worked part-time. This compared with 7 out of 21 at Community (33 per cent) and 6 out of 37 at County Psychiatric (16 per cent). All of the part-time staff were women, and all were catering assistants. This pattern was common to all the hospitals, with only one cook throughout the three hospitals working part-time. One important difference was the period covered by part-time staff. At County Psychiatric, part-time staff were employed only on the evening shift, while part-time staff were employed at all stages of the working day at the other two hospitals.

A further feature of part-time working was that there was a distinct trend away from full-time to part-time working. This was particularly associated with the introduction of bonus schemes and involved a shift for women rather than men workers from full-time to part-time working. There had also been pressure on male cooks to accept cuts in hours with the introduction of new bonus schemes, although this usually meant cuts in overtime working. Nowhere did a male member of staff work less than 40 hours a week. Women's low grade catering work was in the process of being re-constructed as part-time work, although this process was limited to some extent by local factors. Such a process indicates that the nature of change to the organization of work cannot be understood without reference to gender.

Gender divisions in the workplace

Two of the three functional managers of these catering departments were women, although within the departments there was a very clear sexual division of labour. The head cooks, who had supervisory control over the day-to-day running of the whole department, were all men. In every case there were some women cooks, but none at senior levels. All catering assistants were women, all kitchen porters were men. The high level of employment of women in catering seems again to reflect the sexual division of labour in the home. However, within catering there was a highly skilled section of the workforce, that had traditionally been dominated by men.

There were some women of white British origin in higher grade work as cooks. The job of catering assistant was clearly constructed as a woman's job, but this pattern was not so clear in the case of cooks. The occupation of cook or chef is constructed as male or female in different sectors of the labour market. In hospital catering the job of cook was primarily a male job, although some women had entered the occupation.

One feature of employment during the 1990s which should be highlighted is the employment of male school leavers in part-time work. This development challenges traditional patterns of employment in terms of age, sex and hours of work. Such a development is a feature of the increasing disappearance of manual work for men. It is significant, but at present remains exceptional. Bradley (1999) also found evidence of young part-time males working on checkouts, normally a woman's job. It could be argued that this development fits with a picture of the erosion of gender segregation in the service sector (Crompton and Sanderson, 1990). However, as Bradley (1999) points out, they are usually students for whom the work is not permanent.

Racial divisions

There were two main racial groups in the catering departments. These were those of white British origin and those of Asian origin. There were small numbers of staff from Afro-Caribbean origin and southern European origin.

In terms of divisions within the catering departments the main division seemed to be between the women of Asian origin and all other staff. These divisions were reinforced by the policy of making cuts by reducing the hours of catering assistants, the majority of whom were women of Asian origin. The common view expressed by managers, that Asian women were lazy, further fed and emphasized this division. Taking the example of County Psychiatric, it becomes clear that the gender division of labour in the department was mediated by racial divisions. Most senior jobs were held by men of white British origin, and the lowest grade jobs were mostly occupied by women of Asian origin.

The picture drawn here has a number of similarities with that given by Gabriel (1988), where the hospital catering department has a divided staff and management exploit these divisions in the reorganization of work. Being located in London, Gabriel's department had a more heterogeneous staff in terms of ethnic background, including southern European workers. Gabriel (1988) found the main divisions to be between the older foreign and the younger English workers, although the gender divisions were similar to those found in this study. Work is structured by reference to gender and race, but this is not a static process, varying depending on the particular context and location.

Cleaning Work

Domestic Services Departments are responsible for all cleaning inside the hospitals. The defined aim of a domestic assistant is to 'ensure a high standard of cleanliness within the area allocated'. Duties include dusting, sweeping, polishing, cleaning toilets and maintaining provision of soap, towels and toilet rolls. This may include the use of chemical cleaning agents and mechanical cleaning aids. Waste bins have colour-coded bin bags, according to the nature and risk of the waste, and domestic assistants are responsible for the removal and replacement of these bin bags. Although not formally part of their job, domestics frequently assist visitors, offer friendly companionship to patients, and liaise with nursing staff. Williams *et al.* (1977) cite a number of studies which indicate that patient contact, including such activities as re-filling water jugs and attending to patients' flowers, is a crucial factor in terms of domestic staff's work satisfaction. In some hospitals domestics may also be responsible for the service of food on the ward. In the context of a hospital, the importance of cleanliness makes the value of domestic services immediately apparent; cleaning cannot be regarded as peripheral in a hospital. However, it is not always visible and as Coyle suggests (1986: 6), cleaning 'is big business but just as the social value of cleaning is undervalued, and only noticed when it is not done, so cleaning as an economic activity has been considerably under-estimated'.

The most outstanding feature of the organization of hospital ancillary work is its complexity. Even in domestic services departments, where it might be expected to be straightforward, the organization is actually very complicated. Here there are large numbers of women, almost all on the same grade, working on two shifts, but in the 1980s there tended to be a vast number of starting times, a variety of bonus schemes, different staffing levels and different numbers of hours worked. This variety of organization is partly a reflection of difficulties in the past in recruiting ancillary staff, and the need to fit in with workers' other responsibilities such as childcare. However, it also reflects the complex requirements of the hospital sector, with needs changing on the basis of specialty, size and location. It is also affected by managerial policy, partic-ularly the pressures of cuts and privatization which have increasingly pushed management towards a rationalization of work organization. This was made possible in an economic climate in which recruitment of staff was no longer a problem.

Each of the domestic services departments at the four hospitals will be examined in turn. This will be followed by a consideration of the specific features of this work. In each case work organization, shift patterns, hours, managerial policy, and divisions by race and sex will be analysed.

City Centre Hospital

During the 1980s the City Centre Hospital was grouped with two smaller hospitals in the Health Authority to form a unit for administrative purposes. The Domestic Services' Manager was responsible for domestic services at all three sites and worked with an assistant manager, both based at City. The department operated with six supervisory staff. The total number of staff, excluding supervisory staff, was 98 – equivalent to 50 whole time staff. All but one member of staff worked part-time, all but one member of staff were on the bottom grade, all but one member of staff were women. There was one full-time male member of staff, employed on Grade 2.

The shift patterns of the department were divided between day and evening shifts. In the case of the day shift, all 40 staff worked part-time, mostly starting at 7.30 am and finishing at 2.00 pm. The evening shift ran from 5.00 pm to 9.00 pm, all 57 staff working part-time. This department had a much larger number of women employed on the evening shift compared with the day shift. This was because there was a large out-patient department which was closed during the evening, and therefore cleaned during the evening. Most general cleaning was done during the morning, but this was impossible in the busy out-patient areas. Almost all of the women staff were between 30 and 60 years of age. The evening shift were generally slightly younger than the day shift. Women with school-age children were more able to work during the day, while children were at school.

Most staff worked a five-day week, on a four-week rota. There had been a bonus scheme in operation for eleven years at the time of the initial research. The one man employed in the department worked a split shift: mornings and evenings with the afternoon off, except at the weekends when he worked a straight eight-hour day. The staff turnover rate was very low in this department at the time of the research, less than one per cent annually. The absenteeism and sickness rates were also very low, although rising, which the manager thought was related to poor morale resulting from the threat of privatization.

There was a managerial concern with flexible work arrangements. In interviews, the manager stressed the need for flexibility among her 'ladies'. The manager said that because she needed flexibility domestics should not be allowed to remain working on the same section or ward permanently. She was concerned that they would assume a right to work in a particular place. However, because all the staff were the same grade, and since there was no scope or opportunity for promotion or training, there had developed a system of internal hierarchies based on the cleaning of different parts of the hospital. The most highly valued areas to work were those which entailed contact with patients, the wards. Once a domestic had 'made it' to the wards, which could take many years, she would strongly defend her right to stay there. There was also a hierarchy of wards, and when a member of staff left or retired, the remaining staff recognized a strict code of seniority as to who should get which ward. This unwritten code conflicted directly with the managerial need for flexibility.

The conflict over the rights to work in certain areas based on length of service represented a conflict over the control of the work process. In an occupation barren of opportunities, domestics created their own opportunities and career ladders. Working on a ward over a long time not only offered enhanced status within the department, but also the chance to develop relationships with other non-domestic staff on the ward and opportunity to develop the work programme in their own way. Familiarity with a ward offered the chance to become aware of where work could be speeded up or corners cut from time to time, in order to make time for breaks or to talk with patients or other staff.

The manager claimed that she had a departmental 'move round' about every nine months to prevent any feeling of ownership of particular wards or sections. However, a domestic shop steward claimed that this was 'rubbish', and that the manager had tried to move someone once, but that it had caused such trouble that she had to give up and leave everyone where they were. This informally constructed seniority ladder was clearly a focus for struggle between the staff and the manager, who was trying to assert her 'right to manage'. There was also a relief pool of workers who were not based in any particular section, but who were moved in to take care of any particular extra work or where there was a problem through sickness or absenteeism. In this way, some flexibility could be achieved without disturbing territorial 'rights'.

Domestic services in this hospital had been organized around part-time working as long as any staff could remember. More importantly, there was a managerial concern that part-time work be defined as expedient and not necessarily the most desirable way to organize cleaning work. The manager said that she thought that flexibility could be better served by an increase in full-time working, which seemed rather against the trends. She explained that full-time work would only ever be offered on the basis of the split-shift. All of the women cleaners in this department worked on a part-time basis, while the one man worked full-time on a split-shift. The split-shift, common in the hotel and catering industries, was one of the most arduous working patterns. However, it offered the advantage over part-time working of only having staff in for the peaks of activity without the disadvantage of having two separate workgroups.

The one man working in this department was on a higher grade than the women domestics. He was responsible for routine maintenance, including tasks such as floor maintenance and hanging curtains. On the evening shift, he used the large scrubber/drier automatic machine. Although all domestics used cleaning machinery, this particular machine was slightly larger, and was not used by the other domestic staff. In other hospitals, all of these tasks except floor maintenance were performed by women domestics on Grade 1. In other hospitals, floor maintenance was included as part of the work of maintenance staff. Thus the work of this one man was clearly delineated from that of the women. Everyday cleaning tasks were carried out by women.

Two of the domestics were of southern European origin, while the specific origin of the remainder of the staff is not known, although they were all white. This is particularly surprising since the hospital is situated in the city centre with a sizable Asian community close by. The manager felt that the lack of staff of Asian origin could be explained in part by discriminatory employment practices by the previous manager. She argued that since she had been in post, there had been almost no vacancies because they had such a stable workforce and because they had been forced to make some cuts in the numbers of staff. Discussion revealed, however, that Asian women tended to call 'on the off-chance' that there might be a job, rather than apply formally, and the department did not keep records of informal applicants. There was also some disagreement between the manager and her assistant about the importance of spoken and written English for the work.

This example indicates the importance of recruitment practices in excluding groups of workers on the basis of racial origin. The manager attempted to remove 'blame' for discriminatory practices to a previous manager, indicating that there was an awareness of a problem. The explanation that there were no longer vacancies was contradicted by the assistant manager who made clear that women of Asian origin were regarded as 'inappropriate' employees because of language difficulties. The use of language as a means to exclude certain groups of workers and as a form of resistance will be discussed later. That the ability to read and write English was a requirement for the work was challenged by the manager, who showed her awareness of which practices were discriminatory. However, the recruitment system of public advertisements and formal applications continued the exclusion of women of Asian origin, despite the indication of interest in employment through informal enquiries. By 1996, there were still no Asian staff in this department. There continued to be a number of Irish staff and there was a small number of Afro-Caribbean staff.

From 1987 onwards the department had faced periodic 'market testing', but to-date the in-house tender has been successful, although the manager felt that the continual pressure had a negative impact on morale. Total staff numbers had reduced by ten between the 1980s and 1996. These reductions were from the day shift, where there had also been a cut in the length of the shift by one-and-a-half-hours. One person now worked during the afternoon and two staff worked a night shift, enabling 24-hour cover.

It could be argued that among those studied this department had seen the least change. However, it seems likely that senior management were less concerned with work organization at City Centre because they hoped to close the hospital as a part of a Private Finance Initiative (PFI) project. The larger hospital in the trust, Walton, had land potentially available for development and was seeking private partners to develop the site and replace the work of City Centre. The trust defined the 'management of clinical and other related patient care' as its core business. The private sector partner(s) would be able to take over support services, including catering, domestic service, porters, reception, records, computer services, etc. The introduction of the purchaser/ provider relationship into health care has focused management attention on clinical aspects of the health service, and support services are increasingly being seen as peripheral activities, although PFI has yet to take off. Meanwhile, at Walton, generic ancillary services are being developed and there is a move towards harmonization of terms and conditions between manual and white collar staff.

Shire General Hospital

The department at Shire was slightly smaller than the previous one, with five supervisors and a total staff of 69. Of the 69, six were on Grade 2 and the remainder on Grade 1. All of these members of staff were women. There were 64 part-time staff and five full-time, with a whole time equivalent for the whole staff of approximately 45. Bonus schemes had been in operation for several years, with a different bonus on the day and evening shifts. Of the total, eight women worked a split shift, that is they worked some day shifts and some evening shifts. However, only one of the split-shift workers worked over 30 hours a week. There were 50 staff on the day shift, 45 of them part-time, mostly starting work at 8.00 am and finishing at noon or mid afternoon. There were 27 staff on the evening shift, all part-time, working from 4.30 pm to 7.30 pm. The total number of staff seems to add up to more than 69 because the eight split shift workers will appear on both shift totals.

This department had a wide range of starting and finishing times on the day shift compared with the previous department. However, the evening shift was more regular. To get a better idea of the complexity of the arrangements, these are the working weeks of the eight women who worked a split shift:

A worked one day shift and one evening shift for a total of seven hours a week.
B, E, G and H worked one day shift and five evening shifts for a total of 19 hours a week each.
C worked five day shifts and two evening shifts for a total of 28 hours a week.
D worked five day shifts and one evening shift for a total of 31 hours a week.
F worked four day shifts and three evening shifts for a total of 29 hours a week.

When work is organized on a part-time basis, the only way to earn more is to build up a complex system of extra hours, wherever available. Some workers took second jobs outside of the NHS, while this group worked on different shifts. These examples illustrate the mythical nature of the convenience of part-time working;

> There are a lot of myths about women's work and part-time jobs. One of the myths is that it 'fits in' conveniently with family life and suits the women and the families concerned. Looking at the hours of the cleaners in the interview sample, it was clear there was no question of convenience for the women workers, or for their families. None of those interviewed said that it was convenient, only that cleaning was possible while other jobs were not ... families were fitted around the job, and not the other way. (Community Action 1984: 15)

The findings of Community Action on the fragmented working week were similar to those in this research. A typical working week for the last woman in the above list, F, was divided up as follows:

Monday:	work 4.30 to 7.30 pm
Tuesday:	Day off
Wednesday:	Day off
Thursday:	work 8.00 am to 12.30 pm and 4.30 to 7.30 pm
Friday:	work 8.00 am to 12.30 pm
Saturday:	work 8.00 am to 12.30 pm
Sunday:	work 8.00 am to 12.30 pm and 4.30 to 7.30 pm

It is difficult to see how working Saturday morning and a split shift on a Sunday could be described as convenient. This suggests that Community Action has a strong case in characterizing this work pattern as 'possible', not 'convenient'.

In the past there had been problems of recruitment of domestic services staff and the vast array of different working hours may have represented a way of recruiting staff with children. Management made it possible for women with children to work in hospital cleaning, although it should not be assumed from this that the women liked the hours of work. During the mid 1980s, recruitment became less difficult, enabling management to change work organization. The manager in this department was keen to move away from full-time working and gain the flexibility possible with part-time staff.

As with the previous department, there was resistance from staff being moved from section to section. However, in this department the manager had had greater success in breaking down customary 'rights' of staff to work in certain areas. This had been aided by the general fear of privatization in a Health Authority actively seeking private tenders. That the threat of privatization provided management with a powerful weapon in the struggle over control of the work process will be a theme developed in later chapters.

There were no men employed in this department and the manager felt quite clear that it was not the sort of work men would want. She also added that since she was only recruiting part-time staff, men would not be interested. These assumptions that cleaning is 'women's work' and that part-time work is 'women's work' were very strong throughout the research. The assumption seems to be that only women could take what Siltanen (1994) describes as the component-wage job, where wages are insufficient to support a single adult household.

There was no distinct racial division between the day and evening shifts in this department. However, most of the split shift workers and approximately half of the day shift were of Asian origin. Although the precise origin of the remainder of the staff is not known, they were all white. The staff of Asian origin tended to be slightly older than the rest of the staff. Managerial policy at the time of the research was only to take on staff who could demonstrate an ability in reading and writing English. This had come about because of dissatisfaction with 'the attitude' of the Asian women workers. This view was expressed frequently by various managers during the research and will be discussed in following chapters when considering forms of resistance to managerial control. As with the example from City Centre Hospital, language abilities were used as a means of excluding certain groups of workers.

The department at Shire General had only risen from 69 staff in the 1980s to 71 in 1996, despite the dramatic growth in the hospital. By 1996, three men had joined the department, again young school leavers working part-time. Despite women ancillary workers fitting a picture of a peripheral workforce in many ways, it would be wrong to see them in any sense as casual or temporary. Among the staff were seven women who had been in the department over twenty years, and one who had been there over thirty years. Until the 1990s, despite its problems, the NHS provided a major source of secure employment for women manual workers. Having kept the contact in-house for over ten years, the contract was awarded to a private company in 1996, Mediguard.

Community Hospital

The domestic services department at Community Hospital had been identified as one of the first in the Health Authority which should be considered for privatization. It was in fact taken over by private contractors in July 1985. The manager of the department had been promoted from head porter to domestic services manager two years previous to the research. There was a total staff of 58, all women, with a whole time equivalent of 40. All 58 women were on Grade 1. Of the 58 staff there were 22 staff working full-time. There had been a 20 per cent bonus on the evening shift since 1977, and a 10 per cent bonus on the day shift since 1982. There were five supervisory staff.

There were 33 women working on the day shift, two-thirds working full-time. The shift started at 7.30 am with part-time staff finishing at 12.30 pm and full-time staff finishing at 4.00 pm. All of the 25 women on the evening shift worked part-time, mostly from 5.00 pm to 8.00 pm. Regular starting and finishing times had been established in this department. What was most significant about work in this department compared with that previously described, was the use of full-time working by women on the day shift. There was also a high proportion of women of Asian origin in full-time work. On the day shift 13 of the staff were of Asian origin, four of southern European origin, and one of Afro-Caribbean origin. All staff on the evening shift were white, although they included four staff of Irish origin. Eleven of the 13 members of staff of Asian origin worked full-time. The manager described himself as 'stuck with' full-time workers on the day shift. He had tried, unsuccessfully, to persuade the full-time staff to move to part-time working. He argued that with so many full-time staff, he could not produce an in-house tender which would compete with private firms using cheap part-time labour, when it came to privatization.

The bonus scheme had recently been introduced on the day shift, which had reduced staffing levels through 'natural wastage'. However, these cuts were seen by the manager as inadequate in order to be competitive. The fact that full-time staff were regarded as the problem, and that many of the full-time staff were of Asian origin encouraged the manager to identify this group as the main cause of threats to the department, in terms of the impending privatization. Partly because many of the women of Asian origin were also friends outside of work, their husbands also working together, they appeared as a cohesive group. The manager was critical of the work of these women, although his comments referred more to them than their work. He argued that they 'pretend not to understand English when it suits them, but when they have a problem with their wages they seem to understand English.'

This again indicates the importance of language, in this case being used as a form of resistance. Generally morale in this department was very low, and absenteeism and sickness were the highest found in the research. Future events were to show that the feeling of pessimism about the future of the department was not misplaced. The contract for cleaning was awarded to a private company in 1986.

County Psychiatric Hospital

County had the largest single domestic services department included in the research. The department was run by a male manager who was approaching retirement, and an assistant manager. There were a total of 106 staff plus seven supervisory staff. In addition there were also three more staff, men who did not operate under the supervisory structure. Despite a large staff, this department had very regular starting and finishing times. On the day shift there was a total of 60 staff, including the three men, and all worked full-time. The 49 evening staff were all part-time, working 5.00 pm to 8.00 pm.

This department had a significantly higher proportion of full-time staff than any of the other hospitals in the research. There were two reasons for this situation. Firstly the hospital was situated in a remote area where there was no adequate public transport system. Most staff travelled to and from work on hospital transport, which required some uniformity in terms of starting and finishing times and meant that there were difficulties attracting staff for short periods of time to cover peaks in demand. Secondly, this was a psychiatric hospital with a considerable number of day patients as well as a secure unit. The nature of the hospital created extra forms of cleaning which needed to be dealt with throughout the day, and the hospital day did not precisely resemble acute services with visiting during the afternoon in the wards.

In this department, flexibility was not an issue. The manager had no desire to shift to part-time working, suggesting that it was difficult to complete the work with a full-time day shift. Despite the comparatively secure position of this department, the manager suggested that absenteeism and sickness were at high levels. This may have been in part due to what appeared to be very bad relations between manager and staff. The manager made clear that he disliked the women staff of Asian origin, identifying them as a distinct group whom he felt tended to work less hard. He disliked the bonus scheme system which did not allow for managerial decisions about individual incentives, and gave him little control over the payment of the bonus. This scheme had been in operation since 1968, one of the first productivity schemes introduced in the Health Service. Bonus rates were also comparatively high, with a bonus of 33 per cent on the day shift and 25 per cent on the evening shift.

There were only three men in the department, with the remainder women. These men did not work with the women staff, but were defined as 'team cleaners', and mainly worked on polishing the floors. In a department with much full-time working, the employment of men was made more likely. However, the men operated outside of the usual supervisory system, and therefore did not have a woman supervisor over them. Their work was clearly delineated from the rest of the women staff, although it was the sort of work frequently carried out by women at other hospitals. They were also on a higher grade than the women domestics and they were given a different title – team cleaners. Thus even where men carried out similar work to women, they were separated off from the position of women in a variety of ways.

Because of the nature and location of this hospital, recruitment of domestic staff was still difficult at the time of the research despite rising unemployment. Although precise figures were not available, the manager estimated that over half of the domestic staff were of Asian origin. The hospital had tried an experimental English class previously, half in work time and half in the lunch break. However, these had been stopped because management claimed that too little progress had been made. It was unclear whether these classes were seen as a means to improve staff recruitment or as a general part of staff training. It may have been in part a management response to the practice of the women of Asian origin of talking among themselves in Punjabi. Since this did not necessarily result from an inability to speak English, language classes held few benefits for management.

As described previously, the move to St Stephen's enabled a transformation in the organization of ancillary work. Functional departments were abolished in favour of generic support workers, Service Assistants, responsible for cleaning, service of food and various aspects of patient contact. Flexibility was achieved through multi-tasking. Service Assistants are based on the ward, under the supervision of the ward manager, and they appear as a part of the ward head count. Since the domestic service department no longer exists, it is difficult to establish precise numbers of staff. Certainly the number of ancillary staff was dramatically reduced, accounting for only 2.4 per cent of all staff in 1996. The Service Assistants are all female and mostly work part-time. Existing staff from County Psychiatric were invited to apply for the jobs, although they did not get automatic transfer.

Comparison of domestic service departments

As with catering, cleaning has undergone enormous change. Of the four departments studied in the 1980s, one has gone completely, one is now run by a private company, one has been replaced by generic working and the future of the last, City, looks unpromising. The move away from clearly identifiable functional departments towards generic working under ward control has potentially contradictory implications. On the one hand, there seems likely to be a threat to the group consciousness, albeit limited, that came from membership of the large functional departments. On the other hand, it is claimed by management that the multi-tasking involved in the new generic posts is potentially job enhancing, giving opportunities to learn different skills and provide for career development. Certainly the rationale for introducing generic working is to cut costs; it has been suggested that it is the only way for in-house organizations to win bids in the market place (Friend 1995: 8). Interestingly, Hart argues that women domestics who had worked on the ward in the early 1970s viewed the emergence of functional departments as bringing an erosion of their status; as part of the ward team they had had a valued role in patient contact (Hart 1991: 99). The aspects of service work which involve 'emotional labour' may not be recognized financially, but may bring a feeling of job satisfaction (Macdonald and Sirianni 1996).

As with catering, it is possible to identify a number of differences and similarities between the departments in the research. Some of these will be discussed briefly as a lead into the next chapter where a broader analysis will be constructed. Six features of employment in cleaning work will be examined: shift patterns, bonus schemes, grading structures, hours of work, gender divisions and racial divisions.

Shift patterns

All of the hospitals operated the same basic system of a day shift and an evening shift. It was evident that there was some managerial disagreement as to the efficiency of having domestic staff on duty during the afternoon, the quiet time of the hospital day. Even so, the most important trend was towards more part-time staff, and fewer staff on duty during the afternoon. Generally, those sections of the hospital which were in use only during the day were cleaned during the evening.

There were considerable differences between the proportions of the whole staff employed on the day and evening shifts. Only at City Centre Hospital did less than half of the staff work on the day shift. This was because of the large outpatient department which was cleaned during the evening when it was closed. An important feature of the shift systems was the resulting lack of possible contact between workers on each of the shifts. Only where there were split shift workers was there any contact between day shift staff and evening shift staff. Even where there were full-time staff, they finished before the evening staff started. At Shire General Hospital there were some split shift staff; additionally, some day staff finished at 4.30 pm and some evening shift staff started at 4.30 pm. Here there was some possibility for contact between the two shifts. At City Centre Hospital there was one man who worked a split shift, but otherwise there was a complete break of three hours between the two shifts. At Community and County Psychiatric Hospitals there was a complete break of one hour between the two shifts.

A sense of separation between the day and evening staff was found at all of the hospitals. The result was that, where there was extra work to do on one shift, the tendency was to blame staff from the other shift. Where equipment was broken and where materials were short or missing it was assumed to be the fault of the other shift. This division was made more distinct by having different bonuses on the different shifts. This meant that the two sets of staff had a different negotiating position in relation to management. The two sets of staff were then placed in opposition to one another: if there was only so much cake, both wanted to ensure that the other did not get the bigger slice. In her study, Hart found a similar situation, with evening staff feeling particularly marginalized (Hart 1991).

Bonus schemes

All of the departments in the research had bonus schemes in operation. There was no clear pattern as to the size of the bonus on each shift. At Community the day shift were on a bonus of 10 per cent and the evening shift on a bonus of 20 per cent. At County Psychiatric the day shift were on a bonus of 33 per cent and the evening shift on a bonus of 25 per cent.

As discussed earlier, there had been various moves since the 1960s to introduce bonus schemes in ancillary work as a means of both reducing costs and improving recruitment. The bonus scheme at County Psychiatric was one of the earliest of the productivity schemes, introduced in 1968. In contrast, the scheme for the day shift at Community had been introduced by management as recently as 1982 in an attempt to resist privatization. Certainly recent schemes represented little more than a method of persuading less staff to do more work, for slightly more money each. The assumption of the schemes was that more money would be saved by the cut in staffing levels than would be spent in paying remaining staff higher pay.

Bonus schemes in NHS ancillary work were based on group targets. Each shift had a required amount of work to carry out, which had been previously calculated through work measurement. If the work was completed, all members of the shift received the bonus. For a bonus scheme to be efficient in managerial terms, it needed to be re-measured at regular intervals of time. After a scheme had been in operation for some months, workers self-regulated and adapted in order to cope with increased workload, and as time went by it became an 'accepted normal' workload. Management savings were made only once, at the introduction of the scheme when the numbers of staff were reduced. In these circumstances 'scientific' management required continually increased pressure on the staff to speed up and continual reductions in staffing levels to provide continual cuts in costs.

Continual scrutiny of this kind would be expensive, and the functional management in the departments in this research did not have the managerial expertise to carry out such a scheme. In short, bonus schemes only really offered the 'one-off' opportunity to cut staff, as had happened at Community Hospital. Staff were initially enthusiastic about additions to their wages, but found that work was significantly more demanding and the bonus in real terms not very great.

Grading structures

At all of the hospitals, routine, non-supervisory work was carried out by women domestics employed on Grade 1, the lowest grade within hospital ancillary work. The only hope of promotion lay in the possibility of becoming a supervisor, a possibility which could only be a reality for very few staff. This meant that the inequality between men and women was compounded. With little formal hierarchy, staff attempted to maintain a form of internal hierarchy based on the status of areas of work. This attempt to superimpose some control over the organization of work was generally under attack from management as preventing flexibility. Only at City Centre Hospital had the domestic staff retained a strong sense of this internal hierarchy. Since there were few opportunities for promotion, the internal hierarchy enabled staff to feel a sense of progression. The next chapter will develop an argument that the struggle to maintain the internal hierarchy formed an important aspect of worker resistance to managerial control.

Hours of work

At all four hospitals the evening shifts were composed totally of part-time staff. However, there was considerable variation over the use of full-time and part-time staff on the day shifts. City Centre was the only department based almost completely on part-time working, with the employment of one man on a full-time shift. County Psychiatric had the only department with one shift based completely on full-time working. The departments had different methods of coping with the need for weekend working – six-day weeks, permanent weekends and rotating shifts. City Centre had used the split system to enable the single man employed there to work full-time in a department otherwise based completely on part-time working. Shire General had eight split-shift staff, although this system had developed on an *ad hoc* basis to allow women to expand their number of hours without working full-time.

There was considerable variation in the number of hours worked by staff in the four hospitals. This varied not only from department to department, but also within departments. Numbers of hours worked a week varied from seven up to forty for the full-time staff, and included almost every figure in between. Evening shifts tended to have more regular hours. Generally workers on the evening shift were younger with younger children, indicating the importance of age and the life cycle to women's employment (Hart 1991). For the day shift some departments had a regular starting time, while others had many different times. Most had a variety of finishing times. Only at City Centre were there regular starting and finishing times for both shifts, and it had the least variation in terms of numbers of hours worked a week. Domestic services at City Centre had gone furthest in terms of rationalizing work organization and the lack of internal differentiation made the internal hierarchies of greater importance to workers in this department.

The key issue raised by all managers except the one at County Psychiatric was that of flexibility. They desired a flexibility of working hours which would enable the employment of large numbers of staff over short periods of time. The main route to flexible working was regarded as the use of part-time labour. Since part-time working was regarded as possible only with women workers, this is quite clearly a gender-specific route to flexible working. The drive for flexibility by employing part-time labour was also very closely linked to the introduction or updating of bonus schemes. However, the example from Community demonstrated that the introduction of bonus schemes does not guarantee that full-time staff will accept part-time working.

There was also a general feeling that recruitment of staff to ancillary posts had become easier, again with the exception of County Psychiatric. This had given managers greater choice over who they employed. The clear trend was to limit recruitment of women of Asian origin through particular recruitment practices as at City Centre Hospital, through requirements of abilities in English as at Shire General Hospital, or through overt discrimination as at County Psychiatric and Community Hospitals.

An issue affecting all of the departments in the research was the potential threat of privatization of domestic services. All managers were having to consider the development of in-house tenders in order to compete with private contractors. This issue was in the background to all the efforts to achieve flexibility. Fear among staff of losing their jobs led to low morale, and managers appeared to have gained power vis-à-vis employees.

Gender divisions in the workplace

As shown previously, domestic services departments were almost exclusively female. Only at City Centre and County Psychiatric were any men employed in this department. Where men were employed, they worked full-time, were on higher grades, and performed different work. They were involved in work which was carried out throughout the hospital rather than being tied to one section or ward. They always used machinery, and especially larger machines than were used by the women. They carried out 'odd jobs', reflecting a widespread aspect of the sexual division of labour in the home. They worked outside of the supervisory system, being responsible directly to functional management.

In an area of work such as cleaning, which is generally regarded as 'women's work', the employment of men results in the development of specific jobs which are constructed around the need to differentiate men from women. Cleaning in the four hospitals had been constructed as women's work. Where men were employed, aspects of the work were separated off and awarded greater value. If no men were employed these tasks remained part of women's work on Grade 1. This suggests that the value of work is linked to the sex of the worker, and management develops ways of differentiating between the actual tasks performed by men and women. However, as with catering, at one hospital there had been the recent introduction of male school leavers on the same basis as the women staff, suggesting the possibility of some realignment of gender divisions.

Racial divisions

In all of the hospitals in the research there appeared two main racial groups, those of white British origin and those of Asian origin. There were small numbers of staff of southern European origin, one of Afro-Caribbean origin, and some of Irish origin, although there was no distinctive division between these groups and those of white British origin. There did appear to be divisions between the staff of white British origin and those of Asian origin.

At City Centre, the staff was almost completely of white British origin with no staff of Asian origin, despite the location of the hospital very close to an area with a large Asian population. At Shire General most of the split shift workers were of Asian origin, evening shift staff were predominantly of white British origin and the day shift were equally divided between the two groups. At Community there seemed a very clear division, the day shift staff being mainly of Asian origin and the evening shift all of white British origin. At County Psychiatric there was less of a division, with over half of the day and evening shifts being of Asian origin. Generally women of Asian origin were more likely to be working full-time. As discussed, management frequently identified the women of Asian origin as the main 'problem' in their departments, for wanting to work full-time when the trend was towards part-time working, and for not working hard enough. These attitudes from management served to enhance the racial division between shifts, increasing the lack of unity between workers on the two shifts, an aspect discussed earlier. A discussion of the implications of these divisions will be developed in later chapters.

Summary

This chapter has demonstrated that within NHS ancillary work the organization of work discourages the development of unity among groups of workers. Divisions develop around shift systems and work hierarchies. Attempts to reorganize and achieve flexibility indicated the centrality of part-time working to an understanding of women's labour. The developments of the 1990s are likely to further undermine collectivity as generic working removes ancillary departments and locates staff on the ward, an interesting return to the pre-1960s situation. Equally, the use of private contractors, often with anti-union traditions, makes collective organization much more difficult. In particular, the case studies have highlighted divisions based on gender and race in work, themes which are developed in the next two chapters.

5 GENDER AND DIVISIONS IN THE WORKPLACE

This chapter will be concerned to show the centrality of gender to the construction and reconstruction of work; to demonstrate the adaptability of the gendering process; to identify interests specific to women ancillary workers; and to assess the development of a group-consciousness around those interests, drawing on the material presented in the previous chapter. The next chapter will consider issues of race and divisions in the workplace.

It will be argued that the concept of 'sectional interests' is inadequate in the context in which work is constructed around gender, that it is a gender-blind concept. Where the construction of work is based on gender divisions, women will have specific interests in the workplace. While these interests may be termed sectional, there are two problems with using this concept. Firstly, it obscures the gender-specific nature of the interests. Secondly, it obscures the way in which women's workplace interests reflect more general shared interests over the hierarchical division of the labour market by sex. There are, however, limitations to the development of a collective consciousness around these interests. It will be demonstrated that the organization of work militates against this development. The next chapter will show that a key factor limiting the development of a collective consciousness among the women ancillary workers in this research was the racial division of labour.

In Chapter 2 it was argued that there is an underlying limitation to the ability of trade unions to represent the interests of women workers in the overall labour market. In this chapter this general theoretical argument is linked to the actual process of gendering of work in individual workplaces. This chapter and the next are concerned with the identification of interests and processes which promote division among workers. The third section of the book will go on to consider the representation of these interests within local union organizations, and the extent to which trade unions challenge or reflect and reproduce division among the workforce.

Gender and the Construction of Work

In this section the general debates concerning the gendering of work will be considered first, followed by a discussion of the relationship between gendering and skill definitions and part-time working. These, it will be claimed, are the two major aspects of ancillary work that illustrate the process of gendering of work relative to the women in the hospitals. The strict sexual segregation of jobs in hospital ancillary work indicates a high level of gendering of jobs in this area. It is often accepted rather uncritically that women perform those waged jobs in the labour market which they perform unwaged in the home, for example cooking and cleaning (Beechey and Perkins 1987). Women make 'attractive' employees in those areas of work which reflect women's domestic labour in the home, where training is socially invisible (Elson and Pearson 1981). Through assumptions of 'natural' abilities certain forms of employment have been constructed as women's jobs. Routine catering and cleaning work offer prime examples of this process. However, as the previous chapters have shown, men also work in catering and domestic service departments. Cockburn argues that where men do find themselves working alongside women, they will attempt to move out of the area 'contaminated' by women.

> We may assume that men as a sex have an interest vested in maintaining superiority over women, a situation they must secure in a system where they themselves, as workers, are subject to domination by capital. Individual men therefore are under some social pressure to locate themselves in situations not only where they have greater bargaining power relative to capital but in which they are not directly comparable to women. He may be seen to do the job less well. He may, in the logic of things, find himself answerable to a woman supervisor or forewoman. These things are uncomfortable for the individual male and bad for the relative stature of the sex. (Cockburn 1988: 33–4)

A similar process was evident in the domestic services departments at City Centre and County Psychiatric Hospitals, as described in Chapter 4. Separate jobs were devised which were constructed as men's jobs and placed outside of the normal, female, supervisory structure. Cockburn was talking specifically about the process of differentiation when women move into men's jobs. However, the evidence from this research suggests that similar processes occur when men establish a place in women's jobs. At County Psychiatric the rationale was that large polishing machines require strength, and therefore, men had to be employed. A particular form of work organization followed from this. A short distance away at Shire County using the same machines was a normal part of the women domestics' job: they were not considered to require extra strength. Such a situation could be explained in two possible ways – either when women use strength as part of a job it is not acknowledged, or when men are employed assumed requirements for strength may be used as a way to differentiate them from women workers. The gendering of work is not static, with men always doing certain jobs and women other jobs, but a dynamic process continually defining and redefining appropriate roles for men and women (Bradley 1999).

That men are entering women's work at all is a feature of male unemployment. The nature and rewards of the job follow the gender of the people that occupy it, and where men do enter these occupations, management collaborate in redefining the job both in terms of organization and pay rates. The same pattern was found in the catering department at County Psychiatric, where kitchen porters were employed. The job of kitchen porter, a man's job, was differentiated from that of catering assistant, a female job.

The recent recruitment of small numbers of young men into part-time work suggests some redefinition of the boundary between women's work and men's work. In her study of the clothing industry, Kaye (1994) suggests that the masculinity of male migrant workers is being challenged where they take jobs usually done by women. Age is also significant. Male school leavers may be less threatened by the loss of masculinity implied by doing women's work because of their youth, although this area requires further research. Equally, generic working may be shifting the boundary between women's and men's work. In this research, generic posts were created by combining jobs previously done by women into new jobs, still done by women. However, Friend (1995) suggests that in some cases service assistants undertake cleaning, catering and portering, a traditionally male activity. Again more research is required to establish who is recruited to such jobs and how their recruitment is explained.

The general field of catering provides some fascinating insights into the process by which work is gendered. Unlike cleaning, there is a wider range of occupations, skill levels and pay in catering. Not only are broad occupational groups gendered, but specific jobs within occupations are strictly gendered. Senior waiting staff in restaurants are frequently expected to be men. In contrast, waiting/waitressing in hospitals has been constructed as a woman's job. In catering the employment of men is associated with status and prestige, and nowhere is this more clear than in the process of cooking. The peak of the cooking hierarchy is the chef, a term itself which is usually recognized as masculine. All of the senior cooks in the departments examined in my research were men. A survey found that in the private sector, where women are employed in cooking, it is as the breakfast cook or cook in the staff canteen (Counter Information Service undated). A similar picture prevails in hospital kitchens, where the job of diet cook is usually held by women.

The greater the degree of differentiation between men's and women's jobs in the workplace, the more likely was the development of a conflict of interests along sex lines. These interests could be described as sectional. However, to see them only in terms of sectional interests is to fail to recognize their gender specificity. Cockburn (1988) identifies two routes for men to achieve differentiation, to segregate the workplace, through vertical or horizontal moves. The case of the cooks and chefs is an example of vertical movement – certain areas of cooking are defined as more skilled and retained as male preserves. In 'unskilled' manual work, the focus of this research, differentiation was achieved through horizontal movement. As in the case of the kitchen porters and the team cleaners, similar but separate jobs were constructed as men's jobs. This process of gendering cannot be understood without reference to definitions of skills; therefore the next section will consider the concept of skill and how it is formalized in grading structures.

Skill Definition and Grading Structures

Two arguments will be advanced in this section. It will be argued that firstly the concept of skill is a socially defined concept and one in which gender is a key factor, and secondly that even where men's and women's jobs are notionally on the same skill level, women's jobs will be ranked lower on grading structures. This is made possible by the collaboration of management in the horizontal movement of men into jobs specifically constructed as men's jobs.

Beechey suggests that there are three aspects to the concept of skill:

> First, the idea of skill can refer to complex competencies which are developed within a particular set of social relations of production and are objective competencies (in general terms, skilled labour can be objectively defined as labour which combines conception and execution and involves the possession of particular techniques); second, the concept of skill can refer to control over the labour process; and third, it can refer to conventional definitions of occupational status. (Beechey 1987: 83)

As Beechey points out, these different aspects of skill are not necessarily conterminous with one another. It is the third aspect of skill which both indicates the likely financial rewards of the job, and is rarely found in association with manual jobs carried out predominantly by women. Although this aspect of skill has been traditionally linked to collective organization, the association between gender and skill has become so strong that the gender of the worker will have an impact on the assumed skill level of the job independent of collective organization or objective competencies. In the same way that the gendering of work is continually changing, skill boundaries are not static, being continually defined and redefined in relation to gender and race (Kaye 1994).

The argument is that if a man becomes employed in the domestic services department, he is given duties which enable him to be differentiated from the majority of women in the department. This may be achieved by organizing a slightly different pattern of work or work tasks or through the use of slightly different equipment or machinery. By examining specific workplaces and jobs, it is possible to identify the actual means of differentiation. This argument can be substantiated by the example of team cleaners at County Psychiatric, where the manager laid out the basis for 'skill differentiation'. He regarded them as separate to the bulk of the cleaning staff, but when asked about them, he explained that they worked outside of the normal supervisory structure, reporting to and responsible to the departmental manager and not the supervisors. The need for male employees was explained by the need for strength in the use of the larger polishing machines. This further was used to explain the placing of the men on a higher grade than the women staff. A number of important points come from this example, which need separate attention.

Machinery and strength

The use of machinery is of major importance in skill definition. As Cockburn indicates, the process of gendering of jobs is a two way process:

> People have a gender, and their gender rubs off on the jobs they do. The jobs in turn have a gender character which rubs off on the people who do them. Tools and machinery used in work are gendered too, in such a way that the sexes are expected to relate to different kinds of equipment in different ways. (Cockburn 1988: 38)

In the case of the male cleaners at County Psychiatric, the larger polishing machines had become associated with male workers. It had become accepted in the department that they were not suitable for use by women. However, these machines were used by women at Community and Shire General Hospitals as a part of their normal duties on their normal rates of pay. This suggests that there was nothing about these machines that made it essential to employ men to use them. At County Psychiatric they had acquired a gender by association with their users. Four miles away in another hospital the machines had acquired a different gender association, which indicates the adaptability of the gendering process.

Whatever the realities of individual men and women's differing strengths, strength itself is associated with men. Beechey and Perkins (1987) point out that when women's jobs involve heavy tasks, that requirement for strength tends to be ignored. They document a case in the baking industry in which requirements for strength were introduced into job descriptions at the implementation of the Equal Pay Act 1970, in order to differentiate men's jobs.

The requirement for strength to use large cleaning machines at County Psychiatric created a 'need' to employ men to use them (Cockburn 1983 1985). However, this analysis suggests that strength is not a prime requirement of the larger polishing machines, but a key label in the gendering of a job. The defined requirement for physical effort in a job is used in assessments of pay and grade. There seems to be a clear indication that it is not the nature of the work which defines its status and rewards but the sex of the worker.

It should be noted that there was not sufficient evidence to make firm suggestions about why management collude with the gendering of jobs. In their example, Beechey and Perkins indicate that segregation may provide a strategy to avoid the payment of equal pay to women. It may be used as a conscious strategy to maintain division among workers, although this implies considerable management sophistication. The general point to make in explaining this process is that managers exist in a general ideological framework in which gender roles are firmly entrenched. To most managers it seemed 'natural' that cleaners and catering assistants should be women. Even so, there are clues that indicate why jobs may be structured according to a gender order. There were specific advantages to management in having certain jobs constructed as women's jobs, and these may be important in explaining why managers collude in differentiating men from women workers. These advantages included the use of part-time working and particular forms of reorganization, issues which are developed later in this chapter. This, however, still does not provide an adequate explanation as to why managers encouraged the employment of small numbers of men. It may be that the employment of men adds status to the department, although there needs to be further research on this topic.

Job title and grading structures

Where segregation occurs along gender lines, differentiated job titles tend to become the norm. The differentiation between men's and women's jobs is formalized through the application of a different job title, so the male cleaners at County Psychiatric were known as 'team cleaners' rather than domestics, which the women were called. They were further separated off from the women by not operating under the women's supervisory structure. Managers were then able to claim that the men did a different job to the women, used specific machinery and had specific requirements for the job, which legitimated the placing of the men on a higher grade point. In this way job titles acquire a sanctity in terms of gender specificity, even though the same job elsewhere may be performed by a person of a different sex.

Segregation takes place not only between men and women employed in the same department, but throughout the ancillary departments. Catering and domestic services assistants' jobs are classed as unskilled. There are in the ancillary services a number of jobs performed almost exclusively by men which are also classed as unskilled, for example labourer or porter. However, as indicated previously, in public sector grading structures women's unskilled occupations are always positioned below men's unskilled jobs. Changes to these grading structures have served to maintain and conceal this situation, not to challenge it. It is for these reasons that women ancillary workers have a shared interest in challenging this discrimination, the allocation of women's jobs to a lower point on the grading structure.

A further feature of the grading structure which is not initially apparent, is the lack of mobility associated with the jobs predominantly done by women. Unskilled male workers entering the grading structure near the bottom would not expect to remain at that level, but would expect opportunities for rising within the grading structure without actual promotion. All of the male ancillary jobs had this potential. However, women catering and domestic services assistants, who entered the grading structure at the bottom, had almost no opportunity for advancement. In the ancillary jobs carried out by women, there was no possibility for movement up the grading structure without an actual promotion. In domestic services departments all staff except for the supervisors were on the lowest grade, which meant that there were very few opportunities for promotion. In catering departments there was no career ladder between catering assistants and cooking staff, which left no route for promotion. In the study there were many examples of women who had been on the bottom grade for over twenty years.

An important feature of women's manual work generally is the lack of routine movement within and between grading structures and the absence of possibilities for improvement in terms of pay. Women's manual work is not only undervalued and placed below men's work in grading structures, but there are fewer opportunities for women to move off the bottom grade. Therefore women ancillary workers share a further interest in terms of the lack of possibilities for training and promotion associated with their work. Training for basic-level cleaning and catering staff is mostly non-existent. When they begin the job, the only training is 'on-the-job'. This reflects the assumption that these forms of work are 'natural' to women. Training has been limited to hygiene-related procedures, which have come about as a result of a number of food poisoning cases.

In the hospitals studied, women's ancillary work was undervalued in as much as the conventional status of the work did not reflect the complex competencies involved. There was an assumption that cleaning and catering work was 'natural' to women. Further, even where the skill content of jobs carried out by men and women was nominally the same, men were differentiated from women by job title and position on the grading structure. Of particular importance in this process was the way in which the use of certain machinery and claimed requirements for strength were linked to gender. Thus, women ancillary workers have a shared interest in challenging the skill definition of their work, which is defined by the gender of the workers.

It was indicated earlier in this chapter that the construction of certain ancillary jobs as women's jobs has particular implications for the organization of work and benefits for management. These implications were identified as the potential for the use of part-time working and for specific forms of reorganization. These will each be discussed in turn.

Part-time Working

The majority of domestic services and catering assistants in this study were working part-time, but not all. The fact that the majority worked part-time is important, since it is sometimes argued that women's work is marginalized because it is part-time. However, it is more plausible to argue that it is marginalized and part-time because it is women performing this work – it is seen to be women's work. The construction of certain jobs as women's jobs enables employers to pursue particular strategies in terms of work organization and reorganization, and these are only possible in the context of women's work. Only in work constructed as women's work is the use of part-time labour a possible strategy. There is no inherent reason why hospital cleaning should be organized on a part-time basis, but since hospital cleaning has been constructed as women's work, it offers the possibility of being organized in that way.

Part-time working increased dramatically in women's ancillary work at a time when hospitals found it difficult to recruit sufficient numbers of staff. Part-time working was seen as a way of attracting married women into the service, but it was never regarded as an option in those jobs regarded as men's jobs. There were also problems of recruitment in men's jobs in hospital ancillary work, although here answers to recruitment difficulties were identified in terms of the low pay on offer. Therefore the response was in terms of identifying productivity deals which would attract more men into the service – the NBPI Report in 1966 recommended the use of productivity schemes to improve the pay of male ancillary workers. There seemed no necessity to improve the pay of women ancillary workers because, although low, it compared well with the wages which women could achieve in the private sector. However, as was discussed, the actual introduction of productivity schemes was patchy. The initially warm reception from trade unions waned as it became apparent that management were actually using them to cut staffing levels and thus wage bills.

Nonetheless, different methods were identified to attract labour in a period of labour shortage. Male labour was to be attracted by higher pay, and female labour was attracted by flexible hours. This accounts for the vast array of starting and finishing hours which were found in women's ancillary work, especially domestic services, which was discussed in the previous chapter. However, flexibility may be used to the benefit of the workers or the employers: in periods of labour shortage, flexibility may mean that working hours are organized to suit the convenience of the employee, although in the 1980s and 1990s flexibility has little to do with employee convenience.

While there is nothing inherent in catering and domestic services assistants' jobs that makes them part-time, management found that part-time working in these departments represented an efficient use of labour. In many hospitals these jobs have become 'part-time jobs'. Part-time working represents an efficient and effective use of labour from a managerial point of view, since it enables peaks of activity to be covered and is cheaper than the use of full-time labour. It is, however, a strategy only used in those occupations identified as women's work. Although the initial growth of part-time working can be linked to the need to attract women, especially married women and women with children, into the labour market, its centrality to the capitalist economy in Britain had little to do with women's convenience. Part-time workers have a number of specific interests related to their entitlement to employment protection, the ability of employers to organize their work more intensively without breaks, and the extent to which they are required to work unsocial hours. However, the use of part-time working also raises a number of specific issues related to restructuring, which will be discussed in the next section.

Up to this point it has been argued that there are three areas in which women ancillary workers share interests, in relation to definition of skill; placing in the grading structure; and as part-time workers. It has been shown that women's ancillary work cannot be understood without reference to gender, and that the nature and construction of such work cannot be separated from the gender of the workers. This will necessarily lead to different interests in the workplace, although to describe these interests as sectional would be to ignore the gender-specific nature of the interests, and the way in which they reflect more general interests in relation to the hierarchical division of the labour market by sex.

Gender and Restructuring

During the 1980s there were two main routes to restructuring in women's ancillary work, the introduction of bonus schemes and the development of competitive tendering. Not only is it necessary to consider gender in an understanding of the construction of work, but it is also necessary to see the restructuring of work in the context of gender. Beechey and Perkins draw attention to the gendered aspect of restructuring, and also to the issue that women's work may be restructured in more subtle, less obvious ways than men's work:

> It must be emphasised, however, that calculations of job losses and gains, so favoured by economists, do not begin to capture the variety of ways in which work is being restructured. Part-time jobs may not have disappeared as fast as full-time ones but there is a variety of other ways in which they have been adversely affected by the recession and the restructuring of work: the cutting and reorganization of hours, part-timers being sent to work in other workplaces, the abolition of retainers paid during the school holidays and the deregulation of employment contracts through privatization, for instance. (Beechey and Perkins 1987: 39)

Bonus schemes

As was discussed earlier, bonus schemes are not new developments in hospital ancillary work, although there was a push during the 1980s to introduce new schemes, and to update schemes. To fund a bonus payment it is always necessary to cut staffing costs in some fashion. In men's jobs, the only way to achieve this is by an actual loss of jobs, an obvious cut which workers often find unacceptable. A male shop steward from City Centre Hospital described how management had attempted several times to introduce bonus schemes in the portering department. He explained that each time the proposals had been rejected by the porters because they were aware that it would really mean more work and a loss of jobs.

This example illustrates the ongoing struggle that had been taking place between management and the portering staff over attempts to introduce new working practices which the porters had resisted. They collectively sought to resist a scheme because they had access through a senior steward in the department to information about the effects of bonus schemes. The senior steward was able to counter management's argument for more pay, with evidence that this would mean a loss of jobs, and therefore the same amount of work would be done by fewer people. Furthermore, the portering staff had a common interest in resisting the scheme's introduction, unlike the situation in County Psychiatric's catering department, where most staff stood to gain at the expense of the catering assistants. In the porters' department there were no divisions based on sex or race. This example not only illustrates that restructuring may be more overt in men's jobs, but also links into the ability of men to organize collectively to resist restructuring, a matter that will be discussed later.

Women's work, however, presents the possibility of cutting hours, by moving from full- to part-time working, or by reducing the hours of part-time workers. There tends to be an assumption that this is both feasible and acceptable regardless of the individual circumstances of the women concerned. As part-time working becomes the norm for women, to refuse to work part-time is often seen as unreasonable. An assumption that women should work part-time was found in the catering department at County Psychiatric, where the full-time catering assistants refused to move to part-time working and thus allow the rest of the staff to increase their wages through the bonus scheme.

This example illustrates how workers frequently identify another group of workers as the cause of their problems rather than considering the underlying cause of the problem. Armstrong describes such a situation in his research at ChemCo:

> ... whilst the men's hostility towards the women had its basis in fact, a deeper analysis would have led them to the conclusion that their real conflict of interests was with their employers. If the women seem to be a nuisance it is because the management have promised benefits and laid down rules

which make them seem a nuisance. If the men had remained aware of this, of the fact that however uninvolved they may seem, the management have a hand in practically everything that happens at work, none of the issues discussed here need have led to a breakdown of solidarity – let alone to the kind of antagonism which exists in ChemCo's Cement works. (Armstrong 1976: 97)

What is significant in this situation is that, as suggested previously, the sectional interests are divided along sex lines. The continual reaffirmation of sectional interests on gender-specific lines makes the achievement of solidarity particularly difficult. Managers use male and female labour in different ways, and therefore men and women frequently have different sectional interests in the workplace. As these interests, however, reflect underlying conflicts of interest between men and women in the wider labour market, conflict between men and women workers cannot be dismissed as false consciousness, since men frequently benefit from the gendering of work. As will be argued in the next chapter racial divisions also give rise to these kinds of conflict in the workplace.

In this study, the introduction of bonus schemes was speeding up the general trend towards part-time working. The domestic service department at City Centre had already established itself as completely part-time, and the manager of Shire General's domestic services was only employing part-time staff. This form of restructuring could only happen in women's work, where part-time working is regarded as legitimate. Hospital cleaning and catering assistant work were in the process of being reconstructed as part-time jobs.

Competitive tendering

Managements' desire to seek cost-cutting initiatives, such as work study linked to bonus schemes, was encouraged by government directives to subject ancillary services to competitive tendering. Health Authorities, reflecting the political make-up of their respective Local Government Authority, reacted at different speeds to proposals for competitive tendering. City Centre's Health Authority resisted this pressure until compelled, but the Shire Health Authority, which covered the other three hospitals, entered the process at the earliest possible time. Domestic services at Community Hospital were privatized in 1985, being taken over by Crothalls Ltd. Fourteen staff were made redundant, although seven of these were taken on by Crothalls, and twelve staff took early retirement. Many of the cleaning staff at Community had been working in the department for over twenty years.

The implications of competitive tendering were felt long before its implementation. For both private contractors and in-house tenders the only means to offer a cheaper service is to offer lower rates of pay, and/or expect the same amount of work to be done in fewer hours. Employees are faced with the choice of participating in the worsening of their own conditions through an in-house tender or risking the loss of their jobs, with the vague possibility of insecure employment with the private contractor. The domestic services manager described how he had hoped to produce an in-house tender by persuading the full-time staff to move to part-time working. He had been unable to convince them and therefore the tender he produced could not compete with one from a private contractor. He also described how the part-time staff resented the full-time staff for refusing to accept a reduction in their hours. This resentment was increased since most of the full-time workers were of Asian origin.

The manager had identified a shift to part-time working as the only means to produce an in-house tender, a strategy that would only be contemplated in the case of women's jobs. The private firm, coming in fresh with 'new' staff, was able to construct private hospital cleaning as part-time work. Since the manager wanted the in-house tender to receive the contract, and thus maintain his own job, he unsuccessfully put considerable pressure on full-time staff to move to part-time working. He attempted to mobilize pressure from part-time staff, utilizing existing divisions between full- and part-time staff and between staff of Asian and white British origin. The result was discontent and conflict. This state of affairs seems to suggest that the pressure of competitive tendering serves to highlight these divisions.

It is not coincidental that within hospital ancillary work, those departments under the most serious threat of privatization are the departments which are predominantly female. Female labour presents greater potential for rationalization and flexibility. In the case of Community Hospital, although there was high union membership in the domestic services department, the department was bitterly divided, and this precluded a collective response. The union branch secretary also felt that there was little chance of resisting the private contractor. Similarly, in local authority CCT (Compulsory Competitive Tendering), the highest proportion of contracts awarded to private companies has been in cleaning (Escott and Whitfield 1995). Reasons for this include the low level of investment required for this labour-intensive work and the ease with which costs can be cut through reducing pay and conditions. Significantly, Escott and Whitfield (1995) found that CCT had the effect of reducing trade union membership among part-time workers who had previously been union members.

Whilst private cleaning firms have been keen to enter hospital cleaning

there has been less enthusiasm from the private sector over catering departments. Hospital catering offers less opportunity for profit making. Private
cleaning firms can be cheap because they have lower staffing levels (Leonard
1992). Although the result may be unsatisfactory, the effects are felt more in
the long term. With the immediate consumption linked to catering, low
staffing levels would be felt immediately through the lack of meals. Furthermore, with the employment in catering departments of full-time male
workers, there are limited possibilities of moving to completely part-time
working. In short, catering staff appeared to be in a more powerful situation
than domestic services staff. During the 1980s the catering departments in this
research did not appear to be under the same imminent threat of privatization
as the domestic service departments. However, this power is not evenly spread
within catering departments. Management are still concerned to cut costs
wherever possible and this may be focused on the catering assistants through
either cutting their hours or replacing them through the introduction of new
processes. Within the catering departments studied in the research there were
discussions around a number of potential cost-cutting initiatives, such as self-
service canteen facilities, increased use of vending machines, and
pre-prepared frozen meals and cook/chill, the last of which was introduced at
St Stephen's.

The establishment of jobs as women's jobs makes them particularly suscepti-
ble to restructuring through the substitution of part-time labour. This happens
in women's ancillary work with the introduction of bonus schemes and/or
tenders for contracts. This form of restructuring can take place with relatively
little visibility, as moves towards part-time working are seen as natural and
acceptable for women. Once jobs are established as part-time jobs, it serves to
reproduce labour market segregation, since men are even less likely to enter
them. In addition, where generic working introduces aspects of patient contact
and relating to visitors, a caring or 'mothering' approach associated with
femininity may be deemed appropriate or even necessary to do the job, which
would further discourage men. In a similar way Macdonald and Sirianni
(1996) argue that for front-line service workers, the 'emotional proletariat',
personal characteristics are linked to their suitability for certain occupations.

Flexibility

Flexibility has become a key concept in both management and industrial
relations literature and practice, and all but one of the functional managers
interviewed as a part of this research identified the importance of achieving a

flexible workforce. They linked the need to achieve flexibility to both the introduction of new bonus schemes and the attempt to put together in-house tenders. The major concern of catering managers was to be able to move staff from one task to another, thus requiring flexibility in terms of the tasks carried out. This was particularly focused on the catering assistants, who were expected to move, for example, from food preparation to waitressing.

In domestic services, managers were more concerned with being able to move staff from one working area to another, and with being able to change shifts and hours. Since all staff did broadly the same work, managers required flexibility in terms of time and location. The domestic services manager from Shire County Hospital explained that she felt that she had the right as the manager to change the number of hours worked, the time of shifts and areas of work with comparatively little consultation with staff. In this example, the process of achieving the flexibility desired by management was linked to the fact that these were women's jobs. Management's right to change the number of hours worked could not have been contemplated in the portering department. Fairbrother has pointed out that managers in the public sector are looking at means of reorganizing the hours of male staff.

> Proposals to calculate working time over a longer period than a week are currently the subject of negotiations in several areas of employment such as parks, road maintenance and gardens where it would be possible to relate employment numbers to fluctuations in work routines. Similar re-arrangements of the working week would have advantages to employers where some element of weekend working is a requirement of the job.
> (Fairbrother 1988: 21)

These examples are drawn from jobs predominantly carried out by men. In men's jobs flexibility is more frequently achieved through the use of overtime working or the rearrangement of full-time hours over longer periods of time than the traditional unit of the week. In women's work, particularly in part-time work, changing hours is an established and relatively invisible practice. This means that in occupations constructed as women's jobs, flexibility may be achieved in gender-specific ways through the use of part-time labour.

In this section it is evident that not only the construction, but also the reconstruction of work occurs in the context of a gendered labour market. The gendering of the labour market results in gendered sectional interests in the workplace. However, the gendered nature of work organization makes it more difficult for women to organize collectively around their shared interests, as discussed in the next section.

Working Patterns and Limitations to Collectivity

It is important to stress that working patterns in women's ancillary work may militate against collective organization. This was evidenced in both domestic services and catering departments.

As pointed out in the previous chapter, the result of discrete day and evening shifts in domestic service departments was division and a lack of identity between the two groups of workers. A major problem arose from the fact that day and evening shifts operated on different bonus schemes and therefore saw their interests as in conflict. It was also noted that each shift tended to blame the other shift for shortages of materials and damage to equipment and machinery. A domestic services assistant from City Centre described how many of the day shift staff felt that the evening shift left equipment cupboards untidy, used excessive amounts of cleaning materials and left machinery uncleaned. However, a member of the evening shift at the same hospital made similar complaints of the day shift. There seemed to be a general problem of shortages of materials and equipment, with 'blame' being placed on workers from the other shift.

Although any shift working situation presents a possibility for division, the form of shift working found in domestic services departments enhances this likelihood. The particular form of shift working with a permanent part-time evening shift can only be understood in terms of the sex of the workers. The total lack of overlap between shifts in domestic services resulted in no contact between workers. Workers on the other shift remained an anonymous blur rather than real individuals with similar problems. The two shifts also tended to attract women of a slightly different age. The day shift attracted women with children at school, while the evening shift attracted younger women with pre-school age children who could be left with their partners while they went to work. One of the main problems for the women on the day shift was found to be one of how to cope when children were off sick from school.

One implication of this form of shift pattern is that it enhances the problems of getting together for informal discussion. Evening shift staff who worked a small number of hours had no breaks in which to talk to one another. Staff working a variety of shift patterns were working with different staff on different days. In the larger hospitals, the mere geographical separation prevented staff getting together when they did have breaks. It was easier to stay on the ward to have a cup of tea. These problems were enhanced by the frequent lack of rest room facilities where domestics could take breaks together.

In their research Coote and Campbell (1982) found that both men and women stressed the importance of informal 'chatting' for the development of unity and union consciousness in the workplace. In domestic services women work on separate shifts, they are geographically isolated from one another, and work tends to be intense and demanding. One advantage of part-time working for employers is that they can expect greater intensity of work over shorter periods of time, and gone are the communal tea breaks. This compares with the porters, who moved around the hospital as part of their job and had many opportunities for talking to one another, and also had tea and meal breaks in which to discuss any issue arising. This suggests that a major factor in underwriting a division in the domestic services departments was the shift system. These divisions were further emphasized where women of Asian and white British origin were working on different shifts.

As shown earlier, unlike domestic services departments where all staff were on the same grade, catering departments were divided between the catering assistants and all other catering staff, staff classed as skilled. In the extremely hierarchical atmosphere of the catering departments, much emphasis was placed on status and position. While domestic services departments were divided horizontally, catering departments were divided vertically. Staff in catering departments were not separated in time through a shift system, or geographically through working in isolation. The main limitation to the development of a collective identity found in catering departments in the research was that based on racial origin, that between women of Asian origin and all other staff. To a large extent this coincided with the division between catering assistants and the skilled staff, but not completely. This also reflected the sexual division of labour in as much as the catering assistant job has been created as a female job, although some women were found in the skilled positions as cook. Thus the development of a collective identity was hindered by the kitchen hierarchy, in which staff had different sectional interests. This was most obvious in the case of County Psychiatric. As with domestic services, divisions were emphasized most strongly where women of Asian origin were working full-time. This will be considered in more depth in the next chapter.

Controlling the Mop – Worker Resistance

Despite the obstacles to collective organization among women ancillary workers, it would be wrong to assume they constitute a submissive and passive workforce. Attempts by workers, however, to maintain some degree of control over the work process have to be seen in the light of the divisions discussed.

> On the shop floor of many factories the division between the supervisor and the men can be characterized as a 'frontier of control' – management's rights

on the one side and those of the workers on the other. It is in this way, in disputes over control at work, that the class struggle has been fought out by the British working class during this century. At the lowest, and most fundamental level, it has involved a conflict over how much work the men do and how much they get paid for it. At its most developed level it has produced an ideological conflict over who runs the factory and why, to a questioning of the essential nature and purpose of production within a capitalist society. (Beynon 1975: 129)

Although there are limits to the comparisons to be made between a hospital and a car factory, there was significant evidence of a 'frontier of control' within women's ancillary work. In women's hospital ancillary work the frontier of control was between the domestic services assistants and the catering assistants, and their supervisors and managers. As ever increasing pressure was placed on functional management to operate efficient, cost-effective, competitive services, so the struggle became more intense. One aspect of this struggle was the attempt to maintain internal hierarchies in domestic services. It will be argued that the forms of resistance resulted from the nature of women's ancillary work, and contained contradictions and limitations to collective organization.

As was pointed out in the previous chapter the development of internal hierarchies within domestic services, based on the cleaning of different parts of the hospital and informally operated by the women themselves, was felt to be very important by the women domestics. This code of seniority offered the women potential for advancement in a job with few opportunities. The operation of such a hierarchy conflicted directly with managements' desire for a flexible workforce and their 'right to manage'. On the other hand, such a hierarchy enabled a domestic assistant to work in the same area for some time and develop efficient practices and good relations with other staff. Hart (1991: 107) also found strong resistance to forms of flexibility which disrupted such relations, describing internal hierarchies as giving 'shape to the otherwise flat horizon of unskilled work'. Although the attempt to maintain this internal hierarchy presents a challenge to managerial control, the hierarchy in itself has contradictory effects on group unity, since it is actually based on forming and maintaining divisions among the workers. The hierarchy is attractive only to those workers at the top and those that might soon expect to be at the top.

Beechey and Perkins in their research were informed by trade union representatives that

... one of the consequences of the introduction of work study had been an increase in managerial control over the organization of domestic work; thus the women had very little control over their hours or conditions of work. Cleaners, for instance, had been moved from cleaning wards to cleaning offices without management taking into account whether they liked the contact with patients which working on the wards gave them. And hours of work had been changed at little or no notice. (Beechey and Perkins 1987: 88–9)

In this research, although the trends appeared to be in the direction of greater managerial control over the work process, it had not advanced as far as Beechey and Perkins found in their research. In particular there seemed to be differences between what managers claimed had happened and how domestic assistants experienced the changes. A cleaner from City Centre Hospital said that the manager's claim that she moved all staff on to different jobs every nine months was 'rubbish'. She suggested that there would have been a considerable outcry if some staff had been moved from their wards to less attractive areas.

The first implication of this example is a methodological one. There needs to be considerable caution in taking management assessments of developments in their departments as evidence that these developments have in fact taken place. Managers may be defensive of their own practices and present a picture of how they would like to see the department operate, rather than a picture of how it does operate in practice.

The operation by workers of an informal internal hierarchy of jobs in domestic services indicated that the workers were actively involved in exerting their own control over the organization of work. Women domestic staff could not be seen as a purely passive workforce simply accepting management initiatives. They believed that they had a right to work in certain areas of the hospital and were determined to retain that right. Domestic assistants claimed to have retained greater control over hours and allocation of work than managers had suggested was the case. Both management and staff at City Centre were aware that there was a struggle for control being carried out and wanted to present 'their side'. Despite the pressures for re-organization in domestic services, the example of these internal hierarchies indicates that women ancillary workers are not a passive workforce, but actively defend their position. Indeed it could be argued that it is a measure of the success of women ancillary workers to resist work intensification that this has led management in the 1990s to reconsider the use of private contractors or pursue the break-up of functional departments through the introduction of generic working.

Summary

This chapter has illustrated the gendering of work and the continued significance of job segregation by sex. However, it also shows the flexibility and adaptability of the gendering process, where a job in one location is established as a woman's job, yet the same job elsewhere can be established as a man's job. Nonetheless, clear distinctions are maintained between men's and women's work and this is reflected in the way in which work is constructed and reconstructed, which results in women having specific interests in the workplace. While these interests may be regarded as sectional, they reflect underlying divisions in the labour market as a whole. The women's ancillary work studied in this research was organized in such a way as to hamper collective organization, but women ancillary workers did resist attempts by management to extend control over the workplace. In the next chapter, these themes will be extended by looking at the implications of racial divisions in the workplace. This provides the foundation for considering the role of local union organization in accommodating women ancillary members.

6 RACE AND DIVISION IN THE WORKPLACE

In the previous chapter, the focus was on the features related to gender which may promote or prevent the development of a collective identity among women in the workplace. In this chapter, this focus will be extended, showing that it is not only gender that is central to the construction and reconstruction of work, but also race. This results in certain interests in the workplace being defined with reference to and perhaps by racial divisions. A consequence of this is that the concept of sectional interest is inadequate, not only because it is gender blind, but also because it is race blind. Gender and race interconnect in the workplace in a complex way, and this chapter begins to consider how they interconnect in the development of a collective identity. It will be suggested that even where women workers have shared interests, racial divisions are crucial in hindering that development. The argument is that racial divisions result in specific forms of response and resistance to managerial control. This chapter is divided into five main parts, firstly considering race and employment in the NHS, followed by discussions of the role of race in the construction and then the reconstruction of work. The fourth section identifies the importance of working patterns to limiting collectivity, and the final part considers specific forms of worker resistance. Firstly, however, it is necessary to give a brief review of race and employment in the NHS.

Race and Employment in the NHS

The way in which the term 'race' is used in this book, as a social construct, has been discussed in the Introduction. In this study workplace divisions were not based on a distinction between workers born in this country and those born overseas. Rather the key divisions were based on a distinction and separation of a specific group of workers, in this case women of Asian origin. This has methodological and theoretical implications. From a methodological point of view it means that a study of the country of origin of workers will not necessarily illuminate the importance of racial division to the development of a collective identity. From a theoretical position this indicates the importance of maintaining an analytical distinction between race and immigration. Immigration policies have been significant to employment in the NHS, although the focus here is on the way in which race is constructed in the workplace and its implications for the development of a collective identity (Miles and Phizacklea 1984).

During the 1970s and 1980s important research was carried out on migrant workers in the NHS (Doyal *et al.* 1980, 1981, 1983 and Williams *et al.* 1977). One of the main differences found in this research compared with that of Doyal *et al.* is the high level of employment in this study of women of Asian origin. Doyal *et al.* found that 38 per cent of domestic staff in the hospital they studied were Afro-Caribbean, which they compare with 22 per cent Afro-Caribbean in the study by Williams *et al.*. They found as few as one per cent of domestics were Asian. In this study over half of the domestics at two of the hospitals, County Psychiatric and Community, were of Asian origin, and there were no domestics of Afro-Caribbean origin. Similarly in catering, Doyal *et al.* found 32 per cent, and Williams *et al.* 69 per cent, of catering workers were southern European. In this study there were only three catering workers of southern European origin at County Psychiatric. The key group was again women of Asian origin. This was surprising given the generally high levels of workers of southern European origin in catering work. These figures indicate the reliance of NHS ancillary services on black workers, particularly black women workers, although they also indicate how dramatically regional variations may alter the pattern of employment. In this study there were also indications of high levels of employment of women of Irish origin (this category includes both immigrants and those born in Britain). This was not surprising, since the region had a large Irish population. However, it was difficult to establish precise numbers of staff of Irish origin. This in itself suggested that differentiation and divisions were not based directly on immigration. It was for this reason that the focus of the research was on examining how jobs become 'racialized', while immigration is seen as only one facet of this process.

This study, in considering the interconnections between race and gender divisions among working-class women, focuses particularly on women of Asian origin. Some of the issues raised in this chapter may be generalized to other groups of workers. However, the strategies for differentiating groups of workers analysed here such as the use of a particular racial stereotype and the forms of resistance are specific to Asian women workers.

Recruitment to the NHS

Despite the focus on race, it is important to outline the significance of immigration to recruitment in the NHS. There are specific reasons for the generally high level of employment of staff born overseas in the NHS. To understand this, it is necessary to study the implications of general immigration policies and then local recruitment strategies. Doyal, Hunt and Mellor point out that overseas recruitment to the health service began as soon as the establishment of the NHS:

> This initial scheme marked the first systematic introduction of colonial recruits into British hospitals and from the early 1950s until the first Commonwealth Immigration Act of 1962, labour from the colonies was actively sought after. The two areas which achieved particular attention were the Caribbean and the Indian subcontinent. (Doyal, Hunt and Mellor 1981: 55)

Despite the restrictions of the 1962 Act, skilled labour was still able to enter the country. This enabled doctors and nurses to continue to enter the country, but unskilled workers were only able to enter if they were able to obtain a work permit. However, the NHS was made a special case and hospitals were allowed to recruit unskilled overseas workers (Doyal, Hunt and Mellor 1981). After the 1971 Immigration Act removed automatic right of entry to Commonwealth nonpatrials, restrictions on work permits stopped this flow of unskilled overseas workers into the NHS. In this way patterns of recruitment into hospital ancillary work have been directly affected by successive governments' use of immigration legislation.

The women of Asian origin in this study were recruited in this country. In general the women in the study were from the Sikh community, whose families had mostly come from the rural Punjab area of northern India. Wilson (1985) describes how men from the Punjab came to Britain in the 1950s and their wives began to join them in the 1960s. Although these women were not directly recruited in India, they entered a country in which hospital ancillary work had been formally identified as appropriate work for immigrant labour, as appropriate work for black workers. Not only were certain ancillary jobs constructed as women's jobs, but they were also constructed as 'suitable' work for black women workers, whether of Afro-Caribbean or of Asian origin. Mama (1992) argues that NHS ancillary work has tended to recruit Afro-Caribbean women rather than Asian women. However, large numbers of Sikhs from the Punjab settled in the areas covered by this research. For this reason, it was likely that more women of Asian origin might be expected to be present in hospital ancillary work than in southern England, where most studies have been carried out.

That regional variations are so great indicates again the adaptability of the process by which certain jobs can be constructed around race, as well as gender. Doyal's work suggests that, particularly in the London area, hospital cleaning has been established as 'appropriate' work for women of Afro-Caribbean origin and hospital catering has been established as appropriate work for women of southern European origin. In contrast, at three of the hospitals in this study, Community, Shire County and County Psychiatric Hospitals, both areas of work had been established as appropriate work for women of Asian origin.

If the local area is examined in detail, then it becomes apparent that there are particular historical explanations for the concentration of Asian staff in ancillary work in the areas covered by this research. Ancillary staff were mostly drawn from housing areas situated close to hospitals in which they worked. In this case there were a considerable number of women of Asian origin who had been recruited when they came from the Punjab in India in the 1960s to join their husbands, attracted by the prospect of work at a large Ford Foundry. This pattern of immigration fits precisely with the national picture described by Wilson (1985).

Since the women in this study were recruited in this country, it is necessary to consider the recruitment practices of individual hospitals. Smith (1974) found that those employers who had larger numbers of 'minority' (his term) employees had used a wider range of recruitment methods. He found that employers tended to use a wide range of methods when they had difficulty finding labour, especially in low level, low paid work. Although in his later research, Smith suggests that overt discrimination in recruitment was declining, this study found very marked racial divisions of labour (Smith 1977).

Given the general patterns of recruitment, the most significant feature was the lack of employment of women of Asian origin at City Centre Hospital. While there was no definite explanation of the absence of black workers in the domestic services department, the manager explained the situation by reference to past discrimination. Although it was impossible to find evidence to substantiate this suggestion, the example indicates that where employers have been able to recruit white staff, they do so. One explanation for the availability of white staff at City is the generally high economic activity rate of women in the city, linked to a shift in women's employment from manufacturing to the service sector in the 1960s. There may have been more white women seeking employment in the 1960s than in many other towns and cities. This would then give managers greater choice and therefore greater opportunity to discrim-inate in recruitment.

Managers may not be overtly refusing to employ black applicants, but they may be using those recruitment methods which are least likely to result in having black applicants. For example, in his discussion of mainly male manu-facturing work, Wrench (1986a) argues that the common practice of word-of-mouth recruitment works against black applicants. Similarly, in local authority cleaning work, Escott and Whitfield (1995) found that word-of-mouth recruitment resulted in lower levels of recruitment of black workers. If, as suggested by the managers at City Hospital, black applicants were more likely to call at the hospital seeking employment, then the practice of only recruiting through advertisements in the press may also have discriminated against potential black applicants. Using a recruitment practice which is commonly regarded to be fair, may actually involve a more covert exercise of discrimination.

Race and the Construction of Work

In Chapter 2 it was suggested that racial divisions in women's work tend to be horizontal rather than vertical, as in the case of gender. Race, in British capitalist society, does not have the same implications for skill level as gender. While the skill level of a particular work process may be defined by the gender of the workers who perform it, this is not the case with race. This, however, is not to deny that in a society with institutionalized racism, black workers are over-represented in lower grade work (Phizacklea 1988, Owen 1994). In hospital ancillary work, there is an over-representation of black workers in the lower grade work. Nevertheless, the ancillary grading structure is defined primarily around gender, and the precise way in which race interconnects with gender varies very much by location.

Racial stereotypes

The previous section described how, when the NHS was unable to attract staff to ancillary jobs, it sought labour overseas. It also recruited the labour of wives and families of male workers who had immigrated to Britain. However, the example of City Hospital suggests that black workers are seen as less attractive workers and recruited only when there is no alternative supply of labour. This suggests that individual managers base their recruitment practices on racial stereotypes about the suitability of different groups of workers.

The application of stereotypical labels plays a key role in the construction of race in the workplace. As Parmar (1982) points out, work is constructed in terms of racially defined gender roles. She begins to indicate the racial stereotypes which define the employment position of women, and explain features such as the lack of black women in secretarial and other jobs which 'present women as visibly attractive to men. It is precisely these jobs from which black women are excluded because in such instances it is white femininity which is required to be visible' (Parmar 1982: 258–9).

It is important to remember that the construction of women's work around race is based on stereotypes of all women, not only black women. Hoel indicates a stereotype used by Asian employers in her study:

> ... the Asian employers had developed a view of English women workers as undesirable, perhaps dangerous, to employ. While two thought that English women worked harder and would be best suited as forewomen, on the whole they felt that English, unlike Asian women demand higher pay and better conditions, and spend a lot of money on clothes, cigarettes and general entertainment for themselves. (Hoel 1982: 82)

Stereotypes of white British workers tend to be less frequently heard than the expression of white British racism, in terms of stereotypes of black workers. Stereotypes may in certain cases be based in part in fact, for example, there is a strong stereotype of Asian women as passive, and Hoel's research seems to support this. However, what her research also shows is that Asian managers may be able to use family connections to maintain greater control over Asian women workers in certain circumstances. This does not mean that women of Asian origin are inherently passive, or always constitute a passive workforce.

In my research there was some evidence that even within the NHS the family structure may be being utilized as a means of controlling women of Asian origin. The branch secretary from COHSE at County Psychiatric described a case where one of the supervisors felt that one of the Asian cleaners was not working hard enough and contacted the woman's husband, who beat her, and offered to beat her again if her standard of work did not improve. This example suggests that the family may be seen as an appropriate means to control women workers of Asian origin. However, the example was given as an extreme and unusual case. Nonetheless, as Parmar points out, there is much evidence to suggest that the stereotype of Asian women as passive should not be assumed to cover all Asian women.

This discussion does not intend to suggest that racism can be reduced to the application of stereotypes. The argument is made, however, that stereotyping plays an important part in the distinction and separation of groups of workers in the construction of race. This argument will now be developed in relation to the hospitals involved in the research.

Stereotypes used in the hospitals

A key stereotype that emerged in this research was of Asian women being 'slow' and/or 'lazy' and/or 'stupid'. These were views expressed openly by functional managers in the research. An example of this was the domestic services manager at County Psychiatric who, as was discussed earlier, wished to restrict the bonus to white staff. This manager was firstly treating all women staff of Asian origin as a homogeneous group in which individual background and effort were irrelevant. His reasons for wishing to remove the bonus from the women of Asian origin was that he believed that they were 'lazy and slower' workers. Significantly, he was unable to present actual evidence for these beliefs.

Of the seven departments studied, only two managers believed that Asian women workers were no different to any others. In the other departments the functional managers described Asian women workers as problematic in some form or other. The view expressed by these managers was that they had been 'forced' to employ Asian women in the past because they had been unable to recruit anyone else. This suggested that women workers of Asian origin were regarded as the 'last resort' when no other sources of labour were available. During the late 1980s, County Psychiatric was still experiencing difficulties with recruitment, but managers from Shire General and Community felt that increasing unemployment had given them greater choice over who they recruited. In this way increasing unemployment had given them greater opportunity to discriminate against women of Asian origin. This was justified by the need to employ staff who could 'demonstrate adequate use of English'.

While some managers made convincing arguments for the need to read English in relation to the hazards of chemicals used in cleaning, it was obvious that this had not been considered a problem in the past. Further, it should be noted that non-employment of anyone with language difficulties is only one response. During the 1970s many hospitals, including County Psychiatric, organized classes for staff in English, using half their own time and half work time. Equally, chemicals could have been labelled in more than one language. This suggests that this argument had been developed for the sole purpose of excluding women of Asian origin from hospital ancillary work, and to legitimize that exclusion.

Up until the early 1970s low pay and unattractive work made recruitment to hospital ancillary work difficult. Successive governments facilitated the recruitment of overseas workers through immigration legislation. Hospital ancillary work was constructed as appropriate work for black workers and widespread recruitment also took place among black populations living in Britain. Where alternative sources of labour were available, as in City, white workers were recruited in preference to black workers. There seems some evidence from this research that with increasing levels of unemployment in the 1970s and 1980s, hospital ancillary work may have been reconstructed as unsuitable work for black workers. This process appears to be legitimized through the application of racial stereotypes to black workers.

Race and Restructuring

Part-time working is more usual among white women (Beechey and Perkins 1987, Bruegel 1989). If Asian women are significantly more likely to be working full-time, and the main impetus of the restructuring of women's jobs has been the shift from full-time to part-time working, then restructuring cannot be understood without reference to racial divisions. Immediately, new questions are raised. To what extent does the restructuring of the labour process mean the substitution of part-time white women workers for full-time black women workers? To what extent are black women workers taking the brunt of recession in women's manual work? Significantly, in her study, Hart (1991: 90) indicates that some Afro-Caribbean cleaners felt that 'the shortening of working hours was tending to make the job less attractive to them and more attractive to younger white women'. My research can offer some tentative conclusions with reference to hospital ancillary work.

In this study the majority of full-time women staff in both catering and cleaning departments were of Asian origin. The main exception was of more senior cooking staff in catering departments who were more likely to be of white British origin. The previous chapter identified two main forms of restructuring, the introduction of bonus schemes and competitive tendering. The introduction of a bonus scheme required a cut in staffing costs in some fashion, and reducing women's hours of work was regarded as the 'rational' means to achieve such a cut. The women of Asian origin were a potential target as the workers who should absorb this cut.

The example from the catering department at County Psychiatric raises a number of issues relating to some of the complex relationships between race and gender divisions. Only men were doing overtime, which was regarded as acceptable. White full-time women cooks were not expected to take a cut, their jobs being regarded more as 'career' jobs. Part-time white women staff were not expected to take a further reduction in hours. If the Asian women had not been in the department, it seems probable that another strategy would have been sought. However, in this situation they were identified as the first target for cuts, and all of the other staff united in supporting this strategy.

Competitive tendering created the same impetus to cut staffing costs. Again the prime means to create a competitive in-house tender was identified as substituting part-time for full-time staff. As illustrated in the case of the domestic services at Community Hospital, almost all the full-time staff were of Asian origin. The women of Asian origin refused to accept a shift to part-time working and divisions between workers became obvious. The patterns of full-time and part-time working among women mean that black women may be most under threat from the restructuring of women's employment. The examples from this research also suggest that there may be a long-term substitution of white part-time workers for black full-time workers.

During the 1990s two main management strategies were developing in relation to ancillary work, the move to generic working and the use of private contractors. Both developments hold potential threats for Asian women workers. The demands for communication and language, and the demands for patient contact in generic working were being used as a means to legitimate the removal or non-employment of the women of Asian origin. In the previous chapter it was argued that certain generic care jobs require femininity; furthermore the new roles require a public form of femininity which was not seen to fit with the image of the older Asian women, who previously worked in a less public arena. In this way divisions of race may be emphasized in service work (Macdonald and Sirianni 1996). In addition, anecdotal evidence suggested that the private contractors were trying to remove the women of Asian origin. It appears that the various developments of the 1990s serve to reinforce the redefinition of hospital ancillary work as inappropriate for women of Asian origin.

As a result of these developments, the Asian women have specific interests in the workplace relating to restructuring. Different interests in the workplace along racial lines serve to prevent the development of a collective consciousness among staff. These interests may be perceived as sectional, although they reflect more general issues traditionally excluded from the restricted trade union agenda.

Working Patterns and Limitations to Collectivity

Moving from the argument about stereotypes and the implications for restructuring, it will be argued that those divisions identified in the previous chapter which resulted from the patterns of working were reinforced by coinciding with racial divisions. It has been suggested that in domestic services the shift patterns prevented collective identification among the workers. In those hospitals where women of Asian origin were employed, there tended to be a racial division between the shifts. The women of Asian origin were more likely to be employed on day shifts, the most extreme example being at Community Hospital, where the evening shift was completely white. There are a number of reasons which could combine to explain this. Since women of Asian origin were much more likely to be working full-time and evening shifts were always completely part-time, it would be more surprising to find Asian women on the evening shifts. Women of Asian origin may have been able to utilize family networks to care for children during the day, enabling them to work on the day shift. There were often sizable friendship groups on the shifts, and women tended to apply for jobs where they had friends working, reinforcing the racial divisions.

Where antagonisms between shifts reflected racial divisions, these divisions obscured the real problems. For example, at Community Hospital domestic services department the problem relating to the competitive tender was defined racially. Many white British staff held the women of Asian origin responsible for privatization because they would not accept part-time working. The Asian women became 'the problem', a view which was reinforced by the attitude of the manager. In all of the domestic services departments there seemed to be some antagonism between day and evening shifts, with each blaming the other for lack of materials and equipment. Where the shift pattern reflects racial divisions, this antagonism also took on a racial dimension.

As already noted, catering departments were divided vertically and women of Asian origin were employed disproportionately at the catering assistant grade. They were more likely to be working as kitchen assistants than as dining room assistants. This distribution of the workforce was associated with particular tensions in the catering department at County Psychiatric Hospital, where the key division seemed to be between the Asian women and all other staff. This was illustrated by the hostility over the refusal by the women of Asian origin to take a cut in hours. Once again the remainder of the staff seemed to identify the women of Asian origin as 'the problem'. The women of Asian origin were seen as preventing everyone else getting an increased bonus payment. This attitude again seemed to be reinforced by the attitude of the manager.

However, Westwood (1984) is correct to warn against reading from such examples purposeful 'divide and rule' strategies by management. There was little evidence in this research that the functional management had developed strategies as such at all. However, it does not take much sophistication to blame the workers with least power for any problems faced in the department. Where the organization of work results in horizontal segregation based on race, interests of particular workgroups are more likely to take on a racial dimension. This further prevents the development of a collective identity among women ancillary workers who, as was discussed in the previous chapter, have certain common interests.

Asian Women and Resistance

In the previous chapter the struggle over the 'frontier of control' between women ancillary workers and their managers was discussed. In this section it will be suggested that struggle also takes on a particular form in a racially divided workforce.

In her work on women workers during World War Two, Summerfield (1977) suggests that sexism was used by women as a form of resistance to factory discipline. She indicates that where male supervisors assumed that women could not work hard or well because they were women, the women took advantage to play out the stereotype. In this context Summerfield argues that unionization could act as a form of discipline, through channelling random and haphazard forms of resistance into accepted forms of struggle.

Westwood identifies a similar form of resistance based on a shop-floor culture which embodies both resistance and subordination:

> It is an oppositional culture, providing a focus for resistance to managerial authority and demands, while forging solidarity and sisterhood. ... That version of womanhood is tied to Western, romantic idealisations of love, marriage and motherhood, which promote a subordinate definition of woman founded upon weakness and division. (Westwood 1984: 230)

Westwood identifies such strategies as culturally specific. This research supports Parmar, who argues that Asian women have developed their own forms of resistance:

> ... first, that the ways in which patriarchal relations affect Asian women in the workplace take a distinct form that is determined by a racist patriarchal ideology based on common-sense ideas of Asian sexuality/femininity; and, second, that these differing modes of femininity are manipulated by the women to their own advantage (albeit limited). They give rise to specific forms of resistance in the workplace. (Parmar 1982: 258)

This research supports this argument in two particular areas. Firstly, the continual criticisms by management that Asian women refused to hurry in their work suggests that they were more resistant to any speed-up of their work. While such an attitude might usually be identified with good union practice, in this context co-workers, managers and union officers cited this as an example of 'laziness', which they suggested was common to all Asian women. The manager at Community domestic services said that one of the main problems with the Asian women was that he couldn't get them to work any faster, and if he asked them to do anything differently they just pretended that they didn't understand. That he believed that the women were pretending not to understand his requests indicates that he saw their responses as a challenge to managerial control. Secondly, there was evidence to support Parmar's argument that language can be used as a form of resistance:

> One common-sense image of Asian women is that they do not speak English and it is frequently used as an excuse to explain their low position within the labour market and their low participation in trade unions. Many Asian women are well aware that there is always an assumption made that they are dumb because they cannot speak English ... Many Asian women whom we have interviewed have a good grasp of English and can understand it well. Yet, because they are usually expected not to utter more than a few words and are spoken to by management in a patronizing manner, they deliberately let them believe that they don't understand very well. (Parmar 1982: 264–5)

This seemed to be the situation at Community Hospital. The domestic services manager was convinced that the Asian staff did in fact understand English and were being non-co-operative on purpose. This manager saw the women workers of Asian origin not as a passive workforce but as purposefully disruptive. A vigorous management/worker struggle was being enacted in an almost covert fashion, and one into which trade unions organized by white males could not link.

Parmar recognizes the limitations of such forms of resistance, reinforcing the very divisions to which they are a response. However, it is important to recognize that despite divisions, specific groups of women ancillary workers did have a sense of unity and were resisting attempts to increase managerial control over the work process.

Summary

The very reasons which enabled some groups of women of Asian origin in ancillary work to develop a degree of unity with one another served to reinforce divisions between them and other workers which were based on racist stereotypes. Divisions between full- and part-time workers and between day and evening shifts often coincided with divisions between women of Asian origin and women of white British origin. The forms of resistance which were used by the Asian women not only alienated management but also their co-workers, who argued that the result was more work for themselves. As more pressure was placed on domestic services and catering departments to cut costs there was evidence of management and workers of white British origin identifying the women of Asian origin as the major problem – they could not achieve efficiency as long as the Asian women insisted on working full-time, while the Asian women refused to work harder.

It is clear from this research that the women of Asian origin have specific workplace interests, which relate to both gender and race divisions. It is also evident that the women of Asian origin developed their own response and forms of resistance to managerial control, albeit in a limited way.

Hospital ancillary work is in the process of dramatic reorganization. There has already been an enormous loss of jobs in this sector. Many of the changes do not specifically relate to the development of NHS trusts, although local financial accountability results in continual pressure to cut costs. Day surgery, community care and cook/chill food production have all had major effects on the levels of staff for hospital-based ancillary work. The two key developments in progress at the moment are the continual 'market testing' of ancillary departments, and the shift to generic working.

Managers in the NHS disagree as to the effect of trust status on their own power. They are still limited by central government finance, yet they do have considerably more autonomy over how they utilize budgets, and this has given managers more scope to pursue different strategies. The move to generic working is particularly attractive. It means the removal of the big functional ancillary departments, so active in industrial action in the 1970s and 1980s. It also fits well with a general shift towards 'care teams', with an emphasis on patient or consumer satisfaction. Finally the emphasis on training and development, which is integral to most moves to generic working, fits well with the desire of many trusts to become 'learning organizations'. The form of work reorganization is affected by the gender and race composition of the workforce, and these management strategies may, in turn, serve to change the make-up of the workforce.

This part of the book has analysed the changing situation of women's hospital ancillary work, highlighting the way in which a labour market which is structured by reference to gender and race results in specific interests for specific groups of workers. While it is possible to identify generalized interests relating to women or black workers, in specific workplaces interests may emerge in various ways depending on the way in which division or solidarity is manifested in the particular context. The resulting interests expressed by particular workgroups may be identified as sectional, although they reflect more generalized interests. These might be contrasted with the trade union agenda, generally regarded as representing wider class interests, but which has been defined in terms of the interests of white, male, skilled workers. Bradley (1999) suggests that there is now a potential to redefine class interests to reflect the experience of women. The next part of the book examines the articulation and representation of interests in trade unions and assesses how far it may be possible to transform the trade union agenda.

PART THREE
ANCILLARY WORKERS' TRADE
UNIONS

7 WORKPLACE UNIONISM

Through a study of workplace trade union organization, the third part of the book examines local union democracy and assesses how enduring the trade union agenda has been in the context of the formation of UNISON and the changes to the structure of the health service. In particular, the move towards decentralized collective bargaining in the NHS, even if slower than at first envisaged, has placed much greater importance on lay branch officers and shop stewards, while potentially changing the relationship between them (Bryson, Jackson and Leopold 1995, Terry 1996). Further, it has been suggested that local collective bargaining may provide a climate for a more participative form of unionism (Fairbrother 1996, Lloyd 1997). These issues are addressed through an analysis of workplace union organization focusing on the activities of stewards and the role of union meetings.

Central to this chapter is an argument that within the union branches studied there was considerable centralization of power at the level of branch officers. It will be suggested that an essential counter-balance to branch officer power is the development of an effective shop steward system providing a link with members in the workplace, alongside local union meetings. Paradoxically, because of the way meetings are organized they may serve to reproduce the restricted union agenda. Meetings often failed to provide appropriate opportunities for the development and articulation of interests, yet they are an essential basis for workplace democracy. Hyman (1979, 1989) indicates some of the contradictions involved in the concentration of power at branch level. Power may be used to develop and extend participation, or it may be used to contain and limit participation. These contradictions will be examined through a comparison of the union branches covered by the research.

An underlying argument in this chapter is that certain structures may increase opportunities for participation, although they cannot guarantee it. The chapter will focus on union structures at the level of the branch, and assess the degree to which these structures encourage or inhibit the participation of women members. It is maintained that while union structures have implications for the participation of all members, there are specific implications for the participation of women members. Linked to this, it is suggested that women's ability to take a role in union posts is limited by the nature and organization of their work. While it is not suggested that there is an ideal type of local union structure, it is claimed that union structures enable or inhibit the participation of women ancillary members. One specific feature of this is the importance of key branch or union officers in determining access to the structures of participation as well as control over the definition of interests.

Shop steward Systems

This section firstly examines some of the recent debates concerning workplace trade unionism and describes the shop steward systems and union organizations at each of the hospitals in the research. The shop steward holds a key position in local union organization, providing the link between members and the wider union. In Chapter 3 it was demonstrated that women are proportionally underrepresented at the level of shop steward. Through a discussion of various aspects of the shop steward's role, it will be argued that the nature of women's ancillary work makes it more difficult for women ancillary workers to carry out the role of shop steward.

The job of the shop steward and changing workplace unionism

The precise role of a shop steward varies enormously from union to union, and from industry to industry. Coates and Topham outline a range of activities which research suggested formed the main parts of this role:

> (1) spokesman for the workgroup, (2) disseminator of information between the organisation and the group, (3) minor bargaining over grievances, (4) monitoring of information, (5) liaison, with other groups and with managers, (6) exercising leadership, to strengthen the cohesion and therefore the bargaining power of the group, (7) decision making, (8) formal negotiation with senior management. (Coates and Topham 1988: 157)

Evidence from this research suggests that shop stewards in the NHS vary greatly in terms of the degree of their involvement in the activities described. In the 1980s, with pay and conditions set nationally, there was no immediate local role in the negotiation over these issues. Negotiations at the level of District Health Authority and at the hospital level were carried out by branch officers and/or full-time union officials. Negotiations at the level of department were carried out by branch officers and/or stewards who had been identified within the branch as senior stewards. In larger branches small numbers of stewards were identified as potential branch officers and informally recognized as 'senior stewards'. This left only the first three of the spheres of activity identified by Coates and Topham for the other shop stewards. In particular, the main role of shop stewards included in this research was dealing with individual members' grievances and disciplinary cases.

Manson (1977) argued that the introduction of productivity schemes in the 1960s provided a basis for a growth in trade union activity among ancillary workers. The move towards local collective bargaining in the 1990s was initially feared by trade unions as they envisaged less well organized branches being unable to match the new aggressive management. However, research has indicated that those branches which seemed to be handling local bargaining most effectively were those which emphasized workplace organization and representation, and actively recruited and developed activists (Labour Research 1996d). In this context a more optimistic view is possible, where local bargaining creates an opportunity for the development of a more participative trade unionism (Fairbrother 1990, 1996). There is, therefore, a renewed interest in the nature of workplace organization, which forms the focus of this chapter.

Fairbrother (1996) and Fosh (1993) are two major advocates of a union renewal thesis. Fosh argues firstly that there is more workplace participation than is commonly thought, and secondly that there are fluctuations in the degree of participation over time (Fosh, 1993: 579). A suggestion is made that membership participation may rise when issues of direct concern are being discussed, but that the level of participation is mediated by: local leadership style; the industrial relations atmosphere; past experience of the union; and the structure of the local union (Fosh 1993: 581). Fosh emphasizes the role of local trade union leadership, arguing that where they adopt a collectivist and participatory approach it is possible to build on 'surges of participation and interest' (Fosh 1993: 589). In this context a participatory style stresses the importance of the involvement of members, and a collectivist outlook relates problems to shared situations rather than treating them as individual grievances (Fosh 1993: 581).

Fairbrother (1996: 112) has developed a broader discussion about the wider context of state policy in which unions are 'changing both structurally and ideologically, with the development of new forms of unionism becoming a distinct possibility'. The key to this change is the development of a more participative form of trade unionism alongside managerial decentralization in sectors where trade unions have historically been highly centralized, although there is nothing inevitable about this for Fairbrother. Central to this form of unionism is membership participation in the workplace. In this context Fairbrother accepts the importance of branch leadership in these developments, but argues that this cannot be seen as the defining feature of change.

In comparison Colling (1994: 142) presents a cautious approach to the renewal debate, arguing that unions will need to move resources from national to local levels to 'build and invest in workplace organization'. He identifies limitations to renewal in a context in which workplace structures may be weakened in the present public sector industrial relations climate, resulting in over-stretched stewards, limited to a narrow bargaining agenda. Colling also highlights the 'uneven and gendered distribution of bargaining power' which may undermine moves to recruit and represent women (Colling 1995: 143). However, bargaining over equality issues may provide a stimulus to union activity. Significantly, Labour Research (1998a) has found that decentralization has pushed more shop stewards into negotiating over equal pay and equal value cases. As indicated in the previous chapters, detailed information about the make-up of the labour force and pay and grading structures is necessary to assess gender inequalities. Using the Equal Opportunities Commission's guidelines as a lever to gain information from employers could promote workplace activity (Labour Research 1998a).

Colling (1995) also suggests that decentralized bargaining may intensify the pressures towards the bureaucratization of local organizations. Both he and Fairbrother emphasize the continued role for national organization to balance tendencies towards parochialism (Colling 1995) and to provide the landscape in which renewal will take place (Fairbrother 1996). In contrast, Hyman (1997) has placed greater emphasis on the national centralized role of trade unions in a context of the globalization of capital. While it is beyond the scope of this work to develop a general assessment of the potential for union renewal, it can contribute towards these debates.

Steward structures in the four union branches

A prerequisite for any such contribution is an understanding of the forms of union organization which currently operate. The four case study hospitals were introduced in Chapter 3 and this section gives a brief summary of their steward systems There are a number of significant variations between the branches and over time, which are examined through discussions of constituency formation, recruitment to the shop steward role and the range of shop steward activities.

UNISON/NUPE – City Centre Hospital

In 1983 the NUPE branch which included City Hospital had 78 shop stewards, a comparatively large steward body, of whom over fifty were women. At this time there were ten NUPE stewards based at City Hospital itself. Of these, four were men – two from portering, one from domestic services and one from the works department. There were six women stewards – two from nursing, one from the dining room and the remaining three from domestic services.

Proportionate to membership there were fewer shop stewards at City Hospital compared with Walton Hospital, where the branch secretary was based. However, among these ten stewards were the deputy branch secretary (a porter), and the branch chair (an auxiliary nurse who subsequently briefly became branch secretary). Also, when the branch tested the idea of having senior stewards to represent administrative units within the Health Authority, one of the women stewards from the domestic services department was proposed. Although the hospital was numerically short of shop stewards, it was well-equipped with active and experienced stewards. All of the shop stewards at City, indeed all of the stewards in this branch, were white. This branch, as the largest branch in the study, made the greatest use of the senior steward position when compared with other branches. There were poor relations with the full-time official, who was in effect excluded from branch activities, and branch officers operated with considerable autonomy.

By 1996 there had been a dramatic change to the shop steward system, there now being only 12 shop stewards, four based at City Centre and eight based at Walton Hospital. One of the stewards at Walton was a woman, while at City Centre there were no women stewards and no stewards from the porters' department, although a woman domestic was elected during the field research. Shop steward meetings had ceased to operate and the branch secretary, now having been in post for ten years, dealt with all case work and local negotiations.

UNISON/COHSE – County Psychiatric – St Stephen's

The County Psychiatric COHSE branch had a total of 12 shop-stewards at the time of the initial fieldwork. Of these, 11 were nursing staff and one an occupational therapist. There were eight male and four female stewards. One of the male stewards was of Asian origin. Despite the fact that there were no ancillary stewards, branch officers estimated that the branch recruited approximately half of the ancillary staff at the hospital. The remaining ancillary staff were members of the small NUPE branch. The COHSE branch officers were all young, white, male student nurses.

Shop stewards in this branch, despite the young age of many, had considerable experience of unions. Five had at some point held other union posts as well as being shop stewards, although five had only been shop stewards for under a year. This branch was also particularly active in local campaigns against the potential privatization of services.

By the 1990s a degree of stability had been achieved at this branch despite the dramatic changes to work associated with the move to St Stephen's and the large reduction in staff numbers. Branch officer posts were now held by permanent staff, and the eight shop stewards represented most departments. With the formation of UNISON, there has been an increasing move towards regional and national responses to pay negotiations, even where management have attempted to decentralize bargaining. Branches such as St Stephen's and Shire General below, where branch officers feel themselves to be relatively inexperienced, have found this particularly helpful.

UNISON/NUPE – Shire General Hospital

As was explained in Chapter 3, this branch of NUPE was based around Shire and another hospital in the south of the county. At Shire General Hospital there were seven shop stewards, five ancillary stewards, one member of the administration and clerical staff and the senior steward from the works department (who become branch secretary towards the end of the first period of research). One of the shop-stewards was of Asian origin.

With the formation of UNISON, branch officer posts were taken by staff from a range of constituent unions, professional, nursing and administrative. There were in 1996, ten shop stewards, including five from ancillary services: two domestics, one from catering and two porters. There were no Asian stewards despite Asian staff accounting for 75 per cent of domestic staff and 50 per cent of catering staff. Three of the ancillary stewards were women. At the time of the research a convenor post was established to liaise with all unions, a management appointee, a woman from an administrative job. Union recognition had been agreed with the private contractors who had taken over ancillary services.

COHSE – Community Hospital

There were six shop stewards in total at this branch of COHSE. The branch secretary, a man from the works department, did not allow access to the stewards at Community Hospital, although interviews were carried out with three stewards from other small local hospitals covered by this COHSE branch. One of the shop stewards interviewed was an auxiliary nurse and the wife of the branch secretary. The other two were another auxiliary nurse and a domestic. All three were women and all had been shop stewards for over five years. Since Community was closed in 1994, it was not revisited along with the other case studies.

Constituencies

The shop steward is the elected representative of members of the union. However, there is a great variety in the number and location of members whom the steward is expected to represent. In some cases stewards have specific groups of workers to represent. These may come only from their own work-group, or from several work-groups. In other cases stewards may be in a less formal structure in which any steward may be expected to act for any member in the branch. In this way union branches vary in the degree to which stewards have distinct membership constituencies. However, there did appear to be an attempt to move towards constituencies, and a move towards defining constituencies around individual work-groups.

A constituency system had been in operation for the stewards at City Hospital during the 1980s, each steward having a specific group of staff in their own work area to represent.

> 'I represent twenty-one members – twenty of them are men and there is one part-time woman.' (Male porter shop steward – NUPE City)

> 'I represent twenty members, all women, all part-time cleaners.' (Female domestic services steward – NUPE City)

> 'I represent twenty-four nurses. They are all female and eight of them work part-time.' (Female nursing steward – NUPE City)

Each of these stewards knew exactly who and where their members were. In each case the steward constituency was made up of the immediate work-group in which the steward worked. These comments also indicate the usual size of steward constituencies in this branch, averaging between twenty and thirty. In this branch shop stewards only dealt with issues relating to their own immediate work-group. Any problems in areas without a clear constituency were dealt with by one of the branch officers.

With the reduction in size of the steward body by the 1990s, it became impossible to operate a constituency system as such. The branch secretary increasingly took on all individual representational work as well as trust level negotiating. Shop steward meetings ceased to be held, only to be replaced by surgeries held by the branch secretary.

During the 1980s the COHSE branch at County Psychiatric Hospital were trying to organize constituencies for shop-stewards. As a result there was some confusion over whom each of them represented. Some stewards were able to name and number the precise group of staff they represented, while others said that they did not have specific constituencies.

'I am steward for the school of nursing so have special responsibility for student nurses.' (Male nursing steward – COHSE County Psychiatric)

'In theory we try to have a steward for each department but in practice most stewards are responsible for nursing and ancillary staff.' (Male nursing steward – COHSE County Psychiatric)

Although this COHSE branch aimed to organize specific constituencies, it could not match constituencies to work-groups because of the many areas in which there was no shop steward, including the ancillary membership. This resulted in the practice of ancillary staff being represented by nursing stewards. This situation had improved considerably by the 1990s, when all departments had their own stewards. However, as will be demonstrated later, having stewards does not always guarantee that interests are adequately represented.

The stewards interviewed from the COHSE branch at Community were not precisely sure how many members they represented. The domestic steward said that she represented fifty members, including three men, and approximately thirty of the fifty worked part-time. In this branch, and in the NUPE branch at Shire General Hospital, steward constituencies were blurred and not necessarily linked to work-groups. Steward representation of all work groups had improved at Shire County by the 1990s, although, significantly, they had not been able to recruit Asian women stewards from the ancillary departments.

In the case of steward constituencies which are formally organized, there are advantages to both stewards and members, who are clear about who is the appropriate person to carry out representational work and deal with issues arising in the workplace. Where the constituency is also based on the work-group this enhances close contact with members and issues related to the work of the members. In this way it is possible that unions can come to articulate the diverse and specific interests of members. In the NUPE branch at City, with its steward constituency system, the stewards represented the most clearly delineated work groups. However, it was here too that the greatest decline in steward organization was observed. This provides a valuable reminder that union democracy is not a simple tale of progress, as even apparently well-organized branches require some nurturing to maintain their organization.

Becoming a shop steward

Having pointed to the importance of the shop steward system, it is necessary to consider the process by which members become shop stewards. The explanations given for becoming shop stewards were like those found for shop stewards in the private sector. Most shop stewards are persuaded to take the job by the work-group or by branch officers, while those that seek the position may be motivated by the need to solve workplace problems or by political commitment (Coates and Topham 1988). In this study the stewards from COHSE at County Psychiatric Hospital were more likely than stewards from the other branches to have actively sought the position:

'I consider myself to be a socialist and therefore use trade unionism as a medium for expressing my political point of view.' (Male nursing steward – COHSE County Psychiatric)

'Guilt! I felt I should do something to help, which I suppose is not a very popular idea these days.' (Male nursing steward – COHSE County Psychiatric)

'To be a representative for staff, my colleagues, and to negotiate a fair deal for them.' (Female occupational therapist steward COHSE County Psychiatric)

'Personal egotism!' (Male nurse – branch secretary COHSE County Psychiatric)

Stewards from the other three branches tended to come from the 'pushed' category, many being able to give no reason for becoming a steward except that 'somebody had to do it'.

'There was no COHSE steward . . . after the death of Mr B. and I was just voted to become shop steward.' (Nursing steward – COHSE Community)

'I became shop steward because I was asked to.' (Domestic steward – COHSE Community)

The stewards from the COHSE branch at County Psychiatric Hospital were distinct from the other groups of stewards in that they were predominantly male, young and in professional posts. They also worked in psychiatric nursing which has a longer history of union organization (Carpenter 1980, 1988). These features are likely to explain the greater confidence found among these stewards about their own abilities. In the other branches the women stewards, and in particular the ancillary stewards, were the most frequently 'pushed' into becoming a shop steward.

It can be argued that the most important requirement to becoming a shop steward is the self-confidence to believe that it can be done. Many of the writers discussed in Chapter 1 argue that an important limit to women's participation in unions is their lack of confidence, and the interviews with shop stewards support this. This research indicates that the most important route to gaining sufficient confidence to take the post was the support of branch officers. None of the stewards in the study had been elected without the active support of their branch secretary. This suggests that the increased participation of women at the level of shop steward appears to require active recruitment strategies and support from branch officers. Only branch officers from NUPE City Centre and COHSE County Psychiatric claimed to be involved in this process, and giving particular attention to the recruitment of women ancillary stewards. Even so, for COHSE success was slow and limited.

During the 1980s the NUPE Branch at City had, in contrast, recruited shop stewards among women ancillary workers, roughly proportionate to their membership. This provides an example of centralized control being used to extend membership participation. Although most of the stewards from NUPE City had become stewards because 'no-one else would do it', one woman had become involved through her own experiences of dealing with management.

'I had a problem with my own maternity leave arrangements. I represented myself because I didn't know I could contact the shop-steward. It went to a tribunal, and eventually I contacted the chief steward here and got interested and became a steward.' (Female domestic services steward – NUPE City Centre)

Significantly, the deputy branch secretary from NUPE City Centre described steward turnover as 'generally high', particularly among women stewards, who he said tended to act as 'post-boxes' rather than carrying out the full steward duties (Fryer, Fairclough and Manson 1978). This view did not seem to match the interview data gathered from stewards, which showed that of the four women stewards interviewed at City Centre Hospital, only one had been a steward for less than one year. In relation to this particular hospital, the deputy branch secretary appeared to overestimate turnover among women stewards. Indeed, throughout the research an impression was gained of the consistent underestimation of women's union activity. This observation is in line with Fosh's (1993) argument that workplace union activity is often underrated. However, it also suggests that such blindness may also be gendered – activities by women union members are more likely to be rendered 'invisible'.

It is difficult to explain for sure the dramatic loss of shop stewards at the UNISON/NUPE branch at City Centre, although it seems likely that the branch secretary was concerned to centralize power and enhance his own position. In this way the different leadership style appeared key to the changes in this branch in a way which supports Fosh's argument (Fosh 1993).

Levels of activity

Since shop stewards vary in the sort of union activities that they carry out, the following activities of the stewards in the branches covered by the research were examined: time spent on union work, participation in union training, steward turnover and the extent of work carried out by stewards independent of branch officers.

Time spent on union work

In all four branches the branch officers, particularly the branch secretaries, spent much longer amounts of time on union work than the shop stewards. Generally women stewards tended to spend less time on union work than their male counterparts.

During the 1980s the deputy branch secretary from NUPE City Centre had approximately ninety per cent time off for union work. Of the ordinary stewards, four women said that they did not normally take time off work for union business unless there was a special issue, while a male steward said he usually took approximately ten hours a week off for union work. This presents a similar picture to the amount of their own time spent on union work, most of the women doing less than five hours a week and this male steward claiming to be doing ten hours a week. There were also varying degrees of difficulty reported in trying to take time off for union work, with departments with predominantly female workforces having more problems. Male stewards tended to have fewer problems with departmental management in taking time off for union work:

'If it's likely to take a while, I will go and ask – I've never been refused.' (Male portering steward – NUPE City Centre)

This steward from the porters' department had no problems with taking time off for union work. However, a woman steward from catering had major problems:

'I have had disagreement with management at local level, harassment and unwillingness to co-operate because of my different trade union activities.' (Women steward, catering department – NUPE City Centre)

Problems among nursing stewards were most frequently linked to staffing levels and their inability to leave the ward understaffed.

'I have never had any problems with time off until the last spell when I was steward. Then I was only able to attend one out of three meetings. I had changed departments and two staff nurses had left and not been replaced. There was nobody to relieve me while I attended meetings.' (Female nursing steward – NUPE City Centre)

This NUPE branch had a local agreement with the Health Authority for three hours' time off a month for all shop stewards for them to attend the shop stewards' meeting. All the stewards interviewed were aware of this agreement and only in rare cases had problems arisen with management over taking this time. By the mid 1990s, however, these meetings had ceased to operate. Local and functional management seemed to respond differently to requests for time off for other union business, branch officers and male stewards having least difficulty. By the 1990s the branch secretary was dealing with most union work, and time off for shop stewards was no longer an issue.

Generally, the stewards from COHSE County Psychiatric took very little time off from work for union business. No-one took more than five hours in a week. Management at County appeared unsympathetic to union work being carried out during work time.

'I have had disagreements with senior staff at ward level. Sometimes I cannot get time off because of a shortage of staff on wards.' (Female nursing steward – COHSE County Psychiatric)

'We have an agreement for an hour off for the monthly branch meetings – in theory any member may have that hour off, but in practice it is often quite different, for example because of holidays, sickness, etc. There are staff shortages at times, it is particularly qualified staff who find it difficult to leave the wards without adequate cover for proper patient care.' (Male nursing steward – COHSE County Psychiatric)

'Usually I am the only trained member of staff on the ward. I get "cover" for meal breaks but would find it hard to get "cover" for union meetings.' (Male nursing steward – COHSE County Psychiatric)

Only the branch secretary from COHSE County Psychiatric estimated that he did over five hours a week union work in his own time. The particular problems with time off at County were because most of the stewards were nurses. In a situation of frequent low staffing levels, they were reluctant to take time off for union work and increase the pressure on their colleagues. This situation has continued much the same in the 1990s.

All three stewards from COHSE Community said that they did not take any time off for union work. The branch had an agreement with management for branch meetings to take place during work time, and shop steward meetings took place in their own time. The senior steward from NUPE Shire General said that he had no problems taking time off for union work, but that the other stewards tended not to take time off. After the establishment of trust status and the partial move to local pay bargaining, management at Shire General became increasingly unhappy about the number of stewards seeking time off for union work and the rationale for introducing the convenor post was to limit time off to one person. In terms of maintaining local activity, ensuring the right of time off for individual stewards may be particularly important. Equally, it appeared that this branch might become more centralized through what was essentially a management initiative.

Coates and Topham (1988) indicate the importance of mobility linked to the nature of work in facilitating stewards' performance of their union work. In a comparison of the porters' department and the domestic services departments in this research, the cleaners had tighter supervision, were more tied to a precise working area and had less availability for cover. A similar comparison could be made between porters and catering assistants. This suggests that the organization of women's ancillary jobs militates against active involvement in union activities (Neale 1983). In the 1980s three of the four branch secretaries in the research came from the works departments, where workers have greater control over the organization of their work. Significantly, the one male member of the domestic services department at City Centre Hospital was also a steward, and spent much more time on union work than the women stewards in the department. This was possible because his job had been constructed as different from the women's jobs in the department. He had greater mobility and was not part of the women's supervisory structure. In short, the specific way in which women's jobs are constructed makes formal participation in trade unions more difficult.

By the 1990s two of the three branch secretaries were women, from professional occupations. Such jobs may make the job of branch secretary easier, in terms of access to telephones and office equipment, self-confidence and opportunity to liaise with other staff, but getting time-off for union activities appears increasingly difficult with the pressure of staffing levels. As with the labour market as a whole, class and gender inter-connect in a complex way. It appears to be in women's manual work that there is least freedom and tightest control over the work process, with distinctive implications for participation in union roles and activity.

Steward training

Attendance at a training course provides another indicator of the level of activity by shop stewards. In NUPE City Centre, most stewards had attended a shop stewards' basic TUC training course, although only branch officers had been on advanced courses. Within the steward cohort it was more likely for men to have attended advanced courses than women. Such a practice suggests that there may have been a tendency to perpetuate the notion of the male stewards as 'experts'. Even so, the deputy branch secretary suggested that attendance on union educational courses was equally divided between men and women stewards, although this meant that women were proportionally under-represented, since the majority of stewards were women. In addition to this, the deputy branch secretary claimed that part-time women workers on evening shifts were the least likely to attend union educational courses. He suggested that there was little the branch could do about this situation since there were not enough stewards to make it viable to put on part-time training courses specifically for morning staff, or specifically for evening staff.

The COHSE branch at County Psychiatric had a policy of sending all newly elected stewards onto the basic shop steward training course as soon as possible, and all those stewards spoken to had been on at least one union educational course. As with NUPE City Centre it was more likely for male stewards to have been on advanced courses. Three of the male stewards, but neither of the women stewards, had been on more than one union education course.

Only one of the three stewards from COHSE Community had been on the stage 1 shop steward's training course. Less emphasis was placed on steward education in this branch, and this tended to reinforce the central role of the branch secretary in union business.

It would appear that in the branches covered by this research, women stewards were less likely to attend any training course, and those who did were less likely to attend an advanced course. Since almost all union training courses are based on full-time working hours, the issue of part-time working in women's ancillary work appears to be important in limiting women's participation as shop-stewards (Munro 1989).

Representation of Women Ancillary Staff

In the light of the problems raised by stewards in the interviews, they were asked if they felt that steward systems were adequate for the representation of women ancillary staff. There was considerable resistance by many of the stewards interviewed to discuss this issue. Many stewards said that representation was adequate and did not wish to discuss the issue further, while several claimed that 'we treat every member the same'. This response was interesting since it suggested that the idea that particular groups of workers might have specific organizational needs had not been discussed by stewards within their branches. Such a reluctance may reflect a degree of defensiveness often found in relation to what is perceived as positive discrimination (Cockburn 1989). Union activists seek a balance, wanting to treat everyone equally, yet being aware of structural inequality in which certain groups suffer specific disadvantages.

Despite the general reticence on this issue, the deputy branch secretary from the NUPE branch in City Centre was able to give a specific example of how the branch had attempted to improve representation. He described how domestics had suffered problems with excessive informal warnings, 'being pulled into the manager's office' for example, after being off sick. He claimed that at the time, sickness levels were actually higher among porters, although they did not have any problems with management over sickness. This was linked to a greater level of supervision in domestic services, with supervisors walking around in pairs, sometimes being quite threatening to the domestic staff. He also said that management had been successfully pursuing a policy of reducing women ancillary workers' hours to below 16 a week, the level of entitlement to many legal rights.

The union branch response to this situation had been to carry out a recruitment drive for shop stewards among domestic staff. The number of stewards had been increased considerably although many of the problems remained. It was surprising given this situation that other stewards said that generally the branch maintained adequate representation for all members.

'I don't think we've ever put the interests of any group first – sometimes we've made conscious efforts to correct imbalances arising from structural reasons. Some groups are able to look after themselves – are protected by good manager, have no tradition of organization, etc.' (Deputy branch secretary – NUPE City Centre)

As the deputy branch secretary himself pointed out, the staff in the domestic services department were facing particular problems which the branch seemed unable to deal with. The branch officers had attempted to develop the branch structure in order to deal with these problems. In this NUPE branch there had been a specific and successful effort to recruit women shop stewards. This is an important example, and the only example in the research, of a steward system being extended specifically to facilitate the participation of women ancillary staff. However, organization can go in both directions, and by the 1990s women's ancillary representation had all but disappeared.

In the COHSE branch at County Psychiatric Hospital there had been no ancillary stewards. The degree of knowledge among shop-stewards of issues within the ancillary departments tended to be low. The stewards admitted that their ability to represent ancillary workers' interests was limited, although the stewards expressed a commitment to protecting the interests of all groups of members. The branch secretary expressed a desire to recruit ancillary stewards, although no action had been taken on this issue. The situation in this branch demonstrated the importance of a workplace-based steward system. Without stewards based in the ancillary departments, there was no route by which issues or problems could be raised or discussed. This situation had improved considerably by the 1990s, but still the women ancillary staff felt that their interests were not always adequately represented. In the negotiations in the lead-up to the transfer to St Stephen's, an agreement was reached without involving the domestic steward, and the Asian women cleaners felt particularly aggrieved about the content of the agreement.

Active recruitment strategies can result in increasing the number of shop stewards in women's ancillary departments. This was clearly shown in the

NUPE branch in City Centre, although the recruitment of women stewards did not lead to a quick solution of workplace problems. Without the development of targeted support once elected, women ancillary stewards appeared less able to carry out all the steward activities and to tackle the particular problems in their departments.

Developing greater involvement

There appeared evidence from these union branches that positive experiences of dealing with issues in the workplace led to greater union involvement and activity. Where a steward had achieved successes within the workplace, it encouraged further activity by members. This could be related to Fosh's description of 'surges of interest' (Fosh 1993). Conversely, the lack of activity within the branch or department appeared to discourage involvement. Where there was no steward or no experience of success, there seemed little point in becoming involved. In this way the dominance of particularly active groups within the branches tended to be reproduced.

This was illustrated by the example of the porters at City Centre Hospital. The deputy branch secretary from NUPE City Centre, himself a porter, described the porters' department as the most effectively organized department in the hospital during the 1980s. He argued that within this department they had used the union not only defensively to protect existing terms and conditions of employment, but also to improve working facilities and conditions. As examples of their successes he suggested the gaining of a proper path to the mortuary, the establishment of a rest room with a shower, and the on-going ability to get equipment replaced. He claimed that no other department had achieved comparable successes. He also said that this department had been particularly active in the 1982 national dispute, suggesting that they had organized around issues which specifically affected their department and carried out their own negotiations directly with management. The deputy branch secretary suggested that the high level of activity in this department could be explained by the fact that it was a comparatively young department, although he had no evidence to support this claim. The branch secretary from COHSE County Psychiatric, in comparison, suggested that the porters' department there was one of the least active. Interestingly in this case, lack of activity was also attributed to the general youth of staff in the department.

There is, however, another possible explanation for the difference between the porters' departments at City Centre Hospital and County Psychiatric Hospital: namely that positive experiences of the union encouraged interest and activity. In a similar vein, Fairbrother (1994b) describes how workers in the Benefits Agency became more supportive of the union after the local branch negotiated improvements for part-time workers. Likewise, Baden (1986) argues that when public sector unions in the USA have addressed equality issues, women's involvement has increased. In the department at City Centre the first important feature was the presence of an active senior steward. The second important feature is that the organization of the work allowed the development of collective identification and action. Together, this led to effective campaigns which in turn raised union awareness and involvement. Management also recognized the potential of union action in this department and afforded the union stewards greater respect. This suggests that once collective organization is established, it serves to reproduce itself through its own successes. This also supports the general argument that workplace-based steward systems are necessary for the development of membership participation. Significantly, by the 1990s, membership had dramatically declined among the porters at City Centre and they no longer had their own shop-steward. They had gone from the most active workgroup to the most inactive, indicating that men's union organization is as fragile as that of women.

In the women's ancillary departments studied in this research, there were few senior stewards, there was no history of successful campaigns and the construction of work militated against both the development of a collective identity and the activities of stewards. Management, recognizing this, afforded stewards less serious attention and made the performance of steward roles more difficult. This served to reproduce inactivity. This is not to argue that there is an inevitability about this process. Major events in a department may challenge inactivity or activity. However, this argument does suggest that the development of active collective organization is likely to be more difficult in women's ancillary departments, which supports Colling's description of an 'uneven and gendered distribution of bargaining power' (Colling 1995: 143).

Centralization

In all of the branches, branch officers played a major role in dealing with members' problems. Rather than stewards processing problems and representing their members, there was a tendency to refer problems to the branch officers. This supports the general argument about a high level of centralization in these branches.

In NUPE City the branch secretary in the 1980s, who was based at Walton

Hospital, had a high profile and was frequently approached directly by many staff, members and non-members, with their problems. More specifically, the deputy branch secretary from City Centre Hospital suggested that particularly women stewards were likely to approach the branch secretary with day-to-day grievances which would normally not go beyond the level of the steward. Although there was little other evidence available to support this assertion, if correct, it may be explained by the lower levels of training among part-time women workers.

When asked if he thought departmental steward meetings might aid women stewards, the deputy branch secretary said that there was no reason why such meetings should be organized specifically for women stewards. Although he identified a number of ways in which women stewards were less involved, for example in problem handling and turnover rates, he did not think this situation indicated the need for any specific organizational changes.

> 'Meetings of groups of shop stewards in similar departments across the DHA [District Health Authority] might be useful – I feel it might originate more demands on the union and management and more thoughts about how to achieve those demands.' (Deputy branch secretary – NUPE City Centre)

There were no plans, however, to set up such departmental meetings. Although this deputy branch secretary identified women stewards as less able to deal independently with individual cases, he did not regard the situation as requiring specific intervention. Interestingly, Terry suggests that such meetings aid the development of stronger steward groups:

> ... the need for a 'key' steward may disappear as steward organisation at lower levels becomes better developed and co-ordinated. The growing use of sectional meetings demonstrated by Fryer and his colleagues and confirmed by these studies show that this is already happening. (Terry 1982: 18)

Fryer indicates that many studies have pointed to the need for membership section meetings, yet progress in this seems slow (Fryer 1989).

By the 1990s the removal of shop steward meetings and the dramatic reduction in steward numbers resulted in the extreme centralization of power in the post of the branch secretary. Similarly, in the COHSE branch at Community all members' problems were referred to the branch secretary, none being dealt with by the shop steward alone.

There seems some indication that women stewards were less likely to deal with members' problems independently. This may be explained by their particular problems of time off for union work and lower levels of training for part-time workers. The evidence suggests that women ancillary stewards may be less involved in formal union representational activities than their male counterparts. However, the evidence also suggests that the nature of the construction of women's jobs inhibits full participation in steward activities (Kessler 1986). Part-time working made attendance at steward training courses more difficult and women stewards tended to have more difficulties with management in taking time off for union work. Further, the activities of women ancillary stewards were restricted by tighter supervision and less freedom of mobility in the workplace.

The NUPE City Centre branch most resembled the description of centralized and hierarchical leaderships found in some of the earlier studies of workplace organization (Terry 1978, Batstone 1988). The paradox of the NUPE City branch in the 1980s was that it was also the most actively involved in extending and developing workplace organization through the shop steward system. This seems to support Batstone (1998) in his argument for caution in assuming that increased centralization necessarily leads to bureaucratization and incorporation. In the case of NUPE City Centre the more complex branch structure was enabling the recruitment of more women ancillary stewards. Although power appeared to be centralized, it was being used to increase participation at the level of shop steward. In Hyman's terms this appeared to be an exercise of the 'power for' membership (Hyman 1979). This may indicate a dynamic relationship in that a degree of centralization is necessary to the development of effective shop steward systems, which in turn limit the tendency towards centralization. By the 1990s this power was being used to curb workplace organization, as the branch secretary delegated fewer responsibilities to stewards, held few meetings and concentrated on cultivating relationships with senior management. The picture had moved closer to one of 'power over' the membership.

In the 1980s all four union branches had shop steward systems in operation. The largest branch in the research, NUPE at City, was the only one to have a fully developed constituency system for shop stewards and the only branch where the branch secretary had full facility time for trade union work. Both NUPE City Centre and COHSE County Psychiatric were in the process of examining their shop steward systems with the stated aims of improving representation and participation. This process, however, was slower in the COHSE County Psychiatric. In this branch power was not centralized in the hands of branch officers, but union activities were limited by the lack of stewards in the ancillary departments. This branch was attempting to develop new non-hierarchical means of organizing, although in a situation in which the branch was completely dominated by nursing stewards they had been unable to find a way to challenge their own dominance. By the 1990s the situation was almost reversed: UNISON/COHSE St Stephen's had had some success with broadening union activity, while at UNISON/NUPE City Centre it had been smothered.

In all of the branches the branch secretary was a key figure. The section on steward recruitment indicated that the branch secretaries' support was important in encouraging members to stand as stewards (Ledwith *et al.* 1990). Cohen and Fosh (1988) indicate some possible problems of this reliance on key individuals, as over-dependence can result in chaos if the person leaves or is ill. The branch secretary at the COHSE Community branch fitted this description. Cohen and Fosh raise major questions about whether such dependence serves to inhibit the development of workplace organization. The example of UNISON/NUPE at City Centre suggests that strong branch leadership can have positive or negative effects, either being used to stimulate or repress membership involvement.

Union Meetings

In the 1980s there was great variety between the branches studied, in terms of where and when shop steward and branch meetings were held. It is now well established that the time and place of any meeting may present particular problems for women workers (Aldred 1981, Ellis 1981, Coote and Campbell 1982, Beale 1982, Cunnison and Stageman 1993, Briskin and McDermott 1993, Lawrence 1994, Colgan and Ledwith 1996). The evidence from this research generally supports this, finding that the meetings held in work time were the best attended.

Shop stewards all commented on the value of both branch and steward meetings. The two reasons given most frequently for this view were the need for contact and for sharing of information:

> 'It prevents a feeling of isolation. It helps me to see hospitals as a whole rather than from a sectarian point of view. It helps me to feel glad there are so few problems for nurses as opposed to other groups.' (Female nursing steward – NUPE City Centre)

> 'It's the only way of keeping contact with some of the members working in a big hospital spread over a big geographical area.' (Male nursing steward – COHSE County Psychiatric)

These examples indicate that stewards tended not to experience union meetings as a forum in which branch officers exert control. Such meetings enabled stewards to get a wider view of issues affecting the branch generally, and steward meetings particularly were seen as a forum for gaining support from other stewards. In COHSE, branch meetings were also seen as giving an opportunity for contact with members. This was particularly important in this branch, which in the 1980s did not have an effective steward constituency system. Stewards generally expressed a view that it was important to have as much information as possible about events in the branch and the NHS generally. At union meetings they were able to find information which they would not have access to elsewhere. Gaining information and knowledge gave stewards greater confidence. Also important for women was the access to information, because their lack of mobility in the workplace prevented them from finding out what was going on elsewhere, even in the same hospital. The importance of these meetings was enhanced for part-time workers who found it difficult to attend union educational courses.

There was considerable variety in the interpretation of the purpose and organization of union meetings. There was a wide difference in the degree of formality, adherence to procedure, and physical organization of the meetings. There were also differences in the purpose attached to meetings, for example discussion forums, educational sessions and information dissemination arenas. In the light of the discussion of the union agenda, it is important to establish whether meetings enabled stewards and members to raise issues, or whether they served to enhance branch officer control.

Purpose of meetings

For the NUPE branch at City Centre, the shop steward meeting was carried out as a business meeting, local issues were discussed and problems were raised by branch officers who also gave out information. In contrast the branch meetings were organized around a visiting speaker, another form of educational session or specific activity. During the late 1980s these branch meetings ceased to be held on a regular monthly basis due to low attendance.

COHSE at County Psychiatric discussed very similar issues at both branch and steward meetings. The main difference was that individual cases being dealt with by stewards were discussed in detail at the steward meeting. In this way it was used for support and advice for case work. Although COHSE's practice of covering similar material at both meetings resulted in some repetition, it enabled members to become involved in general discussions about issues affecting the branch.

Meetings of both branches covered issues relevant to ancillary and nursing members, despite COHSE being dominated by nursing stewards and NUPE being dominated by ancillary stewards. NUPE generally spent more time in discussion of union organization and recruitment of members and shop stewards. This reflects the particular concern shown in this branch during the 1980s for the development of branch organization. By the 1990s, meetings had ceased and membership participation was no longer seen as an issue. Shop stewards became increasingly isolated and the branch secretary took on all case work. Members' problems were established increasingly as individual problems rather than collective concerns, moving away from the collectivist approach described by Fosh (1993).

Of all the meetings observed during the 1980s, most control was exercised over participants at the NUPE Shire General branch meetings. In this case control was exerted by the full-time official over both branch officers and members, as he appeared to foster membership dependence (Heery and Kelly 1990). This relationship was not one in which the full-time official serviced the branch officers and stewards, but one in which he directed them. This picture fits with Terry's description of NUPE branches being dependent on their full-time officials (Terry 1996). The development of this branch since has been in sharp contrast to the NUPE branch at City Centre. Changes in full-time officials and in branch officers have transformed the branch into a more autonomous and active one, with an expansion of the shop steward system.

Participation in meetings

One common and important point was that at none of the meetings observed during this research did stewards raise issues not on the formal written meeting agenda. Meetings did not provide a forum for the articulation of issues beyond the agenda, normally produced by the branch executive. In this way meeting formality may discourage the active participation of members. Participation in meetings was greatest at the COHSE branch at County Psychiatric Hospital. At NUPE City Centre steward meetings, stewards spoke only to ask questions or give points of information on particular local issues. Only a small number of people ever spoke formally during three-hour shop steward meetings.

At the NUPE shop steward meetings neither men nor women were significantly under-represented in terms of contribution. However, there was generally a low level of participation of shop stewards in their meetings. The comments or questions were never more than one or two sentences. Most contributors were listened to seriously by the meeting, although in any debate the position adopted at the end of a discussion was always that put forward by the branch secretary. This could indicate that the branch secretary was either correctly representing the collective view of stewards, or that he was able to control branch policy and decisions. Although it is impossible to be sure which is the correct interpretation, greater confidence, experience and access to information made the branch secretary's view very persuasive.

Although women stewards were not significantly under-represented in the number of comments made at shop steward meetings, in interviews it was frequently suggested that they found speaking at meetings difficult. A typical comment was:

'I don't feel I know enough. I feel nervy – it is difficult for new stewards.'
(Female ancillary steward – NUPE City Centre)

To contribute in meetings required a degree of confidence which women stewards often did not have. While there is no clear evidence to show whether the nervousness described by this steward was primarily a result of being a new steward, or mainly a result of being a woman steward, it seems possible that this nervousness was enhanced by the dominance of men in the senior positions in the branch. Women stewards often felt that contributions should be informed. The meetings were not seen as a forum in which views could be expressed and problems raised. This reflects the general pattern of meetings as arenas for the dissemination of information to stewards rather than for receiving views from them.

The COHSE branch at County Psychiatric Hospital offers a considerable contrast to the NUPE City Centre branch. In branch and shop steward meetings most people present spoke at some point. There are several possible explanations for this contrast, although it seems likely that the small size of the meeting and the fact that many of the participants were friends outside of work may have encouraged participation. In the COHSE branch meeting discussion was conducted informally and freely, with the meeting being moved on by the branch secretary. Everyone who spoke was treated seriously. Stewards tended not to raise issues not on the formal agenda, although with a small branch it was relatively easy for stewards to have issues added to it. Stewards were actually invited to notify the branch secretary of any issues which they wanted to be put on the agenda. It has already been noted that this branch was dominated by male nursing stewards and the contributions at steward meetings reflected this dominance. At branch meetings too, women ancillary members were under-represented. There was, however, a greater level of involvement in the meetings by those who were there. Although this branch had not had a great success in terms of attendance at meetings, it appeared to have had considerable success in enabling the participation of those members who did attend.

The meeting of the NUPE branch at Shire General Hospital had the least participation by members found at any of the unions in the research. At meetings most of the speaking was by the NUPE regional full-time official. This was the only meeting observed where a full-time union official was present, although he regularly attended these meetings. Discussion centred around the official who 'lectured' those present. Contributions were not invited from members, and there were rarely women members present, other than the branch officers who also made few contributions. Participation in this meeting consisted only of formal voting on proposals.

The NUPE City Centre branch had the most extensive steward system and had given most attention to improving workplace organization, yet this had not been matched by member and steward contributions in meetings. This suggests a need for caution in the assumption of a necessary link between the formal appearance of participation in terms of meeting attendance, and the quality of that participation. Questions are also raised about the impact of meeting formality on participation: more formal procedures may serve to limit participation and enhance the dominance of branch officers and full-time officials. This issue will now be addressed in more detail.

Meeting formality

NUPE City Centre meetings were formally chaired with a 'top table' and rows of chairs facing it. At steward meetings women made up approximately two-thirds of those present, reflecting accurately the proportion of women stewards in the branch. The branch secretary, deputy and chair sat at the top table and were all male. The deputy and secretary spoke when they wished, everybody else spoke 'through the chair'.

Men were consistently over-represented at the COHSE County Psychiatric meetings, all branch officers also being male. Because of the small size of the meetings there was a high degree of informality, with no top table and no formal chair. The branch secretary acted more as a discussion leader. All present joined in discussions.

'They are relaxed and very informal – very little usual meeting formalities followed.' (Male nursing steward – COHSE County Psychiatric)

At meetings of NUPE Shire General business was conducted formally, with a top table and formal proposals, seconded and voted on. Here the top table was further removed from membership by being placed on a raised stage. Members literally had to look up to branch officers and the full-time official. Except for the full-time union official everyone spoke through the chair, and he also directed the chair on how to proceed with the meeting. In this branch, formality was clearly used to maintain control and limit participation. In an interview the full-time union official related an occasion when at one branch meeting three Asian women ancillary members attended and sat at the back of the room. Before the meeting went ahead, the secretary asked them to come forward and say what they wanted at the meeting, in order that they could leave and 'let the men get on with the meeting'. The women came forward and stood in a row in front of the top table. Their problem was discussed and dealt with, and they left the meeting. The meeting was then continued. The full-time official, usually so quick to intervene on procedural matters, said that he allowed this to happen at two or three more meetings before pointing out that this was not correct procedure. In this example it was made clear to the women, who were not regular attenders of branch meetings, that they were not welcome to participate in the meeting as a whole. The humiliation of these members ensured that further participation was limited.

Rees argues that women face particular problems with the formality of union meetings because of their 'lack of familiarity with the discourse and procedures' (Rees 1992: 100). It is not merely that women may not be familiar with the formal meeting discourse, but also that conscious attempts to challenge it are not acceptable. This was shown by a particular meeting of members from County Psychiatric/St Stephen's, which was described by a number of different parties. Negotiations had taken place over the procedures for ancillary staff in the move to the new hospital, and an agreement was reached with the union side being represented by a full-time official and a male steward from the catering department, a situation similar to that described by Fosh and Cohen (1990). The women domestics of Asian origin were particularly dissatisfied with the agreement and with the failure to include their shop-steward in negotiations. At a subsequent meeting they loudly made their unhappiness known to management and the union officers. Several people complained about their behaviour. The women's failure to follow appropriate meeting procedure became the central issue, rather than the question of whether or not they had been adequately represented. A different stereotype of Asian women seemed to develop – no longer the passive doormat, but now a loud uncontrollable rabble unwilling to work through procedure. The move to St Stephen's had created a 'surge of interest' but rather than capitalize on it, the union can be seen as containing and controlling discontented members who felt they had not been adequately represented.

Overall, it seems that meeting procedure of a very formal nature hinders the participation of membership, for both men and women. However, meeting procedure may also be valuable for members. Although it may be experienced as intimidating by members and new stewards, it may also act as a useful point of reference, which is in fact easy to learn. There is no pressure on the newcomer to contribute, s/he has time to watch what happens and work out who everyone is. This seemed to be happening in NUPE City Centre. Paradoxically the informality of COHSE County Psychiatric could be experienced as more threatening. At one of their meetings it was very difficult to work out who was who and what was 'normal' practice and behaviour. Total informality may be experienced as intimidating, just as formality may be.

There was a high level of control over meetings by branch officers, which was maintained through the setting of meeting agendas, the physical organization of the meetings and the assumed right not to be bound by the meeting convention of 'speaking through the chair'. In the 1980s, these dominant roles in all of the meetings observed were taken by men. The meetings did not facilitate the development and articulation of members' interests. Where members try to participate, but do not abide by the rules of the accepted discourse, they are labelled as deviant and their views are undermined.

Summary

This chapter has begun to point to the importance of the structure of local organization for membership participation. It has been suggested that certain structural arrangements are necessary to enable participation. It is well established that attention needs to be given to the time and place of meetings. Women's work organization can make office-holding more difficult. Women's manual jobs often lack opportunities for physical mobility or chances to chat with colleagues, and supervision in women's work is often tighter and gaining time off for union work may be more difficult. Related to the latter point, there seems some indication that management may attribute more importance to male union activists, thus further undermining women stewards. Some of these problems may be limited through formal agreements for time off for meetings and union work, and ensuring union training is available to all groups of staff. Where stewards find it difficult to attend training courses, the importance of steward meetings is heightened.

Three particular issues have been highlighted. Firstly, in the continual balance between individual or workgroup interests and wider collective interests, it is essential that diversity of interest is recognized and opportunity is provided for all groups to articulate particular problems or interests. This process may be facilitated by departmental or work-group meetings. Secondly, the support and encouragement of branch officers or senior stewards appear very important to the development of the initial self-confidence to become a shop steward. Branch officers have considerable power to facilitate or squash participation. Thirdly, the general importance of union meetings was stressed. The meetings observed during the research did not facilitate the development and articulation of interests. Meeting procedure of a very formal nature hinders the participation of the membership, both men and women. In particular, where members did not abide by the rules of accepted discourse, they were labelled as deviant and their views were undermined. Despite the make-up of the work-groups, issues faced by Asian women as a result of the racialization of the job hierarchy largely failed to emerge during the study of local union branches; rather, the Asian women themselves were 'problematized'.

This chapter has particularly illustrated the transient nature of specific developments in workplace organization. Higher levels of membership involvement can disappear as well as appear. Union participation in the workplace requires continued nurturing and support. In many ways UNISON appears to be taking up issues of union democracy and how to represent all sections of the membership. This could be seen as a significant shift, although it is not clear how far national policy statements are reflected in union renewal at the workplace level. Certainly in the NHS the poorly organized branches dependent on full-time officials seem to persist. In this context the power base of the branch officers seems considerable. In the light of these findings the following chapters will develop the argument that structural developments alone are not adequate to guarantee participation.

8 REPRESENTATION IN LOCAL UNION STRUCTURES

The previous chapter demonstrated the low level of participation by all shop stewards in the branch structures and the concentration of power at branch level among branch officers. This analysis will be extended in this chapter to consider the relationship between members and shop stewards in terms of representation of interests, and in the next chapter in terms of membership participation in local union structures. Following the arguments presented in earlier chapters, this chapter suggests that there is a trade union agenda which has developed over time and which is not defined and set in the individual workplace. The argument will be developed that both the sorts of issues seen as appropriate to trade unions, and the forms of action seen as appropriate to union involvement, are defined by this trade union agenda. This agenda excludes certain issues, particularly those specifically relevant to women members, although it is accepted and reproduced not only by union officers but also by women members themselves. Furthermore, the agenda is extremely resilient at a local level despite the national developments in UNISON towards proportionality, fair representation and self-organization.

It has already been shown that certain structures are necessary to membership participation and representation. Further, it has been shown that the nature of the organization of work, based on division and hierarchy, inhibits the development of an articulation of group interests. However, this chapter suggests that the trade union agenda presents an underlying and fundamental limitation to the full representation and participation of women members. This argument will draw particularly on the work of Steven Lukes, in which he argues for a three-dimensional concept of power, as was outlined in the Introduction (Lukes 1974).

The key features of Lukes' three-dimensional view of power are that he includes not only decision-making, but control over the political agenda; not only observable conflict, but also latent conflict; and finally not only subjective interests, but also real interests. When applied to the context of trade unions, this three-dimensional view of power provides major insights into the exclusion of the interests specific to groups of workers, in this case women and black workers. It will be shown that there is an important link between the representation of interests and the form and level of participation in local union activities. Where unions appear inappropriate forums for the issues that actually affect workers, participation will be limited, even where there have been structural changes aimed at facilitating participation.

Shop stewards and branch officers have a key role in the articulation of members' interests, a role which was undertaken with varying degrees of effectiveness in the various branches in the study. In the research it is evident that there was a contradictory tendency among shop stewards, who were often able to identify ways in which women workers and sometimes Asian women workers had specific interests, yet were resistant to the idea of local union branches taking up these specific interests. It is argued that this was not a feature of discriminatory practices by individual shop stewards, but a result of the trade union agenda which excludes a range of sex-specific and race-specific interests. This resistance to acknowledge particular interests has continued into the 1990s despite UNISON's equality initiatives. There was little support among senior stewards for proportionality and fair representation, which were seen as impractical.

In order to develop these arguments, the detailed focus is on two of the domestic services departments covered in the research, considering how problems were defined, how they were raised and how they were dealt with. It will become evident that the range of issues regarded as appropriate for trade unions was very narrow. The shop stewards saw their role as representing particular groups in the workforce in particular ways. It is evident that some shop stewards had the ability to stand above immediate workplace divisions, yet were resistant to dealing with issues that specifically affected women workers. It is argued that the contradictory responses from shop stewards result from the disjunction between the experience of the workplace and the trade union agenda.

Representation and Members

In this section it will be demonstrated that there is a limited range of issues raised by women members with their trade unions. This is explained by a limited trade union agenda, which results in women members taking individual action or no action at all about the problems they face in the workplace.

The data for this section is derived from a questionnaire survey of domestic services staff at Community and City Centre hospitals during the 1980s. Although the return rate for questionnaires was fairly low, with a 30 per cent return rate at City Centre and a 26 per cent return rate at Community, the material provides useful indications about the sorts of problems women domestic workers faced in the workplace, and about how they dealt with them. At both hospitals there was a higher response rate among evening staff than among the day staff. These two departments, which were studied in depth, represented two extremes in terms of effective shop-steward organization as discussed in the previous chapter. At City Centre Hospital there was an effective NUPE shop steward constituency system, while at Community Hospital there was a poorly organized COHSE branch. What emerges in this chapter, however, is that looking at the problems at work from the ordinary member's position suggests much more of a similarity between the two situations.

Community Hospital – domestic services department

The key point to emerge from this section is that the domestics identified only a limited range of problems at work, and had different means for dealing with the various problems. The material in this section is based on a response of 15 (26 per cent), of which there were five responses (15 per cent) from the day shift and ten (36 per cent) from the evening shift. Over half the women were over fifty years old, all were married and all had children. Most had children between five and 18 years, and one had a dependent relative – a disabled husband. Of the five women who responded from the day shift, three were of Asian origin and one was of southern European origin. All other respondents were of white British origin. One of the respondents from the evening shift was also a shop steward with COHSE. Of the total, 12 had held their jobs for over five years. The average length of service on the day shift was 14 years, and for the evening shift seven years.

Respondents were asked what they liked and disliked about their job. The most frequently mentioned aspects which they liked were the money, meeting people and doing a useful, rewarding job. The most frequently mentioned aspects which they disliked about the job were problems with equipment, travelling to work and the unsociable hours of the job. It is frequently argued that part-time evening work is convenient for women with young children, since their partners can look after the children. However, these responses support the argument that women take this work because it is all that is available: many evening staff disliked working in the evening. It was convenient only in so far as there was no alternative on offer. The hours were repeatedly described as 'suitable' but not liked.

The issues of 'lack of equipment' and 'amount of work' recur continually throughout the questionnaires.

> 'Work is now getting very hectic because of cut-backs – cutting down on staff and cleaning materials. More work is being given and still only three hours to cover wide areas of work.' (Domestic – Community Hospital day shift)

This indicates an intensification of work linked to the proposals for an in-house tender, as the work of this department was to be put out to competitive tendering. This process had begun through the non-replacement of staff who had left – through 'natural' wastage.

Problems at work

Respondents were asked to indicate what problems they had found at work. The following problems were identified (the number of times each problem was mentioned is shown in brackets):

- Amount of work (6)
- Equipment (5)
- Wages (4)
- Arrangement for looking after children when sick or during school holidays (2)
- Transport to and from work (1)
- Relations with managers or supervisors (1)
- Any other problems (1) – Privatization

The domestics were then asked who they had approached for help with the problem and whether the problem had been sorted out satisfactorily. Table 4 indicates, even from this small sample, that the women had particular ways of tackling different problems, and almost none of these included reference to the trade union. To illustrate, problems with wages were taken directly to the wages staff and all the problems were sorted out satisfactorily. Similarly, problems with equipment were most frequently taken to the supervisor, but tended not to be sorted out.

The types of problem which were not sorted out are illustrated by the following comment:

> 'Never enough cleaning materials.' (Domestic – Community Hospital evening shift)

Table 4. *Ways of dealing with problems – domestics at Community Hospital*

Type of problem	Day or Evening (D/E)	Was it sorted out satisfactorily?	Who did you approach for help?
Wages	E	Yes	wages staff
	E	Yes	wages staff
	E	Yes	wages staff & domestic manager
	E	Yes	domestic manager
Equipment	E	No	supervisor
	E	No	staff nurse
	E	No	supervisor
	E	No	supervisor
	E	Yes	supervisor
Amount of work	E	No	no-one
	D	No	no-one
	E	Yes	domestic manager
	E	No	no-one
	E	No	no-one
	E	No	supervisor & manager
Transport	E	No	no-one
Childcare	E	No	no-one
	E	No	supervisor & manager
Supervisor	E	No	no-one
Privatization	E	No	COHSE Branch Secretary

This quote indicates the type of problems faced by domestics in doing their jobs: they were expected to do not only more work in the same time, but also to do it with fewer materials. The particular pressures in this department were associated with the development of an in-house tender, and many of the problems raised by the domestics related to the attempts to restructure the work. However, they surfaced in terms of what appeared to be small individual petty grievances. The divisions in the workforce described earlier militated against a group response, and each of the individual problems was not seen as appropriate for reference to the union branch.

The most striking feature of the responses was that in only one case was anyone from the union approached. This was a case where the domestic was a shop steward herself and raised the issue of privatization with the branch secretary. There were no cases of a member approaching her shop steward for assistance with a problem, despite a large number of problems not being resolved satisfactorily. In this branch the union representational structures appeared not to be working at all. As was pointed out earlier, this branch did not have an effective steward constituency system although there was one shop steward in the department.

For problems with the amount of work, the women tended to see the domestic services manager or to take no action. In only one case was a problem with the amount of work sorted out.

> 'Extra work in the same two hours.' (Domestic – Community Hospital day and evening shifts)

None of the other problems mentioned were sorted out:

> 'Youngest being poorly, had no-one to look after her.' (Domestic – Community Hospital evening shift)

While problems linked to the intensification of work are not necessarily gender-specific, in this department these problems were linked to an attempt to shift from full-time working to part-time working, a form of reorganization which is gender-specific. As was discussed earlier, such a shift is only feasible in work done by women. The childcare problems they mentioned are also gender-specific in as much as women generally take the main responsibility for childcare. Thus there is some indication that the sort of problems which were not sorted out or for which no action was taken are particularly linked to the gender construction of the work.

City Centre Hospital – domestic services department

At City Centre Hospital there was a distinct pattern to the sorts of problem women domestics faced. The material for this section is based on a response of 30 (30 per cent), of which there were six responses (15 per cent) from the day shift and 24 responses (41 per cent) from the evening shift. All of the women had children and all had been married, although one was divorced and one was widowed. All the respondents were of white British origin. The women were generally younger at City Centre Hospital, the average age on the day shift being 44 and on the evening shift 38 years of age. The age of children was slightly younger than at the Community, five women having children under five years of age.

'I work during the evenings because it suits me while I still have a relatively young child at home, but I do not enjoy going out at night.' (Domestic – City Centre evening shift)

Of the total, 17 had done their jobs for over five years. The average length of service on the day shift was eight years, and for the evening shift six years. Although evening work was unpopular, women often continued doing it for many years. When asked what they liked most about the job, the most frequent responses were 'meeting people' and 'the money'. These were followed by 'doing a useful job' and 'the hours of work'.

'I feel I am doing something worthwhile for the community.' (Domestic – City Centre Hospital evening and day shifts)

The most frequently mentioned dislikes about the job were 'the hours', 'the lack of equipment' and their 'treatment by some other staff':

'Going out to work on winter nights.'

'Going to work on a summer evening.' (Domestics – City Centre Hospital evening shift)

These comments reinforce the earlier point that women do not like working on an evening shift, but do so because they have no alternative. Compared with Community Hospital there was slightly less concern over the pace of work. This may have been because staff at Community were under particular pressure with the in-house tender. At City Centre there were also more comments about the condescending way in which cleaners were treated by medical and nursing staff.

Problems at work

Respondents were asked to indicate what problems they had had at work. Replies were predominantly from the evening staff. The following problems were identified (the number of times each problem was mentioned is shown in brackets):

- Equipment (12)
- Being moved from one department to another (5)
- Amount of work (5)
- Transport to and from work (4)
- Relations with manager or supervisor (3)
- Changes in hours (2)
- Wages (2)
- Taking sick leave (1)
- Injury at work (1)
- Any other problems (1) – Attitude of nursing staff

No-one reported any problems with arrangements for looking after children when sick, which was surprising, since informal discussions had indicated that this was a major problem for many of the domestics who had young children. However, the reluctance to mention this problem may relate to the usual solution, which was for the woman herself to report sick. The implications of this observation will be developed in the later section on 'issues not raised'. The most frequent problems were to do with lack of equipment, amount of work and being moved from one department to another:

> 'The only problem with cleaning fluids is that you practically have to beg for more when you have used it up.' (Domestic – City Centre Hospital evening shift)

This department was not in the process of being restructured as dramatically as at Community Hospital, since work in this department had already been established as completely part-time and there was no imminent requirement to produce an in-house tender. However, there was some pressure to reduce hours and overall staffing levels, which were causing domestics similar problems of fitting the work into less time. The particularly high level of problems with equipment and materials in this department served to highlight divisions between the day and evening shifts, which were discussed earlier. Workers on the opposite shift were often blamed for these problems. That several women mentioned being moved from one department to another as a problem reflects the particular struggle over the maintenance of internal hierarchies which was discussed in Chapter 5.

Table 5 shows that there were three cases where the shop steward was approached for help, and the result was satisfactory in two of these. That some members saw the union as the appropriate route to deal with certain issues may in part be due to the operation of an effective shop steward system. This would

Table 5. *Ways of dealing with problems – domestics at City Centre Hospital*

Type of problem	Day or Evening (D/E)	Was it sorted out satisfactorily?	Who did you approach for help?
Wages	E	Yes	manager & wages office
	E	Yes	manager
Equipment	D	No	deputy manager
	E	No	supervisor
	E	Yes	supervisor
	E	No	supervisor
	E	Yes	supervisor & manager
	E	No	supervisor
	E	No	supervisor
	E	No	supervisor
	E	Yes	supervisor
	E	No	supervisor
	E	Yes	supervisor
	E	No	supervisor
Amount of work	E	Yes	supervisor & manager
	E	No	manager
	E	Yes	supervisor
	E	Yes	supervisor & manager
	E	No	supervisor & manager
Sick leave	D	No	NUPE shop-steward
Injury	D	Yes	supervisor
Transport	D	No	no-one
	E	Yes	supervisor
	E	No	no-one
	E	No	no-one
Supervisor	D	No	no-one
	D	Yes	NUPE shop-steward
Hours	E	Yes	manager
	E	Yes	supervisor & manager & NUPE shop-steward
Being moved	E	Yes	manager
	E	No	no-one
	E	No	supervisor
	E	No	no-one
	E	Yes	supervisor
Attitude	E	No	no-one

re-emphasize the importance of certain union structures to the representation of members. Nonetheless, despite the effectiveness of the steward system, three cases represents a very small proportion of the reported problems. There is some indication that the sorts of problems which were referred to the union were concerned with individual grievances, directly related to workplace issues and not directly of a gender-specific nature. This is illustrated by the following example:

> 'I suffer from bronchitis and catch cold frequently. Subsequently, without antibiotics my cold stays on my chest. I have a slightly damaged lung. I was called in to see the manager in the office. Where I was told about my absenteeism. I am on three months trial. But have had four days off in the three months. No help available at first, but then I contacted my union officer who said it should never have been brought up in the first place and to await the outcome at the end of January. My shop steward is to go with me as a witness if I do have to be called to her office again.' (Domestic – City Centre Hospital day shift)

Despite the steward system, the member above only became aware that she could call on her shop steward for help after she had been disciplined. Thus even in the NUPE City branch there were problems about membership awareness of the union. As at the Community Hospital, problems with wages, although not as frequent, tended to be resolved without union involvement. Problems with equipment were usually taken to the supervisor and most were not sorted out. Generally the domestics at City Centre Hospital were more likely to take some sort of action than those at Community Hospital, although they too tended not to take any action on the other problems such as transport:

> 'No transport of any kind, have to rely on other people or get a taxi.'
> (Domestic – City Centre Hospital evening shift)

Transport is a particular problem for workers in the NHS, working evenings, weekends and public holidays when public transport is less regular. The domestics were especially concerned about the potential for violent attacks at this city centre hospital. Domestics at City Centre Hospital also tended to live further from the hospital than was the case at Community Hospital. As was pointed out earlier, the immediate residential area to the hospital contained a large Asian community. Since no women of Asian origin were employed in this department a greater proportion of staff travelled from more distant residential areas. Problems of transport were regarded as not appropriate to raise at work, and three of the four women who reported having problems took no action.

Like the problems with transport, victimization by a supervisor was regarded by one domestic as an individual problem which she had to cope with on her own.

'One supervisor in particular jumps on me [harassment] the minute I stop working – especially if I have recently had time off for illness. Even when I'm working with someone she looks straight at me – not at the other domestic – and tells me off not her.' (Domestic – City Centre Hospital day shift)

However, another woman with a similar problem did take the issue up with her shop steward and this problem was sorted out satisfactorily.

'On being moved to another department not being shown the method of cleaning that department. Therefore the work is much harder until you sort it out yourself. This problem was too long being sorted out and it really is quite simple.' (Domestic – City Centre Hospital evening shift)

The resistance by the domestics to being moved from one working area to another and their attempt to maintain an internal hierarchy of work were common, yet all of those who reported it as a specific problem dealt with it on an individual basis or did nothing. The general low status afforded to domestics by other staff was seen as a common problem, but one about which nothing could be done:

'The only problem being that most doctors and nurses treat the domestics quite shabby, and use no manners whatsoever.' (Domestic – City Centre Hospital day shift)

Several important themes have been outlined in this section. Firstly, in the light of the interests specific to women ancillary workers identified earlier, the range of issues raised by the women domestics was very narrow. Secondly, within this narrow range of issues, only a tiny proportion were referred to the trade unions. What was also significant was that a similar picture emerged from both domestic services departments, despite very different trade union organizations. Even with an extensive shop steward system at City Centre, few issues were raised with the stewards. Furthermore, there was some indication that issues specific to women workers were less likely to be referred to the trade unions than issues common to all workers.

Dealing with problems in the workplace

In the two hospitals, a pattern begins to emerge over how different sorts of problems are dealt with. Some issues were more likely to be referred to the union, while other issues were more likely to be dealt with on an individual basis, and yet others were not dealt with at all. At both hospitals very few problems were referred to the union. At City Centre, the few problems taken to the shop-steward tended to be those of immediate individual interest, for example harassment over sick leave and possible cuts in hours. The recurring problems of amount of work and lack of equipment, or of being shifted from one department to another, were not being reported to the union. Frequently nothing at all was done about these problems, or about problems related to transport, childcare and the attitude of nursing and medical staff. Where action was taken to deal with problems it was mostly taken on an individual basis. Problems with wages tended to be dealt with without much difficulty, usually with wages staff and to the satisfaction of the women. At Community Hospital, management and supervisors were less successful at dealing with problems than their counterparts at City Centre Hospital, where supervisors were able to sort out half of the problems raised with them, and managers three-quarters. At both hospitals, problems related to equipment were among the most likely to be raised and the least likely to be resolved.

These findings also expose another extremely important issue, that those problems which particularly affect women workers, childcare and evening transport, were regarded as external to the workplace. Although they had a major effect on the women's ability to carry out their jobs, they were dealt with on an individual *ad hoc* basis, and neither management nor the union were expected to assist in these spheres. This suggests that the women themselves were adopting a narrow view of what counted as a workplace problem. There was considerable similarity between the two groups, in how they dealt with different issues and what they defined as an issue appropriate for a trade union. This suggests that the definition of workplace problems and the appropriate means to deal with such problems belonged to a wider context than the local union branch.

There were structural limitations to the representation of interests, and work was constructed in a way which promoted division among workers and hindered the development of a collective identification of problems. Beyond this, the women themselves defined the bulk of their problems as inappropriate to refer to the union. The central argument here is that this process is largely a result of the restricted trade union agenda. By the 1990s, there had been very little change in the nature of the problems raised by the domestics:

issues concerning being moved around, hours of work and rotas, and under-staffing were still the most common problems, and still remained unaddressed to or by the union.

The trade union agenda and issues not raised

Through the detailed study of the organization of work, issues were identified which were of specific relevance to the women ancillary workers, yet these were not raised by the women domestics in the survey. For example, none of the respondents raised the grading structure as an issue. A sexually divided grading structure based on a hierarchy of skills defined by gender was accepted as 'normal' by these groups of workers. The gendered construction of cleaning work is so absolute that while the domestics considered themselves low paid, they did not identify their work as undervalued compared to men's work. Also, no-one mentioned any issue related to racial divisions or discrimination. No-one raised any issue of a broader nature, for example the lack of any workplace cancer screening, even for workers in the health service.

The range of issues about which any action was taken was relatively narrow, and the range of issues which reached the union structure was even more restricted. Even at City Centre Hospital, where there was a union with an extensive and apparently effective shop steward system, few of the issues affecting women's working lives were raised within the union. Childcare and transport problems were not raised through the union and nor was any issue linked to the intensification of work. The sorts of problems that members did refer to the shop steward at City Centre were of an individual and immediate nature, including a problem with taking sick leave, harassment by a supervisor and a change of hours. These issues were dealt with on an individual basis and the wider implications of problems facing women ancillary workers were not discussed within the branch. There was no attempt to build a collectivist approach which might have been used to capitalize on membership concerns (Fosh 1993). At Community Hospital no issues were referred to the union by members. The only issue identified by a respondent which was raised within the union, the problem of privatization, was raised by a shop steward.

As illustrated in the previous chapter, union meetings in general were concerned with branch officers giving out information to shop stewards. In none of the union branches included in the research was there an arena in which broader issues could be raised and discussed by members. This suggests that there is a structural problem in unions, in that they have not developed adequate routes for members to discuss and articulate problems they face. It is not merely a function of the structure of trade unions which prevents the articulation of certain interests. Although representation could have been aided by the development of workplace organization and the development of forums in which problems could be discussed, the accepted trade union agenda prevents the development of potential issues and interests. A similar argument is developed by Charles:

> Clearly the trade unions, along with the world of work in general, are structured to cater for the interests of men, and women's specific interests fall outside what has until now been defined as the proper concerns of the trade union movement. (Charles 1983: 19)

By applying Lukes' concept of power it is possible to build an argument about the development of a union agenda which shapes the identification and articulation of interests within unions (Lukes 1974). The implication of this argument is that structural changes alone cannot ensure representation of interests, in a context in which women fail to identify the trade union as a route for certain workplace problems. Women members fail to regard the trade unions as appropriate for dealing with their problems because they too accept the restricted agenda. It is not only that women accept the trade union agenda, but that the way in which they identify and define issues or problems at work is actually shaped by that agenda. To illustrate this point, the problem of caring for children who were too unwell to attend school was a concern for many of the domestics. However, because this did not seem like the sort of thing that a trade union could help with, it was perceived as an individual problem to be dealt with on an individual basis.

In this context the UNISON initiative for self-organization becomes particularly significant. The articulation of interests requires space in which problems can be aired and issues discussed. If developed at local levels self-organized groups may provide that space. However, as McBride (1998) points out, there has been little progress as yet at the workplace level. Furthermore, where self-organized groups have been established, they have not addressed issues directly related to the workplace and have not significantly challenged the union agenda (McBride 1998).

Representation and Shop stewards

Shop stewards and branch officers may be in a position to transcend sectional workplace interests and develop a more collectivist approach to members' problems. However, there are contradictions in their identification of problems. Many stewards can identify the gender-specific problems related to the grading structure, to the way in which skills are valued and so on. However, this section demonstrates that while shop stewards may be in a position to identify such group interests, they too work within the context of a restricted trade union agenda. This results in the expression of contradictory views about the specific interests of groups of workers and the development of individualistic responses. This argument will be developed in two stages, the first picking up on the previous debates on the specific interests of women, and the second developing the argument in terms of the specific interests of black workers. The data used is drawn from interviews with shop stewards from three of the branches in the study.

Women's interests

Over and over again shop stewards stressed that women workers did not face any particular problems in the workplace:

> 'There are not any differences to what men have to face – depends on
> attitude. Being part-time doesn't affect what they do in the union. It's a
> bread-and-butter job, and we treat it seriously – we all need the money.'
> (Deputy branch secretary – NUPE City Centre)

Yet this same steward went on to give an articulate critique of the grading structure which specified the devaluation of women's skills:

> 'Women are confined to the lower pay groups in the ASC [Ancillary Services
> Council] grading structure by and large. I generally do not sympathize with
> the differentials which undervalue the ordinary worker – but even within the
> exaggerated hierarchy of a hospital, many women's skills are undervalued.'
> (Deputy branch secretary – NUPE City Centre)

Similar contradictory views were expressed by other shop stewards in this branch. Two other stewards stressed that men and women faced similar problems in the workplace, and were treated equally in the union, but then made the following comments:

> 'Senior management, etc. still tend to class women as second-class citizens
> and have no real policy on promotion for women within the health service at
> lower grade level and don't like the involvement of women in the trade union
> movement.' (Woman catering steward – NUPE City Centre)

'All traditional "women's jobs" are low paid. All hospital workers are
expected to get "job satisfaction" to compensate for low pay.' (Woman
nursing steward – NUPE City Centre)

At first these two stewards seemed to be reproducing their union branch
position on men and women in the workplace, but as the discussions pro-
gressed they identified a variety of ways in which women faced quite specific
problems at work. There was, however, no evidence that any of these issues
were being discussed within the union branch or of any action being taken on
them.

As well as identifying particular problems that women workers face, some
stewards identified women workers as a problem:

'Many are part-time workers, are only interested in the money and can "put
up with" conditions for a few hours a week. There is a fairly high turnover of
staff so union continuity is difficult to maintain.' (Male ancillary steward –
NUPE City Centre)

Neither the assumption that women ancillary staff were only interested in the
money nor the assumption that they did not remain in their jobs for any length
of time fitted with any of the evidence gained during this research. This
steward was working with a stereotype of women workers which did not fit with
the reality of his workplace.

At Community Hospital the COHSE shop stewards all said that women did
not face any particular problems in the workplace, and they could not be
persuaded to pursue the issue further. This may have been a result of poor
communication between stewards and members, resulting in a lack of awareness about members' problems. In contrast, shop stewards in the COHSE
branch at County Psychiatric Hospital showed the greatest range of views and
awareness of problems particularly relevant to women. About half of the
stewards were not sure or doubted that women were treated any differently
within the hospital.

'I do not think, in my experience, that there is any discrimination at my place
of work.' (Male nursing steward – COHSE County Psychiatric)

However, some of their colleagues found it easier to identify particular
problems.

'We are paid according to our grade and number of years' experience. The
majority of "top grade" nurses are male. I recently applied for promotion and

in the "declaration of health" questionnaire I was asked to state if a) I had regular periods, b) I suffered any discomfort, causing days off work due to period pain. I would love to see the questionnaire that male applicants received.' (Female nursing steward – COHSE County Psychiatric)

'Most men are usually graded higher although doing the same work but assuming they're "in charge". Domestics are almost all women – very few supervisors and certainly no black women supervisors, although staff must be 80 per cent Asian women workers.' (Female occupational therapist steward – COHSE County Psychiatric)

Shop stewards thus were able to identify the gendered nature of work with the associated undervaluing of women's skills, the hierarchical grading structure with women at the bottom and particularly subject to low pay, as well as the lack of opportunities for promotion and discriminatory management practices. In no case, however, were the stewards expressing these issues within their union branch, or was any branch taking any action on them. There were no attempts to mobilize members around these issues. It appears that, since shop stewards and branch officers also work within the context of the restricted union agenda, these issues were rendered inappropriate for further action.

Representation and race

This disjunction between the experience of the workplace and what was happening in the union branches became even greater when the issues of race, racism and racial discrimination were discussed. Stewards were generally less able to identify specific interests of black workers and in some cases indicated some antagonism toward them. This was in a situation where divisions were based on race in all of the departments and where black workers had specific interests that were not articulated through the union.

As described earlier, City Centre Hospital is situated adjacent to a sizable Asian community, but the domestic services department at the hospital has no staff of Asian origin. However, shop stewards were antagonistic even to being asked about issues related to racial discrimination. The following comments were made by NUPE shop stewards at City Centre Hospital.

'It would almost be easy to say "yes", [that there was racial discrimination in this hospital], since discrimination like prejudice exists everywhere. But by and large, recruitment and promotion seem reasonably balanced.' (Deputy branch secretary – NUPE City Centre)

> 'Racial discrimination has become an outcry among blacks and coloureds. Even normal discipline will evoke this cry. Of course some people discriminate. I have found the worst is among the African and Asian people themselves. There are black people in all sections of hospital life.' (Male ancillary steward – NUPE City Centre)

This was at a hospital where even the domestic services manager accepted that there had been discriminatory recruitment practices 'in the past'.

At Community Hospital none of the stewards believed there was any racial discrimination, and refused to discuss the issue, although the racial divisions in the domestic services department were a key issue. Also, as discussed in earlier chapters, the manager openly discussed Asian staff in a derogatory manner and blamed them for the threat of privatization. Once again the stewards from COHSE Central displayed a wide-ranging awareness:

> 'There are remarks and references about colour, race, religion, physical features, assumptions of intelligence e.g. Irish are thick.' (Male nurse steward – COHSE County Psychiatric)

> 'It is difficult to instance it but one knows by people's attitude it is under the surface.' (Female nurse steward – COHSE County Psychiatric)

> 'No overt discrimination here.' (Male nurse steward – COHSE County Psychiatric)

However, the COHSE County branch secretary was able to describe numerous instances of racism in the hospital. He described the domestic service manager as 'a real racist'. He said that there were many examples of his attitude, the worst being the example described earlier in which the husband of an Asian domestic had been contacted because it was felt she was not working hard enough. The branch secretary claimed that as soon as the union had heard about this case, they had intervened and stopped the practice. This example was the only one in the research that found a union branch taking any action on issues specifically related to race. The structural problems of the lack of an arena in which members could raise issues was more acute with issues related to race. Women of Asian origin were considerably under-represented at the level of shop steward, and less likely to attend union meetings. This is not meant in any way to imply less interest in union affairs among women of Asian origin. The example discussed in the previous chapter, of the NUPE branch meeting at Shire County Hospital which three Asian women attended, illustrated that women were not expected to take part in union affairs. Many of the shop stewards quoted above had little idea about the problems which affected women of Asian origin in the workplace. With divisions in the workplace based on race, the lack of women shop stewards of Asian origin in ancillary departments meant that the members of Asian origin had no route to raise issues of racism within the union.

Furthermore, there is some indication that issues related to race may be even further removed from the trade union agenda than those related to gender. Women ancillary workers of Asian origin in this study had a number of specific interests and problems. However, none of those who responded to the survey mentioned any issue related to race as a problem. This, when linked to the comments and attitude of some of the shop stewards, indicates that neither stewards nor members saw the trade unions as appropriate for dealing with these issues.

Significantly, the situation had changed little by the 1990s. The branch secretary from UNISON/NUPE Shire General felt that there was discrimination in the hospital and reported that a number of members had claimed to suffer from racial harassment. However, she interpreted this on an individualistic basis, and saw the solution in building the self-confidence and knowledge of individuals in order to fight for their own rights. It was not seen as a collective union issue.

The Formation of UNISON

It could be argued that UNISON has challenged the traditional trade union agenda, with policies for proportionality, fair representation and self-organization. These reforms represent considerable change to the 'way things are done', to the process of trade union activity. Changes to the agenda of issues which emerge from such a process are achieved more slowly. The constituent unions of UNISON – NALGO, COHSE and NUPE – had very specific traditions and cultures. COHSE was seen as dominated by nursing staff, particularly those from a psychiatric background. This picture was reflected at County Psychiatric, where in the 1980s most activists were male nurses concerned about how to represent their ancillary members. In contrast, NUPE was characterized as dominated by male manual workers – school caretakers in the education sector, ancillary or works staff in the hospital sector. Again in the 1980s this picture was reflected in the City Centre and Shire General branches. With the formation of UNISON there has been a complex realigning of interests cutting across gender, class and race. Within the UNISON health group there is general agreement that the national and regional agendas are dominated by nursing interests, and that issues affecting women have gained ground. Within the ancillary sector there remains a significant proportion of male staff, the traditional NUPE activists. Yet there continues to be little space for women ancillary workers.

Summary

It would appear that the issues which particularly affect women in the work-place were defined as 'inappropriate' issues for the union to deal with by the women themselves, by the shop stewards (including the women shop stewards) and by union officers. In the previous chapter it was demonstrated that the representation of women's interests requires the existence of certain union structures. In those branches with effective steward systems women seemed more likely to use the representational system to deal with a limited range of individual issues linked to grievance and discipline. However, in this chapter it has been shown that even in those union branches which seem to have an effective representational role, a vast list of issues which particularly affect women never appear on the union agenda and there is no arena in which they could appear. Nonetheless it was more likely that they would be raised in those branches with a representative structure.

Shop stewards, the key people who mediate between the ordinary member and her union, were mostly very antagonistic to any suggestion that any group of workers might have specific interests in the workplace, despite their ability to identify them. Even women stewards who experienced aspects of these specific problems themselves limited their activities to the narrow trade union agenda.

The stated aim of the branch secretary from NUPE City Centre was to 'treat everybody equally', and the branch officers were comparatively successful in this aim. However, treating everyone equally resulted in ignoring inequalities related to the grading structure, failing to take up many of the issues that actually affected their women members in the workplace, and failing to consider any broader issue relating specifically to women in employment. Despite this, it should be noted that this branch had made considerable improvements in workplace organization and had developed the most exten-sive representational system for women ancillary workers during the 1980s.

The situation on race was even more marked. Despite many observations of racist practice during this research there was very little awareness or concern about these issues. There was even more antagonism by many shop stewards to discussing this issue. In earlier chapters it has been suggested that black women have specific interests in the workplace in a labour market structured by race. However, in this research there was no evidence of any union branch taking on any issues related to racism, except for the example given earlier where a husband was contacted by management in order to make his wife work harder.

The argument is that, while the trade union agenda limits the definition of what a trade union issue is, the expectations of members, shop stewards and union officers remain narrowly defined. In this context, the specific interests of women workers and black workers will remain largely unarticulated and unrepresented. It is not the intention to suggest that the trade union agenda is completely static, rather that it is the result of a dynamic process. In Chapter 2 it was argued that the trade union agenda is embedded in the hierarchical nature of the labour market in which the interests of skilled male workers have been prioritized and presented as general class interests, to the detriment of other groups of workers. The agenda has changed over time, reflecting changes in the nature of work and in the make-up of the workforce. It is affected by the actions of individuals and groups within unions as well as external pressures on unions. Despite pressure for change, the impetus within unions is to retain the status quo. The discourse of 'equality and fairness' which is central to trade unions and results in a 'treat everybody the same' approach, paradoxically, precludes the acknowledgement of the diversity of interests. Moreover, the trade union agenda serves to reproduce itself through shaping the expectations and demands of members, of shop stewards and of union officers. A consequence of the trade union agenda is that the increased participation of women in unions does not automatically or quickly result in improved representation of women's interests. Women's expectations are shaped by the restricted agenda, and they too serve to reproduce it. In this context the need to provide space to discuss workplace issues was identified as particularly important. This may be facilitated through membership educational programmes, work-group meetings, or self-organization. If self-organization is to develop at the workplace, it requires resources and commitment from all levels of the union.

9 PARTICIPATION IN LOCAL UNION STRUCTURES

In Chapter 1 the literature on women in unions was criticized for its failure to distinguish between representation and participation. The previous chapter has demonstrated that not only do they need to be analytically separate, but also that they cannot be equated in practice. It follows from this that increased levels in women's participation in unions does not automatically result in improved levels of the representation of women's interests. Representation and participation are the two sides of involvement, the former focusing primarily on the union and the latter focusing primarily on women members. The focus on women members means that the debates around participation have a tendency to pathologize women, and that tendency will be criticized in this chapter.

The key argument of this chapter is that, although there are a number of factors which have some effect in increasing participation, there is an underlying limitation based on the restricted trade union agenda. The previous chapter showed that trade unions appeared to be inappropriate organizations for dealing with the actual problems and issues faced in the workplace. One ramification of this is that there is little reason for women ancillary members, and in particular for those of Asian origin, to participate in union affairs. Their actual experience of trade unions suggests that unions have little to offer them. This argument could be developed in relation to many groups of workers. However, the argument is that because of the exclusion of issues specifically affecting women and black workers from the trade union agenda, unions appear particularly irrelevant to women and black members.

A secondary argument developed in this chapter is that there is a tendency in the literature on women in unions and among trade unionists themselves to underestimate the degree to which women have an awareness of their position within waged labour and act to protect their working conditions. Women do have a work-consciousness, but this may not be translated into recognized forms of union participation. In Chapters 5 and 6 it was shown that the women ancillary workers were involved in workplace struggle, although the particular and contradictory form that these struggles took was not developed within trade union structures. This chapter will argue firstly that women's activity tends to be underestimated and secondly that, because of the restricted union agenda, women are more likely to engage in forms of activity and resistance outside of formal union structures. These forms of struggle tend not to be recognized as such and it is incorrectly assumed that women are more prone to apathy. In order to develop these arguments this chapter will be divided into three main sections. The first two sections will examine women members' participation as revealed in this research, and shop stewards' views of the women's participation. The third section will review the debates around participation, looking at the main explanations in the literature.

Levels of Involvement – Members

This section examines the way in which the women members in this research were actually involved in a considerable range of union activities, despite the fact, discussed in the previous chapter, that they rarely referred problems to the union. Levels of participation in the unions were similar at City Centre Hospital and Community Hospital, despite the considerable differences in branch organization in the unions at these hospitals.

An assessment of levels of involvement was initially based on what might be termed a traditional notion of trade union activities. These include membership levels, office-holding levels, levels of information or knowledge about the union, and participation in specific union activities. Each of these areas will be discussed in this section. However, during the fieldwork it became evident that many of the women were involved in various activities which did not come under any of these headings, and it is important to examine these other forms of activity because they throw a distinctive light on the relationship between interests, activity and 'participation'. They are therefore discussed in a separate section.

The sample

This chapter draws on the survey of domestic service staff referred to in the previous chapter. Of the 15 respondents to the questionnaire at Community Hospital, 13 said that they were union members, although only eight could actually name their union as COHSE. Ten (77 per cent) had been union members since starting their jobs. Of the 30 respondents at City Centre Hospital, all were union members, 28 members of NUPE and two members of the TGWU. Of the 28 NUPE members, 19 (64 per cent) had been in NUPE since they started their jobs. Union density was very high for both groups, which suggests that part-time working and low skill levels are not alone adequate explanations for membership levels.

Office-holding

As an indication of formal participation in terms of post-holding, the women were asked if they would consider becoming a shop steward, and if they would like to be more active in the union. The COHSE Community sample included an existing shop steward and an ex-shop steward. All of the other respondents said that they would not consider becoming a steward, although all of them said that they would like to be more active in the union. Of the NUPE City Centre sample, all 28 said that they would not consider becoming a shop steward, and 27 of the 28 said that they did not wish to be more active in the union. It is important to note the far higher levels of interest in the union at Community Hospital, since it was at City Centre in the NUPE branch that there had been greater attempts at structural changes to improve participation. Thus, in terms of expressed interest in unionism, structural changes seem not to have had an impact.

Knowledge about the union

On the basis that some degree of knowledge about the union is necessary in order to facilitate participation, the women's knowledge about local union matters was sought. In the COHSE Community sample, the domestics said they knew the following about office-holders in their branches.

- 7 (54%) knew who their shop steward was
- 5 (38%) thought the steward understood the problems facing domestics
- 4 (30%) knew who the branch officers were
- 3 (23%) thought the branch officers understood the problems facing domestics

In this branch, despite a claimed eagerness to be more involved, there was a widespread lack of knowledge about basic facts of the union branch. Since the shop steward is elected by members, the number of people who did not know who their shop steward was, was very high. One respondent particularly criticized communications within the union.

> 'Information of union meetings is only passed on by seeing our night supervisor, who passes the message on. She either forgets to tell us or only a few of us get to hear about it. Usually hardly any of us know or the time is very inconvenient when these meetings take place.' (Domestic evening shift – Community Hospital)

At Community, branch meetings were held in work time during the day. However, the evening shift staff found it difficult to attend, which highlights problems discussed in Chapter 7. The lack of a shop steward on the evening shift also meant that there were problems about giving and receiving information. At the City Centre Hospital a different picture emerged:

- 27 (96%) knew who their shop steward was
- 26 (93%) thought the steward understood the problems facing domestics
- 21 (75%) knew who the branch officers were
- 14 (50%) thought the branch officers understood the problems facing domestics

Despite a stated unwillingness to be more involved in the union, these women actually had considerably more knowledge about their union branch. The attempts in the City Centre NUPE branch to improve the structural organization appear to have been responsible for greater knowledge among this group, although as the previous section showed, this knowledge did not lead to a desire for involvement. Nevertheless, such knowledge remains an important prerequisite for involvement. The highly developed steward constituency system at City Centre meant that almost all members knew who their shop-steward was, and felt that the shop-stewards understood their problems. As with the COHSE branch, this group were less confident that branch officers understood the problems facing them.

Union activities

When asked if they had taken part in a number of specified union activities, there was a surprising similarity in terms of activities that each group had taken part in. The only major difference was over strike action. City had been particularly active in the 1982 strike, which reflects the more effective steward structure in NUPE at City Centre. This would indicate that an effective steward system may be necessary to mobilize members in the situation of a strike, although it appears ineffective in terms of maintaining on-going interest. This supports an argument that an on-going interest can only result from a trade unionism that appears relevant to the experiences of the workplace.

Members' union activities at the COHSE Community sample were as follows:

- 11 (85%) had attended union meetings
- 8 (61%) had taken part in strike action
- 4 (30%) had voted in union elections
- 3 (23%) had picketed during a dispute
- 6 (46%) had read the union newspaper

Members' union activities at the NUPE City Centre sample were as follows:

- 25 (89%) had attended union meetings
- 23 (82%) had taken part in strike action
- 11 (39%) had voted in union elections
- 11 (39%) had picketed during a dispute
- 13 (46%) had read a union newspaper

These results appear slightly different from other studies which indicated meeting attendance rates of about 60 per cent, considerably lower than in this research (Stageman 1980a, Kellner 1980). Kellner also reports strike rates of 24 per cent and picketing rates of 5 per cent (Kellner 1980). This is dramatically lower than in this research, and may be explained in part by this research taking place after the 1982 dispute, but also suggests that the women in this research were more active in industrial disputes than many elsewhere. The level of voting in union elections was similar in all of the studies, at between 35 and 40 per cent. Stageman found a much higher percentage reading the union newspaper, 68 per cent, than found in this research.

Based on these figures, the women domestics covered in this study appear to be comparatively active trade unionists. The figures found in this research may be high because of the 1982 industrial action and because of the introduction of bonus schemes and competitive tendering. More research that also considers the regularity of taking part in such activities would be useful. Nonetheless, in terms of formal branch activities these women members had a high level of participation. This indicates that research which is based on post-holding at higher levels within unions may considerably underestimate women's activities in the workplace, and serve to reproduce stereotypes of women members as inactive. This level of participation was achieved despite the majority of respondents working part-time, many on shifts, and all having considerable domestic responsibilities.

Other forms of activity

Two particular workplace struggles have been described in this research which lie outside of formal trade union activities. Chapter 5 described the attempt to maintain internal hierarchies at City Centre Hospital. Chapter 6 described attempts to resist the shift to part-time working, and the resistance, particularly by women of Asian origin, to speed up. Although these examples could be regarded as good union practice to prevent worsening conditions, none of the union branches in the research recognized or supported such attempts. These examples demonstrate that regardless of participation in formal union activities, women ancillary workers are actively engaged in struggle in the workplace. This indicates that it may be inappropriate to apply the term 'apathy' to workers' lack of involvement in formal structures.

After the completion of the members' survey, observation was carried out at meetings and demonstrations of the 'Defence of the Health Service Campaign', which was a joint union campaign covering the area which included Community, Shire General and County Psychiatric. Although the organizers of this campaign were all branch officers, there was a particularly high attendance on demonstrations and rallies of domestics from Community Hospital, especially of women of Asian origin. Since plans for privatization were further advanced at Community Hospital, this is not surprising. However, it is important to note that these members were not inactive and apathetic. They were acutely aware of their workplace interests and prepared to take action in support of them. Here was a situation with enormous potential for the union to involve these members in union activities, yet no effort was made to do so.

Improving participation

Both groups of domestics were asked in the questionnaire to identify which factors would make it easier for them to be more involved in the union. At NUPE City Centre, the results can be summarized as follows:

- 10 (36%) having more confidence in ourselves

- 8 (29%) having fewer home responsibilities
- 7 (25%) changing the times of meetings
- 7 (25%) changing the place of meetings
- 5 (18%) knowing more about how the union works
- 2 (7%) the attitude of managers/supervisors

The replies of the COHSE Community sample can be summarized as follows:

- 3 (23%) knowing more about how the union works
- 2 (15%) having more confidence in ourselves
- 2 (15%) having fewer home responsibilities
- 2 (15%) changing the times of meetings
- 1 (8%) getting more information about when the meetings take place
- 1 (8%) the attitude of managers/supervisors

Although having fewer domestic responsibilities was given a high placing by both groups, it is interesting that they gave a higher priority to having more confidence and knowing more about how the union works. This suggests a need for caution in regarding domestic responsibilities as providing the main explanation for low levels of participation. These findings also suggest that times and places of meetings are also given too high a priority in the literature. Although this was a small sample it produced broadly similar results to those found by Stageman in her much larger survey of women union members (Stageman 1980a). She also found the main factors mentioned were understanding union business and how unions work, and having more confidence. However, she found having fewer domestic responsibilities was higher in the list of factors.

This section indicates the need to be cautious about underestimating women's participation in union activities and workplace struggles. It has shown that assumptions should not be made that there is no activity within the workplace or no interest in trade unions, even if formal participation is low. In addition, there is an indication of a structural problem in union organizations relating to the flow of information to and from members. Insufficient information about the union and how it works goes *to* members, resulting in them feeling inadequate and lacking confidence. In addition the material from the previous chapter indicates that the lack of information *from* members results in the unions not dealing with the immediate concerns and experience of their members. The consequence is that the unions appear distant and their processes mystified.

Shop stewards' Views on Participation

This section focuses on shop stewards' explanations for the levels of participation by the women ancillary members. It shows firstly that stewards from the various branches held surprisingly similar views about membership participation, regarding members as inactive and apathetic. It also demonstrates that the main explanation given by shop-stewards for this perceived inactivity was women's domestic responsibilities. Shop stewards identified particular barriers to participation among women of Asian origin in terms of language and cultural background. The main arguments of this section are that shop-stewards tend to undervalue the activities that the women are involved in, and that their explanations are based on stereotypical images of women rather than the 'reality' of the workplace.

NUPE – City Centre

The shop stewards from City Centre Hospital put much emphasis on domestic and family responsibilities as preventing women from having a greater involvement in NUPE. Although this factor was deemed very important in limiting their participation by members in City Centre, it was ranked as less important than having more self-confidence.

> 'We have a lot of problems with getting women to attend evening meetings, weekend or residential schools and National Conference. Restrictions on women with domestic responsibilities often mean it is difficult to participate within the union.' (Male deputy branch secretary – NUPE City Centre)

> 'Most women have family commitments which tie up a lot of their time.' (Male ancillary steward – NUPE City Centre)

Despite these comments, the stewards when pressed did not think that the union branch should make any particular arrangements or re-organization to involve more women or try to fit union meetings with domestic arrangements.

One of the active women shop stewards in the domestic services department at City Centre Hospital described how problems with domestic responsibilities continue when becoming a shop steward, explaining that she would feel guilty if her housework was not finished before she started her union work, despite having what she described as a supportive husband:

'I'm not very active I'm afraid. But if I feel I'm right, I'll stick to it. My husband doesn't mind my union work, although sometimes he asks if I've taken on too much. I always do the housework before starting paperwork.' (Female domestic steward – NUPE City Centre)

Alongside this, one steward did identify how the nature of work makes workplace organization difficult. She pointed to the particular difficulties of communicating with women domestics, but did not feel this was a major factor in explaining the level of women's involvement:

'They are divided in areas – we're not supposed to go from place to place, but we still do. A meeting place is washing mops.' (Female domestic steward – NUPE City Centre)

One of the stewards from NUPE made an interesting point regarding the issue of women's confidence. She suggested that involvement in the union could actually serve to boost women's confidence in other spheres of life:

'The trade union involvement can give women more confidence in their own ability in making decisions – not only within the union but at home as well.' (Female catering steward – NUPE City Centre)

This woman explained that the knowledge and experience she had gained through her activities as a shop-steward had made her feel more able to deal with other aspects of her life. This positive aspect of trade union involvement could have been used to encourage membership participation. This, however, was the only example in the steward interviews of a positive aspect of women's involvement being identified.

COHSE – Community

Shop stewards in COHSE at Community Hospital dismissed their women ancillary staff for their 'lack of interest'. This contradicts the evidence from the domestics' questionnaire where domestics said that the factor which would most help them be more involved in their union was 'knowing more about how the union works', and the majority indicated that they did want to be more active in the union. This reflects a structural problem in that there was a weak steward system and little communication between stewards and members. However, it also highlights a subjective problem. The stewards were working with a stereotype of the members as apathetic and disinterested, while the members wanted to be more involved but did not know how to go about it. In this way the branch was actually preventing greater participation by not offering support and encouragement. This shows how membership interest can be underestimated, and that stewards' accounts of membership attitudes are not necessarily reliable. Some of the members did find it difficult to attend meetings, but this suggests that meeting attendance is not a good indicator of interest or awareness.

Only half of the domestics knew who their shop-steward was, yet when asked about opportunities for talking to their members, the shop-steward from that department said;

> 'If members need me, they know where to find me.' (Female domestic steward – COHSE Community)

The shop steward thus left the initiative for contact and communication in the hands of the members. This served to reinforce the notion of the union as the appropriate route for issues only in extreme circumstances. There was no conception of the union as involved in day-to-day issues and experiences of the workplace. This in part reflects a structural problem in that there was no forum for issues and expectations to be articulated and developed for the domestics. It could also be argued that the shop-stewards saw this as inappropriate and unnecessary because of the restricted union agenda.

The shop stewards' explanations for a relatively low level of involvement by women members were in terms of features of the women themselves and their lives, in particular in terms of their domestic responsibilities. The shop stewards were reflecting a common view, found in much of the literature, that because of women's activities in the domestic sphere, they give a secondary role to paid employment and therefore to trade union activity. Throughout my analysis, by contrast, it has been argued that there is inadequate evidence to suggest that women do give a secondary role to paid employment, and the evidence from this branch suggests that this group of domestics were actually being held back from greater involvement because shop-stewards assumed they were not interested.

COHSE – County Psychiatric

Shop stewards from COHSE County Psychiatric were prepared to consider issues beyond the home and family, but they too concentrated on aspects of the women themselves.

'Although the majority of COHSE members are women, at union meetings the percentage of men attending is much higher – maybe because many are part-timers and night workers with family commitments.' (Male nursing steward – COHSE County Psychiatric)

This steward indicated that women may find meeting attendance difficult because of their role in the family. The steward quoted below goes further than this and links low meeting attendance and low levels of post-holding to a lack of interest in unions, though this assumption is challenged by the evidence from the membership questionnaires.

'Women occupy very few posts in the hierarchy of the trade union – there are few women officials, this is reflected at branch levels. There is a lack of motivation and awareness among the majority of rank-and-file members and even more so with the female members. Commitment to nuclear family responsibilities, of parents towards children is uneven and biased – can't attend meetings, got to look after children. Husbands won't let them come to meetings – see them as full of lefties.' (Male branch secretary nurse – COHSE County Psychiatric)

'Pressures of family and domestic responsibilities mean most women have far less time or opportunity to be involved. Also some women are shy and perhaps not assertive enough, therefore think of it as a man's territory.' (Female nursing steward – COHSE County Psychiatric)

This steward picks up on the issue of confidence and links it to women's socialization as subordinate and passive. This, however, conflicts with the evidence of workplace resistance discussed in Chapters 5 and 6. This indicates a need to consider why women members may perceive unions as 'a man's territory'. One explanation is that the women were shy in dealings with the union because it appeared remote from the workplace and dominated by men and issues primarily or exclusively relevant to men. This suggests that 'shyness' cannot be taken for granted, but is a function of both structural aspects of unions and the restricted union agenda.

The list of features which might limit women's activities are expanded by this group of stewards to a list similar to the points raised by the domestics themselves, lack of confidence, meeting times and places, part-time and night working as well as domestic responsibilities. There was, however, no apparent attempt to overcome any of these problems. Even where stewards felt they could identify reasons for women's lower participation in union activities, there was little commitment to overcoming any obstacles. The great emphasis on domestic responsibilities led stewards to feel that the main limitations were beyond their control, and women's apathy towards unions was assumed to be inevitable.

Members of Asian Origin

The shop stewards from COHSE County Psychiatric were the only ones to mention specific reasons why Asian women in particular were not active within the union:

'The majority are Asian – there are language and cultural barriers. General reluctance of female trade unionists to be involved in day-to-day running and business of a union organization. Seem to think that it's not their job.' (Male nursing steward – COHSE County Psychiatric)

'The language and cultural barriers make it almost impossible for most Asian women, some are too shy even to come to a meeting unless they have a friend with them.' (Female nursing steward – COHSE County Psychiatric)

'Most Asian domestics do not speak much English, the younger workers who are able to translate for them are reluctant to become representatives.' (Female occupational therapist steward – COHSE County Psychiatric)

The main explanations in relation to women members of Asian origin were seen to be difficulties with language, and a cultural background which did not encourage the development of active trade unionism. However, the particular attention to Asian culture as one which discourages unionism has been challenged by Parmar (1982). Observations at union meetings confirm that very few women of Asian origin did attend; however, there was a high level of attendance by women of Asian origin at various demonstrations and marches organized as part of the 'Defence of the Health Service Campaign'. They were also particularly involved in workplace struggles. This suggests again that there was a tendency to underestimate the activities of these women by the shop stewards, accepting a stereotype rather than the evidence of the workplace.

It was only in relation to Asian members that any of the stewards from any of the branches felt that the union needed to take any specific action, and this was linked to language problems.

'Language is a problem with domestics – they don't always understand leaflets. We have an Asian shop steward – we're going to print leaflets in

Urdu and Punjabi, and he will interpret at meetings. They feel oppressed and discriminated against in the hospital, it discourages them to voice opinions in a branch meeting. They don't want to be seen as obvious or obtrusive.'
(Male branch secretary nurse – COHSE County Psychiatric)

Language was always seen by the shop stewards as a problem but, as suggested in previous chapters, language was also used as a means of resistance. Although the potential of such a form of resistance should not be overstated, the shop stewards were completely unable to perceive the positive aspects of any of the actions by the Asian women. Forms of resistance such as this do not fit with the shop stewards' notions of what trade union activity is. As there is a trade union agenda which defines what issues are appropriate for trade unions, so it also defines what activities count as 'appropriate trade union activities'. This example is particularly interesting because by the 1990s the ancillary staff had become the most regular attenders at meetings. The general complaint was that the Asian women talked all the time, even when business was being done and other people were talking. Either too passive or too noisy, they always failed to find the required behaviour. Participation is difficult for members who never seem to fit the model of a 'trade unionist'.

Debates on Participation

It is important to place these findings in the context of a discussion of the debates which focus specifically on women's participation, and general debates in the context of trade union democracy.

Work-consciousness

The concept of work-consciousness was discussed in Chapter 1. The literature which refers to it was criticized for conflating concepts of work-consciousness with those of union-consciousness, and for ignoring the limitations on the development of a union-consciousness. This conflation of two issues assumes that involvement in trade unions is the only rational response to an awareness of exploitation in wage labour. The level of work-consciousness has tended to be assessed by the levels of participation in trade unions. There are two problems with this form of reasoning. Firstly, levels of participation are usually judged on the basis of formal activity, such as post-holding. This ignores other forms of struggle which may be taking place in the workplace outside of the formal structures of unions (Cohen 1987). Secondly, it ignores the limitations to participation. It assumes that trade union machinery is equally open and equally relevant to all workers engaged in struggle. This chapter suggests that the settled and relatively narrow trade union agenda results in unions appearing inappropriate to certain groups of workers, and therefore serves to limit participation. The previous chapter showed that unions were not always seen as the appropriate means for dealing with women ancillary workers' issues. This lack of relevance of unions to the experiences of the workplace reduces any incentive for participation. This then challenges the idea that lack of union participation is an indicator of membership apathy. It cannot be assumed that lack of participation is a result of apathy, for it may reflect rather a reaction to women's experience of unions.

Union structures and participation

The previous chapter argued that certain union structures are necessary for representation, but do not guarantee it. Similarly this chapter argues that certain structures are necessary for participation, but do not guarantee it. In a discussion of research on the structure of NUPE, Coates and Topham suggest that apathy is primarily a result of structural problems.

> We suggest that the apparent apathy and lack of interest experienced in some of the ways we have described is also engendered by the difficult environment in which the Union operates rather than being the result of individual members or whole sections simply 'not caring' about the Union. In other words, apathy can be understood as a symptom of isolation or remoteness that is caused chiefly by NUPE's environment and partly by NUPE's own structure. But it follows that if this is the case, 'apathy' is amenable to structural modification and may be reduced by changes in structure. (Coates and Topham 1980: 67)

There are problems, however, about the concept of apathy. If this is taken to mean lack of participation, the argument in this chapter is that it cannot be explained by reference to structural aspects of trade unions alone and hence it may be reduced but not prevented by structural modification. The evidence here broadly supports the argument that certain union structures are a prerequisite of participation. Indeed the general argument supports the importance of workplace-based trade unionism with open and democratic structures.

Fairbrother has outlined some of the structural requirements for union

democracy in relation to the development of a workplace based trade unionism (Fairbrother 1986). Furthermore, he points to the need for this trade
unionism to be directly related to the experiences of members:

> At the most general level, for a union to be democratic it should be based on
> the immediate and direct concerns and experiences of members as workers
> enmeshed in complex and particular employment relations. This requires
> that the primary unit of union organization is rooted in the workplace, that is,
> the workplace-based branch. (Fairbrother 1986: 177)

While the present work shares Fairbrother's concerns, it also argues that the
trade union agenda limits the degree to which even workplace-based trade
unionism can reflect the direct concerns and experiences of women members.
In 1989, Fryer wrote that many union studies pointed to the need for membership section meetings, yet by 1996 there was no evidence of such a
development in the branches covered by the research (Fryer 1989). There
seems to have been a general reluctance by unions to respond to research
findings which indicate the importance of workplace organization and meetings.

The formation of UNISON has led to dramatic structural changes. Self-
organization is one of the key equal opportunities developments in UNISON,
yet progress in this has also been slower at the workplace level (McBride 1998).
At the time of the fieldwork, there had been no initiatives in terms of self-
organized groups in the union branches and little awareness about how to
develop them. In contrast, proportionality had made a greater impact,
although feelings were not always positive. At St Stephen's the branch secretary
said that there had been a big change, since previously branch and regional
meetings had been dominated by men. She also felt that having a supportive
full-time official had made a big difference. However, at Shire General the
branch secretary felt that proportionality discriminates and limits their choice
of delegates: '... have it stipulated that one of our delegates has to be a woman,
we would be happy to send two men, the women have children, we end up
sending no-one'. At the other end of the spectrum, the branch secretary from
City Centre felt that the changes had made very little difference to this
branch.

While many of UNISON's policies nationally appear to reflect a dramatic
shift towards acknowledging issues affecting women workers and black workers, there are difficulties about imposing an agenda on local branches.
Significantly, many of the changes are changes to structures and processes.
The UNISON agenda still ignores many of the workplace *issues* directly

affecting the groups of workers studied in this research, the women ancillary workers. There are, however, other initiatives which may provide space in which to address such problems. All branches are required to produce 'Branch Development Plans'. Assistance is provided by the full-time officers and educational programmes have been designed to support the process. To complete the plan, branches need to analyse the make-up of the branch membership and consider the representation and participation of all groups of members. Yet the branch officers still act as 'gate-keepers' to participation in the branch, and their power has, as was discussed in Chapter 7, been increased by the growth of local collective bargaining.

Women's participation

The literature on women's participation was discussed in Chapter 1, where various factors which may hinder participation were outlined. A major theme in much of the literature was that women do not participate in trade unions because they give time and emotional priority to the domestic sphere. While recognizing the additional burdens on women of domestic responsibilities, these arguments were criticized for giving too much emphasis to this explanation. The material from this research suggests that union involvement is possible for women despite such responsibilities, and that women's concern for the domestic sphere does not necessarily exclude an interest in issues related to paid employment. The significance of the life cycle is, however, acknowledged, as many studies have found that those women who are active in trade unions are often older with less dependent children (Cunnison and Stageman 1993, Lawrence 1994, Colgan and Ledwith 1996).

Many of the writers criticize the times and places of meetings, which made it difficult for women to participate. The material in Chapter 7 showed that meetings in work time were much more frequently attended, but it also showed that meetings varied in the degree to which they enabled participation. This suggests that there is a need to distinguish between meeting attendance and the nature of participation within meetings. The way in which meetings are organized may be as, or more important than the time and place of the meeting.

Coote and Campbell (1982) argue that the organization of women's work makes involvement in union activities more difficult. This is supported by the material in Chapters 5 and 6 which indicates ways in which the construction of women's ancillary work militates against the development of collective organization. Furthermore, the material in Chapter 7 indicates that the nature of women's jobs makes the carrying out of duties attached to union posts more difficult.

The central argument of this Chapter, however, adds another dimension to these debates. It is that while women see trade unions as largely irrelevant to their workplace concerns, there is no impetus to becoming more involved in union activities. At the same time, the myth of female apathy is perpetuated so long as definitions of participation rest on formal post-holding. However, there are limits to the degree to which participation can be improved while the trade union agenda excludes issues specifically relevant to women, especially where changes to the union agenda cannot be easily brought about by individual women or groups of women. Particular events, such as involvement in industrial action, may lead members to identify a relevance for trade unions (Lane and Roberts 1971, Heritage 1983). The claim is that participation and representation interconnect in a complex way, and low levels of participation cannot be understood by reference to false consciousness or lack of union awareness. Levels of participation can only be understood in the context of a form of trade unionism which excludes issues specific to women workers, and which women perceive as irrelevant to their experience and concerns in the workplace.

Summary

This chapter has demonstrated that the issue of participation is more complex than indicated in much of the literature. There is some indication that because of the restricted trade union agenda, women ancillary workers are more likely to be involved in workplace struggles which are defined as outside of union activities. The previous chapter showed that, as trade unions appear largely irrelevant and distant, women workers deal with problems on an individual basis. This chapter suggests that the forms of workplace struggle women engage in tend not to be recognized or supported by local union officers.

The degree to which women workers have a work-consciousness is often underestimated. The women in this study were found to be more active in union activities than could have been anticipated from the literature discussed in Chapter 1. Women appeared to find it difficult to attend meetings and hold union posts, although they had high levels of participation in strike action, picketing and attending demonstrations. This suggests that an assessment of the level of participation which relies on meeting attendance and post-holding will further underestimate the actual activities of women members. Women's extra responsibilities in the family, their lack of confidence in relation to trade unions and the nature of work organization all have an impact on women's ability to attend meetings and hold union posts. These explanations are relevant, but they cannot explain the overall form of women's participation.

Shop stewards were found to work on the assumption that women were apathetic, and that it was women's own fault for not being more active in their union branches, because they were more concerned with their families, because they were not interested, and because they did not speak English. The picture painted by the shop stewards was based on meeting attendance and willingness to become a shop steward, and was one which undervalued the actual activities of the women members. The structure and organization of the unions themselves were regarded uncritically by the shop stewards, although this chapter demonstrates that there were considerable structural problems related to participation. There were problems of communication between stewards and members and there was a problem of the lack of a route by which members could become more active.

There were similar problems with participation even in branches which had very different structural developments. This suggests that structural manipulation cannot guarantee increased participation, although it is a prerequisite for it. Underlying these structural problems is a problem about the relevance of trade unions to the experiences of the workplace. The steward who made the following comment did not feel that his comment raised any questions about trade unions:

'The real problem is trying to persuade them that the union is useful.' (Male nursing steward – COHSE County Psychiatric)

The argument of this book is that the real problem is how to make trade unions useful to the experiences and concerns of women workers.

10 Assessment

Based on a study of workplace unionism, this book is primarily about working-class women and the effectiveness of trade unions in representing their interests. It has drawn on, and attempted to link, two bodies of literature which have developed relatively independently. These are the sociological literature on work and unionism, which tends to ignore the specific implications of divisions of gender and race, and the literature on women and trade unions, some of which lacks a general theoretical underpinning. It aims to contribute towards the development of academic debates in this area, and to highlight some of the practical implications for trade unionism.

Three main arguments have been advanced. These are firstly that there exists a limited trade union agenda; secondly that work is constructed and reconstructed by reference to gender and race which results in specific gendered and racially defined interests; finally that trade union involvement can only be understood in the context of both structural organization of trade unions and their ability to reflect the experiences and interests of workers. Each of these will be examined in turn.

The Trade Union Agenda

Drawing on Lukes' work on power, the central argument has been that there exists a trade union agenda which limits the sort of issues which trade unions deal with. In particular, it excludes a number of interests specific to women workers, and interests specific to black women workers. This restricted agenda serves to promote lack of interest in unions, since they appear irrelevant to the experiences of workers and of the workplace. In this way a lack of interest in unions does not reflect false consciousness, but a reaction to the realities of experience. To assume that this lack of interest reflects an apathy towards the process by which workers are exploited within waged labour fails to appreciate the way in which workers' expectations are limited. This argument was illustrated in Chapter 8, where it was shown that women ancillary workers rarely identified the trade union as the appropriate arena in which to raise their interests and concerns. The material from this chapter also suggested that issues particularly relevant to black women workers may be even further removed from the union agenda.

Furthermore, as a result of the limited representation of women's interests, the union agenda serves to discourage the participation in unions by women workers. Chapter 9 showed that where trade unions appeared irrelevant, women ancillary workers either made individual and *ad hoc* responses to their problems or 'put up' with the problems in a fatalistic fashion. In this way participation is linked in a complex way to the process of representation of interests. The evidence of the failure of union officers to acknowledge workplace struggle in hospital ancillary work suggests that such struggles may be channelled away from union organization. In this way the restricted agenda may serve to limit the sort of workplace activities which are regarded as part of union involvement.

It has been argued that the union agenda results from an institutional mobilization of bias, in the context of an historical development of trade unionism based on the maintenance of division and hierarchy, where skilled white male workers have traditionally dominated the agenda. The union agenda develops in a dynamic process in which it is shaped by, but also shapes, the expectations and demands of members. The union agenda provides the context in which workers identify interests, and determines which interests are articulated within the union. It tends to be reflected and reproduced by all actors within the union movement, including those members whose interests are excluded.

Since the agenda is not static, however, it does retain the potential for change. This may come about through changes in the make-up of the labour market which result in changes in union membership. As unions become more reliant on women for membership, arguments for developing the scope of union activities carry greater weight. It may also be challenged by the activities of groups or individual members, as women and black workers organize to assert their specific interests. This may be speeded up within UNISON through such measures as the development of self-organized groups, proportionality and fair representation. However, despite these pressures the union movement retains an immense ability to absorb a changing membership without fundamentally altering the union agenda. As men's interests have been accepted as 'class interests' and women's interests dismissed as 'sectional interests', to promote women's concerns appears to be promoting disunity. At the same time the union discourse of equality promotes the notion of treating everyone the same; any recognition of a diversity of interests would undermine this basic feature of trade unionism. While unions appear to be changing at the policy level, their practice has changed much less. One illustration of this was given in Chapter 5, where apparent challenges to grading structures actually concealed the consolidation of the hierarchy of labour based on sex. This indicates a need for caution in the assessment of changes to the union agenda. While the general national agenda appears to be changing, and is acknowledging issues of importance to women, the workplace interests of working class women and black women are still being neglected.

The Organization of Work

A study which aimed to identify those interests of women workers which do not appear in union activities necessitated a detailed study of work itself. Through the analysis of women's ancillary work in the NHS, a number of arguments were made about the nature of women's work. The main theme was that the crucial division of interest between men and women in the labour market stems from the hierarchical division of the labour market by sex, which is mediated by race. Central to this theme was the argument, made in Chapters 5 and 6, that work is constructed and reconstructed in relation to gender and race. It was argued that the gendering of work draws on stereotypical notions of masculinity and femininity, and is so adaptable that it causes certain tasks to be regarded as 'naturally' women's work in one place, and 'naturally' men's work in another. These arguments were developed in relation to the differentiation of men and women cleaners and of catering assistants and kitchen porters. While there has been research on the gendering process in professional and managerial work (Halford, Savage and Witz 1997, McDowell and Court 1997), there has been less attention on manual work. My research indicates the continuing significance of the gendering of low-paid, subordinate forms of female labour. Furthermore, depending on the available supply of labour, different tasks were defined as more or less appropriate for women of Asian origin. With an increasing supply of white women workers, ancillary work appeared to be in the process of being redefined as inappropriate work for women of Asian origin.

The gendering of work was formalized in grading structures which maintained women at the bottom of the hierarchy of labour. It was demonstrated that apparent attempts to challenge that hierarchy of labour have in fact served to make divisions within grading structures less overt, while maintaining them. It was argued that these grading structures are maintained and legitimated by skill definitions which undervalue the tasks involved in women's work. The boundary between definitions of women's work and men's work is continually shifting and one recent development which illustrates this is the introduction of young part-time male workers into jobs traditionally considered as women's. It was suggested that young men may accept the challenge to their masculinity which results from doing a woman's job, provided it is seen as a temporary occupation. As such, this development does not necessarily indicate the degendering of part-time work.

Work is both constructed and reconstructed in relation to gender. During the 1980s there was a trend towards the substitution of part-time jobs for full-time jobs. Despite the observations above about some male part-time workers, this reconstruction strategy is only feasible in women's work. There was also some evidence that this included the substitution of white workers for black workers. During the 1990s, and in the context of NHS trusts, there has been renewed attention to ancillary work as providing opportunities for cost-cutting. It has been women ancillary workers who have borne the brunt of these recent changes. Two main strategies have been developed, either renewed interest in privatizing the services or a shift to generic working. The former is associated with worsening terms and conditions. Both have been linked to a reduction in job opportunities for black women and both seem likely to result in work intensification.

These arguments suggest that working-class women have a number of specific interests related to the hierarchy of labour. In developing this proposition it was demonstrated that women have a number of other specific interests related both to the immediate workplace and to wider issues. Alongside this, the construction of women's work militates against the development of a collective identification in a variety of ways. Women's jobs frequently lack geographical mobility and opportunities to talk to other workers, the supervision of women's manual jobs tends to be tighter than that of men, and part-time work is generally more intense. In ancillary work discrete shifts meant that many staff never saw each other, while shortages of materials often resulted in workers resenting staff from the opposite shift. Furthermore, the specific organization of women's work hinders active participation in union activities. Nonetheless, despite these restrictions, it should not be assumed that women workers have no work-consciousness. They are frequently involved in workplace struggles over the control of work, and indeed, given the barriers to activity, it could be argued that women are surprisingly active in workplace struggles.

Trade Union Organization

It is evident from this research that the women ancillary workers rarely refer issues or problems at work to the unions; instead they make individual responses, or just make the best of the situation and do nothing. Even where shop stewards and branch officers were aware of issues affecting women members, they rarely took any action. Furthermore, the emphasis on formal types of participation underestimates the degree to which women ancillary workers are involved in workplace and union activities. There is, however, an indication that structural changes in unions, in terms of improved workplace organization, could improve both the representation and participation of women members. There is a problem around the lack of communication with members, and there is a lack of an appropriate forum in which members could begin to articulate issues. The material from Chapters 7, 8 and 9 pointed to the need for certain structural developments as a prerequisite for the representation and participation of women members.

Shop stewards and branch officers were found to have a stereotypical view of women members as apathetic, and this also tends to be assumed in much of the literature on women and unions. This stereotype has been challenged in the research since it does not reflect the experience of the workplace. Stereotypical views of Asian women as particularly passive have also been criticized and alternative forms of activity which are defined as outside of trade union organization were identified. In contrast, at St Stephen's, when the Asian women ancillary staff did try to express their views within the branch, they were criticized for being disruptive in meetings. They believed that their shop steward had been excluded from negotiations, resulting in an agreement which meant many of them losing their jobs, yet the women themselves were presented as the problem. Union procedures were being used to contain conflict.

Explanations for the level of women's involvement in trade unions, by union activists and in the literature, concentrate on women's domestic role as preventing participation. While recognizing that there are additional burdens on women, it is the case that too much emphasis is placed on this factor. In particular, it is used by union activists to justify their own inactivity towards women members.

There is a tendency in some of the literature and among trade union activists to pathologize women members, to blame them for low levels of formal union involvement. This research aims to re-direct debates to consider the role of trade unions themselves, and the way in which the interests of certain groups of workers are excluded from the trade union agenda. It also points to the need for the development of workplace union organization and structures to enable union involvement. Such developments could serve to improve the involvement of all union members. In the light of the discussions of the trade union agenda, however, it becomes apparent that there is a particular need to improve communication and facilitate the articulation of interests among women and black members. The UNISON initiative of branch development plans may provide a context for this articulation of interests, yet this relies on the activities of branch officers.

While the union branches covered in this research varied considerably in the extent to which they had developed workplace organization, there was similarity in terms of the sorts of issues they were dealing with. In all of the branches, shop stewards and branch officers were resistant to the idea of particular groups of workers having specific interests. This was despite their own ability to identify some of the particular problems facing women ancillary workers, and in some cases women of Asian origin. It was argued that the contradictory views expressed by stewards resulted from the disjunction between the trade union agenda and their experience of hospital ancillary work. This suggests the need for an emphasis on the role of the shop steward of relaying members' interests and concerns 'upwards' within union hierarchies, rather than passing 'down' information. Continual change in the NHS has resulted in shop stewards and branch officers feeling weighed down by the pressures of their workloads and unable to address 'extra' concerns of specific workgroups. However, responding to these concerns might actually serve to stimulate workplace organization.

These discussions highlight the need for structural changes within unions to enable the development of expectations and articulation of interests among members. Of the unions in the research, in the 1980s the NUPE branch in City Centre had by far the most extensive shop steward system. The branch had recruited a large number of women ancillary workers as shop stewards, yet still many of their interests were not articulated within the branch. This was also linked to the dominance of branch officers in union meetings and the lack of a forum for discussion. By the 1990s, the shop steward system had all but disappeared, despite the formation of UNISON with its range of initiatives aimed at improving participation. This indicates the fragility of workplace organization.

In comparison, the main concern of the COHSE branch from County Psychiatric Hospital in the 1980s was the extension of the shop steward system. While the branch had no ancillary stewards there were no routes of communication between the ancillary staff and the wider union structures. This situation was exacerbated by the lack of women stewards and particularly the lack of women stewards of Asian origin. This branch had, however, been the most successful in enabling membership participation in union meetings. The shop steward system was extended to ancillary departments during the 1990s, yet the branch had failed to include women ancillary stewards in key negotiations over the reorganization of their work.

In all of the branches centralization of power within branches was identified as a problem. In the NUPE branch at Shire General Hospital this was particularly linked to the dominance of the full-time official, who did little to assist in the development of a participative trade unionism. The branch also had a poorly developed shop steward system and openly discouraged participation in union meetings. Here, major improvements in participation had been achieved by the 1990s, and full-time officials covering all of the branches were regarded in a more positive light by branch officers. The COHSE branch at Community Hospital similarly had a weak shop steward system, in which many staff did not know who their shop steward was. The impetus for communication was left with members. The membership survey indicated considerable interest in the union, yet members did not know where to take that interest. Again the situation was worsened by the absence of shop-stewards of Asian origin.

The key points to emerge from the research were the needs for a line of communication between the branch and all groups of workers, and for arenas in which members' interests could be articulated. These are particularly important in the context of work structured around race and gender, resulting in interests specific to women and black workers. The main implication of this research is that the key to improving women's participation and representation within trade unions is a challenge to the restricted union agenda. In relation to union structure at the level of the branch, a number of developments would assist a challenge to the union agenda. Firstly, a prerequisite of involvement is a workplace-based shop steward system. Without this there is no link between members and the wider union. Secondly, there needs to be improved routes for the flow of information, particularly upwards, from members to shop stewards and branch officers. Finally, linked to this, there is the need for the development of workplace-based meetings or discussions for members and stewards. These would provide a forum in which women members and stewards would feel more confident, and could begin to articulate the problems which they actually face. Branch officers have been identified as a crucial group in enabling or discouraging the involvement of women members. Attention needs to be given to how this group can be encouraged to recognize the variety of contributions which members may make within the branch and how they can encourage and support participation. This has significant implications for resources, for training and the support of full-time officials.

Paradoxically, activists and members in the branches appear the most resistant to national initiatives aimed at improving opportunities within UNISON for women, black workers and other groups traditionally less well represented. This reflects the problem of imposing democracy from above, and results in an agenda which still appears irrelevant to workplace concerns. Links need to be made between the more general equal opportunities issues generated nationally with these workplace concerns – to achieve a balance between 'power over' and 'power for'. It is necessary to acknowledge and tackle the differences of interest and not to dismiss workplace interests as sectional. Within the health sector of UNISON the interests of professional staffs, particularly nurses, appear to dominate the agenda. Issues affecting women generally have moved to centre stage, yet issues affecting women ancillary workers seem as excluded as ever. This highlights the difficulty of defining a feminist union agenda without reference to workplace concerns.

The formation of UNISON provided an opportunity for the development of a truly innovative approach to both the content of the union agenda and the processes of union organization. However, it retains a centralized 'top-down' structure which fails to capitalize on opportunities to stimulate workplace activity. In the subtle realignment between interests of class, gender and race, the voices of many working-class women remain unheard. The continuing challenge facing trade unions is one of transforming the fundamental nature of their role in their representation of members. Some of the changes occurring at present may indicate that the union agenda is entering the process of change. Only a long-term study of the sorts of issues unions are taking up will show whether this is the case.

BIBLIOGRAPHY

Aldred, C. (1981) *Women at Work*, London: Pan.

Allen, M. (1987) 'Less Equal than Others? – Black workers and trade unions'. *International Labour Reports*, issue 20, March–April 1987.

Armstrong, P. (1976) 'Workers Divided: The Case of Six Women' in *Workers Divided*, ed. T. Nichols and P. Armstrong, London: Fontana.

Baden, N. (1986) 'Developing an Agenda: Expanding the Role of Women in Unions'. *Labour Studies Journal*, Winter, pp. 229–49.

Bain, G. and Price, R. (1983) 'Union Growth: Dimensions, Determinants, and Density' in *Industrial Relations in Britain*, ed. G. Bain, Oxford: Blackwell, pp. 3–34.

Balfour, C. (1972) *Incomes Policy and the Public Sector*, London: Routledge and Kegan Paul.

Batstone, E., Boraston, I. and Frenkel, S. (1977) *Shop Stewards in Action*, Oxford: Blackwell.

Batstone, E. (1988) *The Reform of Workplace Industrial Relations*, Oxford: Clarendon Press.

Beale, J. (1982) *Getting it Together – Women as Trade Unionists*, London: Pluto Press.

Beechey, V. (1979) 'On Patriarchy'. *Feminist Review*, vol. 3, pp. 66–82.

Beechey, V. (1983) 'What's so special about women's employment? A review of some recent studies of women's paid work'. *Feminist Review*, vol. 15, pp. 23–45.

Beechey, V. (1987) *Unequal Work*, London: Verso.

Beechey, V. and Perkins, T. (1987) *A Matter of Hours – Women, Part-time Work and the Labour Market*, Cambridge: Polity.

Beynon, H. (1975) *Working for Ford*, Wakefield: EP Publishing.

Bhat, A., Carr-Hill, R. and Ohri, S. (1988) *Britain's Black Population*, 2nd ed., Aldershot: Gower.

Blackburn, R., Jarman, J. and Siltanen J. (1993) 'The analysis of occupational gender segregation over time and place: considerations of measurement and some new evidence'. *Work, Employment and Society*, vol. 7, no. 3, pp. 335–62.

Boston, S. (1980) *Women Workers and the Trade Unions*, London: Davis-Poynter.

Bradley, H. (1989) *Men's Work, Women's Work*, Cambridge: Polity.

Bradley, H. (1993) 'Divided we fall: trade unions and their members in the 1990s'. *Management Research News*, vol. 16, no. 5/6, pp. 15–16.

Bradley, H. (1996) *Fractured Identities – Changing Patterns of Inequality*, Cambridge: Polity.

Bradley, H. (1999) *Gender and Power in the Workplace*, Basingstoke: Macmillan.

Briskin, L. and McDermott, P., eds (1993) *Women Challenging Unions*, Toronto: University of Toronto Press.

Brown, C. (1984) *Black and White Britain – The Third PSI Survey*, Policy Studies Institute, London: Heinemann.

Bruegel, I. (1989) 'Sex and Race in the Labour Market'. *Feminist Review*, vol. 32, pp. 49–68.

Bryan, B., Dadzie, S., and Scafe, S. (1985) *The Heart of the Race – Black Women's Lives in Britain*, London: Virago.

Bryson, C., Jackson, M. and Leopold, J. (1995) 'The impact of self-governing trusts on trades unions and staff associations in the NHS'. *Industrial Relations Journal*, 26: 2, pp. 120–33.

Carpenter, M. (1980) *All for One – Campaigns and Pioneers in the Making of COHSE*, Banstead: COHSE.

Carpenter, M. (1988) *Working for Health – The History of COHSE*, London: Lawrence and Wishart.

Carpenter, M., Elkan, R., Leonard, P. and Munro, A. (1987) *Professionalism and Unionism in Nursing and Social Work*, Coventry: University of Warwick, March.

Cavendish, R. (1982) *Women on the Line*, London: Routledge and Kegan Paul.

Charles, N. (1983) 'Women and trade unions in the workplace'. *Feminist Review*, vol. 15, pp. 3–22.

Clark, A. (1982) *Working Life of Women in the Seventeenth Century*, London: Routledge and Kegan Paul.

Clegg, H. (1979) *Local Authority and University Manual Workers, NHS Ancillary Staffs and Ambulancemen*, Standing Commission on Pay and Comparability, Report No. 1.

Coates, K. and Topham, T. (1980) *Trade Unions in Britain*, Nottingham: Spokesman.

Coates, K. and Topham, T. (1988) *Trade Unions in Britain*, 3rd ed., London: Fontana.

Cockburn, C. (1983) *Brothers – Male Dominance and Technological Change*, London: Pluto Press.

Cockburn, C. (1985) *Machinery of Dominance – Women, Men and Technical Know-how*, London: Pluto Press.

Cockburn, C. (1987) 'Women, trade unions and political parties', *Fabian Research Series*, no. 349.

Cockburn, C. (1988) 'The gendering of jobs: workplace relations and the reproduction of sex segregation' in *Gender Segregation at Work*, ed. S. Walby, Milton Keynes: Open University Press.

Cockburn, C. (1989) 'Equal opportunities: the short and long agenda'. *Industrial Relations Journal*, vol. 1, no. 2, pp. 171–89.

Cockburn C. (1991) *In the Way of Women: Men's Resistance to Sex Equality in Organizations*, London: Macmillan.

Cohen, R. (1987) *The New Helots – Migrants in the International Division of Labour*, Aldershot: Avebury.

Cohen, S. and Fosh, P. (1988) 'You are the Union: trade union workplace democracy'. *WEA Studies for Trade Unionists*, vol. 14, no. 53, WEA, April.

Colgan, F. and Ledwith, S. (1996) 'Sisters organising – women and their trade unions' in *Women in Organisations*, ed. S. Ledwith and F. Colgan, Basingstoke: Macmillan, pp. 152–85.

Colling, T. (1995) 'Renewal or rigor mortis? Union responses to contracting in local government', *Industrial Relations Journal*, vol. 26: 2, pp. 134–45.

Colling, T. and Dickens L. (1989) *Equality Bargaining – Why Not?*, Warwick University/EOC, London: HMSO.

Community Action (1984) 'Special Issue on Cleaners', *Community Action*, no. 67, November.

Confederation of Health Service Employees (undated a) *Information Paper – Introducing COHSE*, Banstead: COHSE.

Confederation of Health Service Employees (undated b) *The Position of Women within the Confederation of Health Service Employees*, Banstead: COHSE.

Coote, A. and Campbell, B. (1982) *Sweet Freedom – The Struggle for Women's Liberation*, London: Picador.

Coote, A. and Kellner, P. (1980) 'Hear this, brother. Women workers and union power'. London: *New Statesman*, Report no. 1.

Corby, S. (1996) 'Keeping a finger on the NHS pulse'. *People Management*, vol. 2, no. 7, April, pp. 30–2.

Corby, S. and Higham, D. (1996) 'Decentralisation of pay in the NHS: diagnosis and prognosis'. *Human Resource Management Journal*, vol. 6, no. 1, pp. 49–62.

Counter Information Service (undated) *Hardship Hotel*, London: CIS.

Cousins, C. (1988) 'The restructuring of welfare work: the introduction of general management and the contracting out of ancillary services in the NHS'. *Work, Employment and Society*, vol. 2, no. 2, June, pp. 210–28.

Cousins, C. (1990) 'The contracting-out of ancillary services in the NHS' in *New Forms of Ownership – Management and Employment*, ed. G. Jenkins and M. Pool, London: Routledge.

Coyle, A. (1982) 'Sex and skill in the organisation of the clothing industry' in *Women, Work and the Labour Market*, ed. J. West, London: Routledge and Kegan Paul.

Coyle, A. (1984) *Redundant Women*, London: The Women's Press.

Coyle, A. (1985) 'GOING PRIVATE: the Implications of privatization for women's work'. *Feminist Review*, no. 21, November, pp. 5–23.

Coyle, A. (1986) *Dirty Business – Women's Work and Trade Union Organisation in Contract Cleaning*, Low Pay Unit.

Coyle, A. and Skinner, J., eds (1988) *Women and Work – Positive Action for Change*, Basingstoke: Macmillan.

Crompton, R. (1997) *Women and Work in Modern Britain*, Oxford: Oxford University Press.

Crompton, R. and Sanderson K. (1990) *Gendered Jobs and Social Change*, London: Unwin Hyman.

Cunnison, S. (1983) 'Participation in local union organisation. School meals staff: a case study' in *Gender, Class and Work*, ed. E. Gamarnikow, D. Morgan, J. Purvis and D. Taylorson, London: Heinemann.

Cunnison, S. (1995) 'Trade unions and women's way of organising: a case from Northern Ireland'. *Journal of Gender Studies*, vol. 4, no. 3, pp. 327–32.

Cunnison, S. and Stageman, J. (1993) *Feminising the Unions*, Aldershot: Avebury.

Department of Employment. *Employment Gazette*, various years.

Department of Health and Social Security. *Health and Personal Social Services Statistics*, various years.

Dimmock, S. (1977) 'Participation or control? The workers' involvement in management' in *Conflicts in the NHS*, ed. K. Barnard and K. Lee, London: Croom Helm.

Dix, B. and Williams, S. (1987) *Serving the Public – Building the Union – The History of NUPE*, London: Lawrence and Wishart.

Dorgan, T. and Grieco M. (1993) 'Battling against the odds: the emergence of senior women trade unionists'. *Industrial Relations Journal*, 24: 2, pp. 151–64.

Doyal, L. with Pinnell, I. (1979) *The Political Economy of Health*, London: Pluto Press.

Doyal, L., Gee, F., Hunt, G., Mellor, J., Pinnell, I. and Parry, N. (1980) *Migrant*

Workers in the National Health Service – Report of Preliminary Survey, Polytechnic of North London.

Doyal, L., Hunt, G., and Mellor, J. (1981) 'Your Life in their hands: migrant workers in the National Health Service'. *Critical Social Policy*, vol. 1, no. 2, pp. 54–71.

Doyal, L., Elkan, R., Gee, F., Hunt, G., Mellor, J., Pinnell, I. and Parry, N. (1983) *Migrant Workers in the National Health Service*, Part 2, Polytechnic of North London.

Drake, B. (1984; first published 1920) *Women in Trade Unions*, London: Virago.

Dromey, J. and Taylor, G. (1978) *Grunwick: The Workers' Story*, London: Lawrence and Wishart.

Elliot, R. (1980) 'Women in unions: the contribution of trade union education'. *Trade Union Studies Journal*, no.2, autumn.

Ellis, V. (1981) *The Role of Trade Unions in the Promotion of Equal Opportunities*, EOC/SSRC.

Ellis, V. (1988) 'Current trade union attempts to remove occupational segregation in the employment of women' in *Gender Segregation at Work*, ed. S. Walby, Milton Keynes: Open University Press.

Elson, D. and Pearson, R. (1981) ' "Nimble fingers make cheap workers": an analysis of women's employment in Third World export manufacturing'. *Feminist Review*, vol. 7, pp.87–107.

Equal Opportunities Review (1993) 'Profile – Gloria Mills – Director of Equal Opportunities, UNISON'. *EOR*, no. 51, September/October.

Escott, K. and Whitfield, D. (1995) *The Gender Impact of CCT in Local Government*, Manchester: Equal Opportunities Commission.

Fairbrother, P. (1986) 'Union democracy in Australia: accommodation and resistance'. *Journal of Industrial Relations* (Australia), June, pp. 171–90.

Fairbrother, P. (1988) 'Flexibility at work – the challenge for unions'. *Studies for Trade Unionists*, vol. 14, no. 55/56, WEA.

Fairbrother, P. (1989) 'Workplace unionism in the 1980s – a process of renewal?'. *Studies for Trade Unionists*, vol. 15, no. 57, WEA.

Fairbrother, P. (1990) 'The contours of local trade unionism in a period of restructuring' in *Trade Unions and the Members*, eds P. Fosh and E. Heery, Basingstoke: Macmillan.

Fairbrother, P. (1994a) 'Privatisation and local trade unionism'. *Work, Employment & Society*, vol. 8, no. 3, September, pp. 339–56.

Fairbrother, P. (1994b) *Politics and the State as Employer*, London: Mansell.

Fairbrother, P. (1996) 'Workplace trade unionism in the state sector' in *The*

New Workplace and Trade Unionism, ed. P. Ackers, C. Smith and P. Smith, London: Routledge.

Forrest, A. (1993) 'A view from outside the whale: the treatment of women and unions in industrial relations' in *Women Challenging Unions: Feminism, Democracy, and Militancy*, eds L. Briskin and P. McDermott, Toronto: University of Toronto Press.

Fosh, P. (1981) *The Active Trade Unionist*, Cambridge: Cambridge University Press.

Fosh P. (1993) 'Membership participation in workplace unionism: the possibility of union renewal'. *British Journal of Industrial Relations*, 31: 4, pp. 577–92.

Fosh, P. and Cohen, S. (1990) 'Local trade unionists in action: patterns of union democracy' in *Trade Unions and their Members*, eds P. Fosh and E. Heery, Basingstoke: Macmillan.

Friend, B. (1995) 'Role Dispersal'. *Health Service Journal*, vol. 21, September, pp. 7–8.

Fryer, R. (1989) 'Public service trade unionism in the twentieth century' in *Industrial Relations in the Public Services*, eds R. Mailly, S. Dimmock and A. Sethi, London: Routledge.

Fryer, R., Fairclough, A. and Manson, T. (1974) *Organisation and Change in the National Union of Public Employees – A Report Prepared for the Special National Conference on Reorganisation*, University of Warwick.

Fryer, R., Fairclough, A. and Manson, T. (1978) 'Facilities for female shop stewards: the Employment Protection Act and collective agreements'. *British Journal of Industrial Relations*, July, pp. 160–74.

Gabriel, Y. (1988) *Working Lives in Catering*, London: Routledge.

Game, A. and Pringle, R. (1984) *Gender at Work*, London: Pluto Press.

Gilroy, P. (1987) *There Ain't No Black in the Union Jack*, London: Hutchinson.

Glenn, E. (1996) 'From servitude to service work: historical continuities in the racial division of paid reproductive labor' in *Working in the Service Society*, eds C. Macdonald and C. Sirianni, Philadelphia: Temple University Press.

Gow, D. (1987) 'Restoring black faith in unions'. *The Guardian*, September 7.

Gurnham, R. (1976) *200 Years: The Hosiery Unions 1776–1976*, Leicester: National Union of Hosiery and Knitwear Workers.

Hakim, C. (1979) *Occupational Segregation – A Comparative Study of the Differentiation between Men and Women's Work in Britain, the United States, and Other Countries*, Department of Employment Research Paper, no 9, November.

Hakim, C. (1981) 'Job segregation: trends in the 1970s'. *Department of Employment Gazette*, December, pp. 521–9.

Halford, S., Savage, M. and Witz, A. (1997) *Gender, Careers and Organisations*, Basingstoke: Macmillan.

Harrison, M. (1979) 'Participation of women in trade union activities: some research findings and comments'. *Industrial Relations Journal*, vol. 10, pp. 41–55.

Hart, L. (1991) 'A ward of my own: social organization and identity among hospital domestics' in *Anthropology and Nursing*, eds P. Holden and J. Littlewood, London: Routledge.

Hartmann, H. (1979a) 'Capitalism, patriarchy, and job segregation by sex' in *Capitalist Patriarchy and the Case for Socialist Feminism*, ed. Z. R. Eisensten, London: Monthly Review Press.

Hartmann, H. (1979b) 'The unhappy marriage of Marxism and feminism: towards a more progressive union'. *Capital and Class*, 8, pp. 1–33.

Hayes, M., Joyce, P. and Williams, J. (1986) *Local Union Organisation: A Survey of NUPE Branches in Local Government in 1982*, Department of Sociology, Polytechnic of North London.

Heery, E. and Kelly, J. (1988) 'Do female representatives make a difference? Women full-time officials and trade union work'. *Work, Employment and Society*, BSA, vol. 2, no. 4, pp. 487–505.

Heery, E. and Kelly, J. (1989) ' "A Cracking job for a woman" – a profile of women trade union officers'. *Industrial Relations Journal*, 20: 3, pp. 192–202.

Heery, E. and Kelly, J. (1990) 'Full-time officers and the shop steward network: patterns of co-operation and interdependence' in *Trade Unions and their Members*, eds P. Fosh and E. Heery, Basingstoke: Macmillan.

Heritage, J. (1983) 'Feminisation and unionisation: a case study from banking' in *Gender, Class and Work*, ed. E. Gamarnikow, D. Morgan, J. Purvis, and D. Taylorson, London: Heinemann.

Hertzog, M. (1980) *From Hand to Mouth – Women and Piecework*, Middlesex: Pelican.

Hoel, B. (1982) 'Contemporary clothing "sweatshops", Asian female labour and collective organisation' in *Work, Women and the Labour Market*, ed. J. West, London: Routledge and Kegan Paul.

Hunt, J. (1975) *Organising Women Workers*, London: WEA.

Hunt, J. (1982) 'A woman's place is in her union' in *Work, Women and the Labour Market*, ed. J. West, London: Routledge and Kegan Paul.

Hunt, J. and Adams, S. (1980) *Women, Work and Trade Union Organisation*, London: WEA.

Hutchins, B. L. (1978; first published 1915) *Women in Modern Industry*, Wakefield: EP Publishing.

Huws, U. (1982) *Your Job in the Eighties – A Woman's Guide to New Technology*, London: Pluto Press.

Hyman, R. (1971) *Marxism and the Sociology of Trade Unionism*, London: Pluto.

Hyman, R. (1975) *Industrial Relations: A Marxist Introduction*, Basingstoke: Macmillan.

Hyman, R. (1979) 'The politics of workplace trade unionism: recent tendencies and some problems for theory'. *Capital and Class*, vol. 8, pp. 54–67.

Hyman, R. (1989) *The Political Economy of Industrial Relations*, Basingstoke: Macmillan.

Hyman R. (1997) 'The future of employee representation', *British Journal of Industrial Relations*, 35: 3, pp. 309–36.

IRS Employment Trends (1993) 'Local bargaining in the NHS: a survey of first- and second-wave trusts'. *IRS Employment Review*, no. 537, June, pp. 7–16.

IRS Employment Trends (1997) 'Organising the unorganised'. *IRS Employment Review*, no. 644, November, pp. 4–10.

Jenkins, R. and Solomos J., eds (1987) *Racism and Equal Opportunity Policies in the 1980s*, Cambridge: Cambridge University Press.

John, A. V. (1984) *By the Sweat of their Brow – Women Workers at Victorian Coal Mines*, London: Routledge and Kegan Paul.

Kaye, A. (1994) ' "No skill beyond manual dexterity involved": Gender and the construction of skill in the east London clothing industry' in *Women, Work and Place*, ed A. Kobayashi, McGill–Queens University Press.

Kellner, P. (1980) 'The working woman: her job, her politics and her union' in *Hear This, Brother*, eds A. Coote and P. Kellner, London: New Statesman, Report no. 1, pp. 25–40.

Kelly, J. (1987) *Labour and the Unions*, London: Verso.

Kessler, I. (1986) 'Shop stewards in local government'. *British Journal of Industrial Relations*, vol. 24, pp. 419–41.

Labour Research (1982) 'Women in the unions'. *Labour Research*, March.

Labour Research (1988a) 'Working for equality in the unions'. *Labour Research*, March.

Labour Research (1988b) 'Are unions working for black members?'. *Labour Research*, July.

Labour Research (1988c) 'Educating Rita to sort out the boss'. *Labour Research*, September.

Labour Research (1989a) 'Unions and part-timers – do they mix?'. *Labour Research*, March.

Labour Research (1989b) 'TUC Reports'. *Labour Research*, October.

Labour Research (1995a) 'Too much trust in the NHS market'. *Labour Research*, April.

Labour Research (1995b) 'On the road to private health care'. *Labour Research*, July.

Labour Research (1996a) 'Getting women in proportion'. *Labour Research*, March.

Labour Research (1996b) 'Women resist union decline'. *Labour Research*, June.

Labour Research (1996c) 'Recruitment – stopping the rot'. *Labour Research*, September.

Labour Research (1996d) 'Union activity goes local'. *Labour Research*, November.

Labour Research (1996e) 'A foiled attempt at a private NHS'. *Labour Research*, November.

Labour Research (1997a) 'NHS faces crisis in morale'. *Labour Research*, March.

Labour Research (1997b) 'Is union decline bottoming out?'. *Labour Research*, July.

Labour Research (1997c) 'Do unions serve black workers?'. *Labour Research*, December.

Labour Research (1998a) 'Equal pay cases – a reps' job?'. *Labour Research*, February.

Labour Research (1998b) 'Are women out of proportion?'. *Labour Research*, March.

Labour Research Department (1985) *Black Workers, Trade Unions and the Law – A Negotiator's Guide*, LRD, October.

Labour Research Department (1998) *Union Action for Race Equality*, LRD, January.

Lane, T and Roberts, K. (1971) *Strike at Pilkingtons*, London: Collins/Fontana.

Lawrence, E. (1994) *Gender and Trade Unions*, London: Taylor & Francis.

Leah, R. (1993) 'Black women speak out: racism and unions' in *Women Challenging Unions: Feminism, Democracy, and Militancy*, eds L. Briskin and P. McDermott, Toronto: University of Toronto Press.

Ledwith, S. and Colgan, F. (1996) *Women in Organisations*, Basingstoke: Macmillan.

Ledwith, S., Colgan, F., Joyce, P. and Hayes M. (1990) 'The making of women trade union leaders'. *Industrial Relations Journal*, 21: 2, pp. 112–25.

Lee, G. 'Black members and their trade unions' in *The Manufacture of Disadvantage*, ed. G. Lee and R. Loveridge, Milton Keynes: Open University Press.

Lee, G. and Wrench, J. (1983) *Skill Seekers – Black Youth Apprenticeships and Disadvantage*, National Youth Bureau.

Leedham, W. (1986) 'The privatisation of NHS ancillary services'. *Studies for Trade Unionists*, vol. 12, no. 45, WEA, March.

Le Grand, J. and Robinson, R. (1984) *Privatisation and the Welfare State*, London: George Allen and Unwin.

Leonard, M. (1992) 'The modern Cinderellas: women and the contract cleaning industry in Belfast' in *Women and Working Lives – Divisions and Change*, eds S. Arber and N. Gilbert, Basingstoke: Macmillan.

Lever, A. (1988) 'Capital, gender and skill: women homeworkers in rural Spain'. *Feminist Review*, vol. 30, pp. 3–24.

Lewenhak, S. (1977) *Women and Trade Unions*, London: Ernest Benn.

Liddington, J. and Norris, J. (1978) *One Hand Tied behind Us – The Rise of the Women's Suffrage Movement*, London: Virago.

Lilley, R. and Wilson, C. (1994) 'Change in the NHS: the view from a trust'. *Personnel Management*, May, pp. 38–41.

Lloyd, C. (1997) 'Decentralization in the NHS: prospects for workplace unionism'. *British Journal of Industrial Relations*, 35: 3, pp. 427–46.

Lloyd, C. and Seifert, R. (1995) 'Restructuring in the NHS: the impact of the 1990 reforms on the management of labour'. *Work, Employment and Society*, vol. 9, no. 2, June, pp. 359–78.

Lukes, S. (1974) *Power – A Radical View*, Basingstoke: Macmillan.

McBride, A. (1996) 'Being there – developing effective representation for women in UNISON', paper presented to the Labour Process Conference, Aston.

McBride, A. (1998) 'The exclusion of men in a liberal democratic organisation', paper presented to the Gender, Work and Organization Conference, Manchester.

Macdonald C. L. and Sirianni, C., eds (1996) *Working in the Service Society*, Philadelphia: Temple University Press.

McDowell, L. and Court, G. (1997) 'Missing subjects: gender, sexuality and power in merchant banking' in *Space, Gender, Knowledge*, eds L. McDowell and J. P. Sharp, London: Arnold.

Mackie, L. and Pattullo, P. (1977) *Women at Work*, London: Tavistock.

McLoughlin, J. (1985) 'A woman's place is in the power house'. *The Guardian*, September 2.

Mailly, R. (1986) 'The impact of contracting out in the NHS'. *Employee Relations*, vol. 8, pp. 10–16.

Mailly, R., Dimmock, S. and Sethi, A. (1989) 'Industrial relations in the

National Health Service since 1979' in *Industrial Relations in the Public Services*, eds R. Mailly, S. Dimmock and A. Sethi, London: Routledge.

Mama, A. (1992) 'Black women and the British state – race, class and gender analysis for the 1990s' in *Racism and Antiracism – Inequalities, Opportunites and Policies*, eds P. Braham, A. Railansi and R. Skellington, London: Sage.

Manson, T. (1977) 'Management, the professions and the unions: a social analysis of change in the NHS' in *Health and the Division of Labour*, ed. M. Stacey, M. Reid, C. Heath and R. Dingwell, London: Croom Helm.

Martin, J. and Roberts, C. (1984) *Women and Employment – A Lifetime Perspective*, London: HMSO, Department of Employment Office of Population Censuses and Surveys.

Marx, K. (1977) *Capital*, vol. I, London: Lawrence and Wishart.

Miles, R. (1982) *Racism and Migrant Labour*, London: Routledge and Kegan Paul.

Miles, R. and Phizacklea, A. (1984) *White Man's Country*, London: Pluto.

Modood, T. (1997) 'Employment' in *Ethnic Minorities in Britain*, ed. T. Modood *et al.*, London: Policy Studies Institute.

Moore, R. (1975) *Racism and Black Resistance*, London: Pluto Press.

Munro, A. (1982) *The Organisation of Women Workers in the Hosiery and Knitwear Union*, unpublished M.A. dissertation in industrial relations, University of Warwick.

Munro, A. (1989) *Developing Women's Trade Union Education*, unpublished report to the West Mercia district: WEA.

National Board for Prices and Incomes (1966) *The Pay and Conditions of Manual Workers in Local Authorities, the National Health Service, Gas and Water Supplies*, Report 29, HMSO Cmnd 3230.

National Board for Prices and Incomes (1971) *Pay and Conditions of Service of Ancillary Workers in the National Health*, Service Report 166, HMSO Cmnd 4644.

National Union of Public Employees (1982) *NUPE Reorganisation – An Executive Council Discussion Document on Union Structure*, NUPE.

National Union of Public Employees (1984) *The Report of the Women's Working Party*, NUPE.

National Union of Public Employees (undated a) *Women in NUPE*, NUPE.

National Union of Public Employees (undated b) *Policy File on Women*, NUPE.

National Union of Public Employees (undated c) *NUPE Women on the Move*, NUPE.

National Union of Public Employees (undated d) *End Poverty Pay – A Strategy for the 1980s*, NUPE.

Neale, J. (1983) *Memoirs of a Callous Picket – Working for the NHS*, London: Pluto Press.

Nicholson, N. (1976) 'The Role of the shop steward: an empirical case study'. *Industrial Relations Journal*, vol. 7, no. 1, pp. 15–26.

Ohri, S. and Faruqi, S. (1988) 'Racism, Employment and Unemployment' in *Britain's Black Population*, 2nd ed., eds B. Ashok *et al.*, Aldershot: Gower.

Owen, D. (1994) *Ethnic Minority Women and the Labour Market: Analysis of the 1991 Census*, Equal Opportunities Commission.

Parmar, P. (1982) 'Gender, race and class: Asian women in resistance' in *The Empire Strikes Back – Race and Racism in 70s Britain*, Centre for Contemporary Cultural Studies, London: Hutchinson.

Partridge, B. (1977–8) 'The Activities of Shop Stewards'. *Industrial Relations Journal*, vol. 8, no. 4, pp. 28–42.

Perkins, T. (1983) 'A new form of employment: a case study of women's part-time work in Coventry' in *Sexual Divisions – Patterns and Processes*, ed. M. Evans and C. Ungerson, London: Tavistock.

Phillips, A. (1991) *Engendering Democracy*, Cambridge: Polity.

Phillips, A. and Taylor, B. (1980) 'Sex and skill: notes towards a feminist economics'. *Feminist Review*, vol. 6, pp. 79–88.

Phizacklea, A., ed. (1983) *One Way Ticket – Migration and Female Labour*, London: Routledge and Kegan Paul.

Phizacklea, A. (1988) 'Gender, racism and occupational segregation' in *Gender Segregation at Work*, ed. S. Walby, Milton Keynes: Open University Press.

Phizacklea, A. and Miles, R. (1980) *Labour and Racism*, London: Routledge and Kegan Paul.

Pinchbeck, I. (1981; first published 1930) *Women Workers and the Industrial Revolution 1750–1850*, London: Virago.

Pollert, A. (1981) *Girls, Wives, Factory Lives*, Basingstoke: Macmillan.

Purcell, K. (1984) 'Militancy and acquiescence among women workers' in *Women and the Public Sphere*, eds J. Siltanen and M. Stanworth, London: Hutchinson.

Rahman, N. (1985) *Pricing into Poverty – Council Manual Workers' Pay*, Birmingham: Low Pay Unit.

Rees, G. and Fielder, S. (1992) 'The services economy, subcontracting and the new employment relations: contract catering and cleaning', *Work, Employment & Society*, vol. 6 no. 3, pp. 347–68.

Rees, T. (1990) 'Gender, power and trade union democracy' in *Trade Unions and their Members*, eds P. Fosh and E. Heery, Basingstoke: Macmillan.

Rees, T. (1992) *Women and the Labour Market*, London: Routledge.

Robarts, S., Coote, A. and Ball, E. (1981) *Positive Action for Women – The Next Step*, NCCL.

Robinson, O. (1988) 'The changing labour market: growth of part-time employment and labour market segregation in Britain' in *Gender Segregation at Work*, ed. S. Walby, Milton Keynes: Open University Press.

Seifert, R. (1992) *Industrial Relations in the NHS*, London: Chapman & Hall.

Siltanen, J. (1994) *Locating Gender*, London: University College London Press.

Sivanandan, A. (1982) *A Different Hunger*, London: Pluto.

Smith, D. (1974) *Racial Disadvantage in Employment*, PEP vol. XL, Broadsheet 544, June.

Smith, D. (1977) *The Facts of Racial Disadvantage*, PEP vol. XLII, Broadsheet 560.

Somerville, J. (1997) 'Social Movement Theory, Women and the Question of Interests'. *Sociology*, vol. 31, no. 4, pp. 673–95.

Stageman, J. (1980a) 'A study of trade union branches in the Hull area' in *Hear This, Brother. Women Workers and Union Power*, ed. A. Coote and P. Kellner, London: New Statesman, Report no. 1, pp. 49–62.

Stageman, J. (1980b) *Women in Trade Unions*, Paper no. 6, Industrial Studies Unit, Adult Education Department, University of Hull, May.

Stamp, P. and Robarts, S. (1986) *Positive Action – Changing the Workplace*, London: National Council for Civil Liberties.

Summerfield, P. (1977) 'Women Workers in the Second World War'. *Capital and Class*, vol. 1, pp. 27–42.

Terry, M. (1978) *The Emergence of a Lay Elite? Some Recent Changes in Shop Steward Organisation*, Industrial Relations Research Unit Discussion Paper 14, University of Warwick, November.

Terry, M. (1982) 'Organising a fragmented workforce: shop stewards in local government'. *British Journal of Industrial Relations*, vol. 20, pp. 1–19.

Terry, M. (1996) 'Negotiating the government of Unison: union democracy in theory and practice'. *British Journal of Industrial Relations*, 34: 1, pp. 87–110.

Trades Union Congress (1987) *Black and Ethnic Minority Women in Employment and Trade Unions*, TUC, February.

Trades Union Congress (1992) *Black Workers and Trade Union Organisation*, Background Paper to the Black Workers' Conference, TUC.

Vulliamy, D. and Moore, R. (1979) 'Whitleyism and health – the NHS and its industrial relations'. *Studies for Trade Unionists* vol. 5, no. 19, WEA.

Wajcman, J. (1983) *Women in Control*, Milton Keynes: Open University Press.

Walby, S. (1986) *Patriarchy at Work*, Cambridge: Polity.

Walby, S. (1990) *Theorizing Patriarchy*, Oxford: Blackwell.

Walby, S. (1997) *Gender Transformations*, London: Routledge.

Wertheimer, B. M. and Nelson, A. H. (1975) *Trade Union Women: A Study of their Participation in New York City Locals*, New York: Praeger.

Westwood, S. (1984) *All Day Every Day – Factory and Family in the Making of Women's Lives*, London: Pluto.

Whitelegg, E., *et al.* (1982) *The Changing Experience of Women*, Milton Keynes: Open University Press.

Williams, A., Livy, B., Silverstone, R. and Adams, P. (1977) *The Recruitment and Retention of Ancillary Staff in Hospitals: A Review of the Literature and Bibliography*, Working Paper 2, The City University Business School.

Wilson, A. (1985) *Finding a Voice – Asian Women in Britain*, London: Virago.

Witz, A. (1992) *Professions and Patriarchy*, London: Routledge.

Wrench, J. (1986a) 'Unequal comrades: trade unions, equal opportunity and racism'. *Policy Papers in Ethnic Relations*, no. 5, University of Warwick Centre for Research in Ethnic Relations/ESRC.

Wrench, J. (1986b) 'Unequal comrades: trade unions, equal opportunity and racism' in *Racism and Equal Opportunity Policies in the 1980s*, 2nd ed., Cambridge: Cambridge University Press.

Wrench, J. and Virdee, S. (1996) 'Organising the unorganised – "Race", poor work and trade unions' in *The New Workplace and Trade Unionism*, ed. P. Ackers, C. Smith and P. Smith, London: Routledge.

INDEX